WITHDRAWN
UTSA LIBRARIES

P9-EEL-394

DEMOCRACY'S
CHILDREN

DEMOCRACY'S CHILDREN

INTELLECTUALS
AND THE RISE
OF CULTURAL POLITICS

JOHN
McGOWAN

Cornell University Press

Ithaca and London

Copyright © 2002 by Cornell University

All rights reserved. Except for brief quotations in a review, this book, or parts thereof, must not be reproduced in any form without permission in writing from the publisher. For information, address Cornell University Press, Sage House, 512 East State Street, Ithaca, New York 14850.

First published 2002 by Cornell University Press
First printing, Cornell Paperbacks, 2002

Printed in the United States of America

Library of Congress Cataloging-in-Publication Data

McGowan, John
    Democracy's children : intellectuals and the rise of cultural politics / John McGowan.
       p. cm.
    Includes bibliographical references (p.) and index.
    ISBN 0-8014-3973-6 (alk. paper) — ISBN 0-8014-8766-8 (pbk. : alk. paper)
      1. Criticism—History—20th century.   2. Criticism—Political aspects—History—20th century.   3. College teaching—United States.   4. Intellectual life—History—20th century. I. Title.
  PN94 .M35 2001
  801'.95'0904—dc21
                                       2001005519

Cornell University Press strives to use environmentally responsible suppliers and materials to the fullest extent possible in the publishing of its books. Such materials include vegetable-based, low-VOC inks and acid-free papers that are recycled, totally chlorine-free, or partly composed of nonwood fibers. Books that bear the logo of the FSC (Forest Stewardship Council) use paper taken from forests that have been inspected and certified as meeting the highest standards for environmental and social responsibility. For further information, visit our website at www.cornellpress.cornell.edu.

Cloth printing   10 9 8 7 6 5 4 3 2 1

Paperback printing   10 9 8 7 6 5 4 3 2 1

Library
University of Texas
at San Antonio

For Kiernan and Siobhan

"Earth's the right place for love:
I don't know where it's likely to go better."

Contents

Preface

> My remarks are addressed to those, who by their use of
> speech and through their explicit formulation of general
> ideas, have been able or are now able to attempt to have
> an influence on how their society evolves and the course
> of history.
> —CORNELIUS CASTORIADIS

This book is about the vicissitudes of intellectual practice, viewed from
a pragmatist and pluralist perspective. Most of the essays concern U.S.
literary intellectuals over the past thirty years. But this provincial focus
is expanded in the last three chapters. In every case, I strive to identify
the aspirations and strategies of those contemporary humanistic intellectuals who want their work to intervene in the political and cultural formations of our time. I am interested in situating such intellectuals within
the institutional setting—the academy—in which they almost all work
and within the more general culture that they wish to influence. And I am
interested in locating their favored method of intervention—cultural politics—alongside other political strategies.

The results of examinations can look dismissive. But I count myself
among these intellectuals whom I am attempting to describe, explain, and
assess. So my emphasis on the difficulties, obstacles, and contradictions of
this enterprise is not meant to belittle it. But I also do not think there is any
self-evident legitimacy or virtue attached to the intellectuals' efforts. There
is nothing pure or simple about intellectual work, from its motives to its

means and consequences, so I am afraid that I constantly take back with one hand what I have given with the other. I hope my book recaptures the tone and intellectual acuity of a book I love—Alvin Gouldner's *The Fate of the Intellectuals and the Rise of the New Class* (1979)—more for the clear, cold eye it casts on its subject than for any of its specific arguments.

My swings between sympathy and criticism, affirmation and rejection, both stem from and help explain my reliance on the essay form here. I am a committed pluralist (I outline some of my reasons for that commitment in the final chapter), which means (among many other things) that a synthetic view of "the intellectual" is not, I believe, possible. The opportunities, concerns, and roadblocks any intellectual faces keep shifting. What worked elsewhere is no sure guide to what will prove effective here and now. These essays each attend to specific sightings of the species in different habitats and base their appeal on an attempted resonance with the reader's own engagements on similar, but not identical, terrain. If the gentle reader keeps in mind that the focus is on humanist, especially literary, intellectuals who hope that their work will have social and political consequences, my to-and-froing may appear more intelligible and less frustrating.

My ambivalence about cultural politics is worn on my sleeve throughout these essays. By cultural politics I mean the attempt to intervene in cultural processes of representation, categorization, and reflexive understanding, with a focus on the ideological production of values and beliefs along with adherence to them. I am willing to recognize the importance of cultural politics as one form of political activism. But I balk at views that make cultural politics primary. Take, for example, Nancy Armstrong's claim that "the most important achievement of 'the sixties' was . . . to shift the theater of political activism from the plane of physical actions, conflicts we call real, to the plane of discourse, conflicts over how our relation to the real should be imagined." What follows from this claim? "Something got permanently turned around in the process, I am suggesting, and the outcome of military actions, hunger, trade policies, as well as elections and, yes, university search committees, began to depend on how those under consideration were represented, how well they managed the information about themselves. . . . To come to this conclusion is to admit that any responsible political action depends on understanding the world so classified as the real and primary one, the one that must be changed if the material conditions in which people live and die are going to improve" (2000, 323–24). I am skeptical that "something got permanently turned around" and think the effectiveness of cultural politics is often similarly overstated. But I hardly think cultural politics—the intervention in discursive processes—has no effects. So I try in the following essays to think about where and how a cultural politics makes sense—and where and how it runs up against limits to its powers. As I explain in the introduction, the rise of cultural politics to its current prominence is overdetermined; the two crucial factors are (1) the academic venue of most intellectual work and (2) the shift since the 1960s from antiliberal socialism to social democracy as the political position of choice among left-of-center Westerners.

A word about the historical origins of the category "intellectual" is in order. The actual word dates from the 1820s, but I follow various writers—most notably Lewis Coser (1965) and Jürgen Habermas (1991)—in placing the origin of the species in the eighteenth century. Intellectuals are democracy's children insofar as they are called into existence in plural societies in which freedom of speech and the press combines with wide-open debate among competing visions of the good life, the good polity, and good art (among other issues). I was tempted to call this book "Democracy's Waifs" because "children" does not quite capture the way in which democracy both creates the intellectual (by providing the public stage for his or her appearance) and trivializes the intellectual's work (by placing it in the context of so much intellectual work and alongside commercial activities that ignore that work with impunity). There is almost always something forlorn about the intellectual, always a sense of being slightly irrelevant, something that motivates the corresponding dream of hooking up with the true source of social power, whether that source be the state or the proletariat. Hence Gramsci's (1971) notion of the "organic" intellectual who is seamlessly woven into a social group. The intellectual rarely, if ever, feels organic. And the contemporary practitioners of cultural politics are no different, as is beautifully caught in Stuart Hall's rueful description of the origins of cultural studies: "[T]here is no doubt in my mind that we were trying to find an institutional practice in cultural studies that might produce an organic intellectual. We didn't know precisely what that would mean . . . and we weren't sure we would recognize him or her if we managed to produce it. The problem about the concept of an organic intellectual is that it appears to align intellectuals with an emerging historical movement and we couldn't tell then, and can hardly tell now, where that emerging historical movement was to be found. We were organic intellectuals without any organic point of reference" (1992, 281). I am interested in the tension between a cultivated ironic distance and a deep desire to belong found in much intel-lectual work.

Although this is a book of essays, their arrangement plots an over-arching argument. The introduction fleshes out the connection of intel-lectuals to democracy, while also suggesting that, as grateful children, in-tellectuals should be the champions of democracy, ever vigilant against the anti-democratic forces in modern societies. That such has not always been the case, both historically and in our own time, garners my atten-tion (especially in chapter 4). Part 1 focuses on the contemporary intellec-tual as academic, while also considering the role and place of the academy within society at large. These chapters move from personal reflections on my own professional activities as critic (chapter 1) and teacher (chapter 2) to broader reflections on changes in the style and aspirations of academic intellectuals (chapter 3) and on changes in understanding the role of the university (chapter 4).

In part 2, I widen the frame. Chapters 5 and 6 look backward to con-sider the intellectuals' relation to modernity, culture, nationalism and other large-scale explanatory terms that were born at the same time (1750–1820) as intellectuals themselves. I agree with Ron Eyerman that "this notion of 'the intellectual' . . . first emerged in the new political context created by what has come to be called the transition to modernity . . . . In-tellectuals were those who wrote or spoke out in public either as active sup-porters or as opponents of what they themselves identified as modernity" (1994, 37). I try to examine this implication of intellectuals with the very idea of modernity, of a transition from one way of being to another that occurs on a grand scale. My final chapter sketches some implications and consequences of the pluralist position toward which the earlier chapters gesture.

The political commitment that motivates my work is to democracy. If I aspire to Gouldner's mordant wit, the gentler tutelary spirits of this en-terprise are John Dewey and Hannah Arendt. My core belief may be stated as the conviction that the cure for many of our social ills is more democ-racy, not less, and that there are powerful blocking forces working against democracy in contemporary society, even if few dare to speak openly against it. The intellectual committed to democracy strives to articulate what that vague and contested term can mean both practically and ide-ally, to lyrically evoke the virtues of democratic citizens and the joys of democratic culture, and to model in his or her own work democracy in action. The somewhat embarrassing whiff of the lay preacher inevitably (unfortunately) haunts the intellectual's work, because the moral cannot be fully expunged from the political, and because exhortation is necessary where more overt forms of compulsion are eschewed. I try to be as hard-headed about democracy's limitations and the ways the term can be used to forestall thought as I am about terms such as "modernity" and "culture." Undoubtedly, I do not fully succeed.

Which brings us back to the question of form. This is a book of essays. I have provided short overviews for each of the book's two parts to orient the reader—and I have cross-referenced topics that are touched on in one essay to their fuller discussion in another essay. But I am committed to the informality of the essay form for a variety of reasons. I want to achieve the plain tone of one citizen speaking to others, and I want to suggest the tentativeness of one person trying out ideas, aiming to provoke various responses as much as trying to convince. These are not particularly personal essays in content (although more personal than standard academic prose), but they are personal in tone. They aim to portray a mind and sensibility at work. Central to my self-image as intellectual is the notion that everything is matter for thought, that my questioning and opining know no boundaries. If this sounds joyless, I can only respond that, on the contrary, it is the only way to keep the vital spark aglow. What's deadly is the curbing of curiosity and the timid assumption of territories from which I am barred that attends too scrupulous a respect for reigning authorities and proprieties.

I contemplated calling this book *Representative Me*, a take-off of a title used by that first great American essayist, Ralph Waldo Emerson. The point would have been that I rely, probably far too heavily, on my experiences and my concerns chiming with my readers' experiences and concerns. The essay as a rhetorical form makes a personal appeal—from one person to another—that scholarly prose tries to escape. The danger is that the reader will weary of the personal tone, the personal appeal, the sensibility ever on display, just as the writer is sometimes weary of self. The gain is a heightened sense of connection, an enlivening of the stakes.

The essay allows for assertion, the direct stating of "here is where I take my stand." (My editor vetoed the title *Pledges of Allegiance*.) I often only sketch in arguments or gesture toward the historical evidence that underlies a position taken. But I trust the reader will catch the point, and I try in the footnotes to point toward works where these questions have been taken up in detail by other writers on whom I rely and by whom I have been influenced. When I presented some of this work to a faculty group in Chapel Hill, a philosopher remarked that he was pleased to see that he and I really did share common concerns, but philosophy went much more slowly, taking issues one small bit at a time. I was chastened—and it was only six months later that I realized that I would never master slowness. The only proper strategy for me was to go faster. The footnotes in this book are a compromise, curbing what is perhaps the over-reliance on allusion or on assuming my readers' familiarity with certain positions. But too many of our academic books are written as if for an audience (our students?) entirely new to the matter at hand. I am trying here to address adults—readers who have funds of knowledge, experience, and beliefs against which they will judge what I have to say. Our overly didactic forms do a disservice, not only by insulting the reader's intelligence, but also by providing a bad model of the opinionated give-and-take that aligns the intellectual with the democratic life. Essays as a genre—and these essays in particular—have no truths to hand over ready-made.

In *Jude the Obscure*, Hardy's narrator tells us, "As you got older, and felt yourself to be at the center of your time, and not at a point in its circumference, as you had felt when you were little, you were seized with a sort of shuddering . . . . All around you there seemed to be something glaring, garish, rattling, and the noises and glares hit upon the little cell called your life, and shook it, and warped it" (1966, 60–61). Chapters 1 and 2 of this book show me taking stock just as I felt that awful movement to the center of my time. I wanted to locate my allegiances amid the warping noises and glares. (Chapter 2 first appeared in *The Centennial Review* 40 [1996]: 5–30; I thank R. K. Meiners, Clint Goodson, and Judith Stoddart at Michigan State, who have been such stalwart supporters of my work.)

I have been luckier than Jude, however. Coming in from the circumference has involved me with others who have solicited my views; all the remaining chapters of this book were written at the request of those others, who also secured audiences for their first airings. I owe much to Regenia Gagnier and Donald E. Hall for the introduction (about half of which appears in Hall's edited volume, *Professions: The Future of Literary Studies* [Champaign: University of Illinois Press, 2001]); to Sharon Oster, who solicited and edited chapter 3; to Tony La Vopa, Gary Wihl, Steve Vincent, and Charles Capper of the Sawyer Seminar on Liberalism and its Cultures at the National Humanities Center, both for the intellectual vitality of that two-year enterprise and for requesting the work that, much revised, is now chapter 4; to John Kucich and Dianne F. Sadoff for making me write, much against my will, chapter 5 and then, even more against my will, making me rewrite it several times (it appears in their edited volume, *Victorian Afterlife: Postmodern Culture Rewrites the Nineteenth Century* [Minneapolis: University of Minnesota Press, 2000]); to John Burt Foster for insisting that I turn a haphazard conference paper for the International Association for Philosophy and Literature Conference at George Mason University into a coherent essay (now chapter 6); and to Allen Dunn, Jim Nelson, Hilde Lindemann Nelson, Jonathan Dancy, and the philosophy department at the University of Tennessee for inviting me to talk on pluralism and then engaging my ideas so vigorously that chapter 7 bears very little resemblance to the paper they heard in Knoxville in early 2000; another portion of chapter 7 comes from a review essay commissioned by Craig Calhoun and first published in *Sociological Theory* 16 (1998): 292–97. Thanks also to the anonymous reader for Cornell and to the press's editorial board, both for their suggestions for revision and for reading the manuscript in the spirit in which it was intended. They gave me hope that my readers will be able to do the same. I also want to praise exemplary editor, Bernhard Kendler, who drives a hard bargain when it comes to titles. But he met his match in my daughter Siobhan.

Much of the time that I spent writing this book came my way through the good offices of two deans with whom I have had the pleasure of working closely at Chapel Hill: Linda Dykstra and Darryl Gless. I also owe time debts to Lloyd Kramer and Ruel Tyson of UNC's Institute for the Arts and Humanities. But my intellectual debt to them is even greater; my sensibility has been shaped by the Institute and its modes of intellectual interaction. Ruel and Lloyd have worked their magic on many UNC faculty, but I think I can safely claim to be their most fervent convert. Special thanks also to the Institute's many generous supporters, especially Janie and Billy Armfield. Large chunks of chapters 4 and 7 were written on the back porch of their Roaring Gap home. Finally, my gratitude to the University Research Council, the English Department, and the College of Arts and Sciences at the University of North Carolina for funds that paid for this book's cover.

The older I get, the more people read my work in the various stages before it gets into print. The list of those who have aided in this book's production is so long that I cannot detail the contribution each made, even though each and every one of them richly deserves a particular word. To all of you: understand that this list says much less than I would say, given pages enough and time. Thanks to Charles Altieri, Bill Andrews, Suzy Anger, Susan Bickford, David Brehmer, Tony Cascardi, Rom Coles,

Jill Craven, Tyler Curtain, Kim Curtis, Randi Davenport, Doug Dempster, Eric Downing, Judith Farquhar, Jim Hevia, Eric Iverson, Nancy Jesser, Gary Johnson, Charlie Kurzman, Laurie Langbauer, Dom Lopes, Megan Matchinske, Carol Mavor, Mary Papke, Kevin Parker, Della Pollock, Bill Rasch, Lorena Russell, Rob Spirko, James Thompson, and Jeffrey Williams. Much of this book almost takes the form of a personal letter because I have so often articulated my thoughts with Allen Dunn and John Kucich as my imagined or actual audience. Every writer should be blessed with friends who blend such complete incredulity with such willingness to read—and even take pleasure in—every word.

Jane Danielewicz has been by my side since even before that night, five months pregnant, she endured two and a half hours in the stalled elevator in the Warwick Hotel. It's often difficult to be married to someone whom everyone loves so unreservedly, but I console myself with the knowledge that her adoring public only sees half her virtues. This book is dedicated to Kiernan and Siobhan McGowan, who are the true children of its title, and who will be blessed in this life if they only garner a small portion of the happiness they have given to their loving father.

JOHN MCGOWAN

Carrboro, North Carolina

DEMOCRACY'S
CHILDREN

INTRODUCTION

Literary Intellectuals in and for a Democratic Society

I am an intellectual, not a scholar. The distinction is not meant to be invidious, nor to mark an absolute divide. My own work would be impossible without scholars, just as scholarly work always has some connection to current affairs. Still, a rough distinction is useful, if only to indicate various positions on a continuum that registers the relation of academic work to the attempt to have an influence on life in the polity right now. What interests me is the desire of many literature professors to address the general public, a desire hardly shared by the chemist who writes to a scientific community of the fifty people in the world able to understand his work, or by the Milton scholar who is tracing the sources of Milton's Latin poetry.

Tzvetan Todorov identifies two "conditions" that define an intellectual. "The first is that the individual in question is engaged in an activity of the mind resulting in the production of a work . . . . The second is that the individual is not content simply to produce a work but is also concerned about the state of society and participates in public debate. A poet shut off in an 'ivory tower' or a scientist in a laboratory is not an 'intellectual' "(1997, 1121). The term "intellectual" is often said to have originated during the Dreyfus affair in late nineteenth-century France. But Raymond Williams (1976, 140–41) places the term's origins in the early part of that century, citing a usage found in Byron in 1813. In the sociological literature on the subject (including Coser [1965] and Habermas [1991]), intellectuals as a recognizable social group are usually said to emerge in the eighteenth century, with the French *philosophes* and English periodical writers as the first examples. My position (hardly unique) is that a pluralistic, secular society with freedom of speech and the press calls intellectuals into existence. The date of this emergence varies from place to place and is dependent on local conditions. This contextual dependence also insures that intellectuals' self-understandings and others' understanding of them are not stable. Thus, any characterization of intellectuals (like mine in this book) is also always a polemical attempt to influence intellectuals to be this rather than that. My efforts here are descriptive; I do try to characterize the current plight and goals of intellectuals in a way that "gets it right." And I certainly expect that I will only convince my readers if I am accurate about current conditions. But this work is also prescriptive; it argues for and models a certain way of doing intellectual work and certain commitments that claim to give that work meaning and value. I have no desire to disentangle the descriptive and prescriptive from one another in my work. So I agree with Todorov when he says "the intellectual cannot be replaced by the expert: the latter knows facts; the former discusses values. It is in their interest not to ignore each other, but there is a difference in their positions" (1997, 1122). I must also admit that I have no further definition of intellectuals to offer. I am certainly not interested in providing necessary and sufficient features for being a member of this group. Instead, this book discusses a number of institutional sites—the professional conference, the classroom, the university—and a number of key concepts—modernity, culture, democracy, pluralism—in or around which intellectual work is done. The plausibility and usefulness of the way I deploy the term "intellectual" will rest on how it focuses or illuminates discussion of these specific matters—and on the light these matters shed back on how we might understand the intellectual.

If this seems cavalier, even irresponsible, I had better 'fess up to another irresponsibility, while I'm at it. The political theorist John Dunn castigates writers who treat texts from the past or present "with varying degrees of attention and patience, simply as repositories of potential intellectual stimulation for a contemporary reader, and permitting themselves to respond, accordingly, just as fancy takes them" (1996, 19). I cheerfully accept that this description fits my own work. Except, of course, that Dunn rather overstates the freedom of the intellectual grasshopper as contrasted to the scholarly ant. The intellectual is rarely so footloose and fancy free. Responsibility is located elsewhere for the intellectual, not nowhere. Working from commitments to present programs and present constituencies, the intellectual might very well envy the freedom of the scholar whose pursuits are less guided by immediate pressures or the desire to address audiences outside a particular specialist cohort. The intellectual articulates concepts, commitments, and visions that legitimate and/or contest the way that we live now.[1]

This work of articulation is eclectic. It requires, among other tasks, elucidation/elaboration/contestation of received and current ideas; the examination of prevailing practices, beliefs, and institutions in relation to stated principles and as indicators of unstated motivations; an engagement with the multiple traditions that traverse contemporary cultures and influence individual agents; and efforts to bring intellectual discourse to bear within a polity which features a plurality of discourses.

To embark on these tasks would be difficult if the intellectual could not name for himself or herself the fundamental commitments that underwrite the work. To what do I feel responsible, to whom do I hold myself answerable? There have been various answers to the "what" over the past two hundred years: art, economic justice, social equality, my ethnic group, my nation, my gender group. Intellectuals have been notoriously prone to opt for package deals that encompass a "what" to be committed to, an analysis of how that "what" has been maligned, and a program for correcting past and current wrongs. Think here of aestheticism, Marxism, nationalism, or whatever other -ism is your personal favorite or personal *bête noire*. Even where the intellectual eschews the rigidity of the Bergonsonian clown which threatens the card-carrying adherent, intellectual positions are almost always charted by way of programmatic signposts. Such programs conveniently provide others with whom to converse and argue, thus offering an audience for the linguistic output that is the final product of almost all intellectual work.

But this audience only partly constitutes those to whom the intellectual feels answerable. There is almost always another group—a group often figured as oppressed—who is to benefit from the intellectual's activities. This

1. Edward W. Said's account of the intellectual starts from a similar place: "the intellectual is an individual endowed with a faculty for representing, embodying, articulating a message, a view, an attitude, philosophy or opinion to, as well as for, a public." But he then connects that articulation to "universal principles . . . concerning freedom and justice" that are often violated by "worldly powers or nations." Thus, the intellectual is to be "someone who cannot easily be co-opted by governments or corporations, and whose *raison d'être* is to represent all those people and issues that are routinely forgotten or swept under the rug" (1996, 11). Said moves too quickly here, I think. Both universal principles and the intellectual's relation to the neglected and to worldly powers are more problematic than he allows.

group isn't seen as directly connected (either through reading or other direct encounters) with the intellectual's work, but is to benefit nonetheless. At the very least, then, the intellectual's discourse is double-voiced, addressed to a peer audience which has similar concerns (and, very often, similar commitments) and to a more amorphous and often unlocatable public.

It is allegiance to an -ism, I take it, that provides both the significance and the agonies of the intellectual's efforts. At the current time, when the intellectual and her peers almost invariably hold university posts, work addressed solely to a peer audience would be entirely academic. By way of the -ism, the intellectual holds onto the aspiration of doing work that extends beyond the academy—and is ever aware of what few resources she has for successfully breaking the barriers between the academy and other social locales. For the pure academic, a discipline serves as the substitute for an -ism; most intellectuals, however, strive to subordinate academic work and academic disciplines to the service of their "larger" commitments. The intellectual struggles to make the university serve his or her program, not *vice versa*. In short, the intellectual's self-understanding usually includes an ironic relationship to academic usages and disciplines, a determination to keep things in perspective, to balance continuously "petty" academic concerns against the needs of the "wider" world. She dreams of being a "public intellectual," of reaching that chimera "the general reading public."

Intellectuals, then, are vulnerable in their allegiance to a program and in their relationship to the university. Every time they make careerist moves or win academic accolades, they can be accused of hypocrisy, of striving strenuously for honors they claim to despise. More pointedly, intellectuals always harbor delusions of grandeur. They could not do their work if they didn't project consequences wildly out of proportion to what they actually accomplish. Modest and reasonable ambitions would render the work pointless. A certain willful blindness is required.

Called upon to explain how their work will effect the transformations it calls for, the intellectual has only comically feeble Rube Goldberg scenarios to offer, a voodoo politics replete with its own versions of "trickle down" influence. There are no palliatives for these vulnerabilities, certainly no *a priori* strategies that insure scaling the academic walls and making an impact elsewhere, anywhere but here. The intellectual is constantly bedeviled, no matter what she is doing, by the thought that she has undertaken the wrong work at the wrong time and in the wrong place. There is no salvation from double-voicedness and double consciousness ("optimism of the will, pessimism of the intellect" in Gramsci's words), just as there is no escape from mixed motives, from writing manifestos with footnotes, from wanting to impress academic peers as we strive to better the world.

All I would ask is that we intellectuals avoid fetishizing and cherishing our dilemmas as we also eschew pronouncements of exceptional virtue, purity, and integrity. We are in the mix like everyone else, although in ways made distinctive by our specific institutional (academic) location. What I am trying to combat is the narcissism of intellectuals, their tendency to find their own ambiguous position in modern societies endlessly fascinating. "This is not about us," I want to scream. Yes, our own perplexities are analogous in ways to those bemusing other social agents. And our institutional positionings do locate us within networks of power relevant to, and sometimes significant impediments to, the larger concerns we strive to address. So we do need to articulate where we stand and what we are trying to accomplish. But to probe continually the difficulties of doing our work is, precisely, not to do the work. And I do not believe that the next (or any) probing will make the work less difficult.

I want to think about the intellectual as ideologue, as a public advocate for a particular set of arguments. *The American Heritage Dictionary* defines "ideology" as "the body of ideas reflecting the social needs and aspirations of an individual, group, or culture." Let's try, for a little while at least, to keep the definition neutral with respect to whether the ideology is true or false, conscious or unconscious, autonomously generated or reflective of some more fundamental set of interests/motives. The intellectual is someone who publicly articulates an ideology—and who makes no bones about his or her support of that ideology, support that often involves refutation of rival ideologies. Intellectual work involves struggling to articulate a position in such a way that I satisfy myself and think I might persuade others. Satisfying myself, from which much of the pleasure and interest of the work comes, entails feeling that I have figured something out, have increased my understanding, have gotten things "right" in both expression and accuracy, and have been faithful to my primary commitments. But achievement of these satisfactions depends on the pointedness my thoughts only assume when they are articulated for a public airing. Whether I persuade a single reader or not, the intended publication of my views is necessary to their being stated in a form capable of satisfying even my private investments in the work. That articulation is mine, but it is a part of me that can only come into existence in the public sphere of published writing.

Like many intellectuals today, I name my primary allegiance "democracy" and want my work to further the cause of democracy. Specifically, that aspiration entails elucidation of the term itself; advocating extension of democratic practices into social sites (the classroom, the workplace) where they are often deemed inappropriate; and considering how commitments to equality and autonomy can be negotiated in concrete situations involving differences and interdependencies (of various kinds) as well as complex, differentiated social structures/institutions.

There is good reason to believe that historically and logically the intellectual is a product of democracy—democracy's child—and feels for democracy all the ambivalent love that ties a child to its parents. To thrive, intellectuals require freedom of speech and of the press; a public sphere in which ideas are aired and debated; tolerance of, even a taste for, multiple, dissenting opinions; the possibility of gaining authority, of winning the assent of others to one's views, through speech alone; and a market that allows cultural capital to be translated into money (a salary). Democracy, especially in its demotion of all traditional established authorities, provides many of these conditions. The autonomy granted to individuals to choose their own course in life leads to an explosion of public speech both because individuals strive to justify their choices to others and because others strive to influence the individual's choices. Of course, the Protestant Reformation with its elevation of individual conscience, the invention of the printing press, and the rise of capitalism all contribute to the appearance of intellectuals in the eighteenth-century, and historians debate how these factors are implicated in the slow (and still incomplete) movement toward democracy in the West from 1750 to the present. My point here is that the conditions that accompany democracy also enable the existence of intellectuals, even those intellectuals who rail against those conditions. The persistent downside of democracy for intellectuals of every persuasion is that their views rarely become authoritative. Economic necessity and interests, nationalism, religion, careerism, consumerism, and mass culture all seem to influence individual and societal choices more than intellectual articulations.

I am a left democrat. I am tempted, of course, to say that it is impossible to be a right democrat, because the right, with its concerns about order and excellence, believes in hierarchy. One fundamental difference between the left and the right is that leftists think that the most vulnerable in any society are those with the least economic resources and/or those who have historically been denied the full rights, benefits, and duties of citizenship. Such leftist concerns are best captured by the term "justice" as in economic or social justice. It is not self-evident that justice and democracy go hand-in-hand, although much leftist writing on the subject nowadays appears to take the connection for granted. More democracy must lead to more justice, these writers assume. The link here is through the concept of equality. More democracy would require more political equality than we currently have, and more political equality would lead to more economic equality, which would be more just. All of these equivalences must be questioned. One task of the leftist intellectual committed to democracy is, as I see it, to think through the tangle of leftist allegiances and the possible synergies as well as the possible incompatibilities among them. Nothing guarantees that all these desired goods must function harmoniously together in some Hegelian fashion. It is much more likely that the opposite is true, that compromises and trade-offs will be required all the way down the line.

Still, we can recognize the right's opposing tendency to think that the exceptional person (whether the writer of genius or the highly successful entrepreneur) is prone to the envy of the mediocre and/or the efforts of the state to rein him in, to regulate his activities. The right worries about the tyranny of the majority and about leveling effects that hamper excellence (either its achievement and/or its receiving due appreciation/reward).

Because the right used the word "democracy" during the Cold War to name its moral superiority to its adversaries behind the Iron Curtain, the left lost the word for a time.[2] But a post-communist left (freed from a continually embarrassing alliance with the Soviet Union and China, an alliance stemming from the fact that their enemies on the international scene were our enemies on the domestic front) is now beginning to relearn the resources that democracy affords a critique of the current form taken by the soi-disant "Western democracies."

At issue then is what relation intellectual activity can have to the project of left democracy. I think there is a form/content split here that is rarely acknowledged. Intellectuals of any stripe make substantive arguments, or content-laden interventions, on specific occasions. Such attempts at direct persuasion are published in various venues—and there is absolutely no way to measure what, if any, impact is made. When the goal is as diffuse as influencing people (as opposed to an appeal directly made to a

2. Compare with Todorov's comment: "In the last quarter century, intellectuals seem to have reconciled with democracy, and when they criticize it, their criticism is founded on the ideal of democracy itself" (1997, 122).

specific few), we cannot know if the goal has been reached, or to what extent. This is as true for those relying on the indirect discourses of the arts as for those who employ a more direct, argumentative discourse. The ability of intellectual activity to generate further intellectual activity is palpable, but its ability to generate political conviction that results in political action is not.

Oddly enough, upon reflection most people with an allegiance to democracy wouldn't have it any other way. Despite postmodern critiques of autonomy and humanist individualism, most academics (even those who are, roughly speaking, postmodernist in their views) think it a fundamental violation of their students to tell them what to think and to require the regurgitation of that content on exams. A basic ethos of autonomy prevails. We can give people the materials for forming an opinion; we can expose them to strongly argued opinions on a topic; we can even express strongly our own opinion (although only carefully when our audience is subordinate to us in a hierarchical institution); but we cannot require others to adopt any particular opinion. Allowing individuals autonomy of belief seems fundamental to the very democracy we would cherish and nurture. Critiques of autonomy, then, usually aim at demonstrating that we shouldn't take the existence of autonomy for granted, that we are continually influenced by forces that are invisible to us; only rarely do such critiques argue that autonomy in opinion formation is not desirable. It is precisely the gap between enunciation of my belief (in whatever guise) and its adoption by my audience that I strive mightily to overcome and am relieved never to bridge successfully. The only thing worse than a world in which no one agreed with me about anything would be a world in which everyone agreed with me about everything.

This substantive failure to persuade all my readers is paired with a formal success. The view of democracy which I am trying to enunciate highlights not only the individual determination of belief, but also transformative interaction. As we strive for a substantive agreement we never fully achieve, we encounter others in a dialogic give-and-take that is potentially transformative. Admittedly, I am stressing (to the neglect of other elements for the moment) the rhetorical component of democracy. A democratic polity is marked by the continual effort of various citizens to persuade their fellow citizens of something. The relative failure of such efforts at persuasion makes democracy look like cacophony. My suggestion is that the cacophony is substantive, while the form of the polity is constituted by these dialogic interactions. The democratic polity is not dependent on agreement; it depends on our continuing to talk to one another. A political community, a functioning public sphere, rests not on whom I agree with but on whom I keep talking to. Intellectual activity is precisely this continuing to talk. By the enunciation of my views, I contribute to the ongoing talk that is a crucial part of a democratic society.

To decenter the notion of substantive agreement in this way suggests that a polity does not possess one public sphere, but any number of smaller spheres, some of which overlap at times, some of which function entirely independently of each other.[3] Any citizen is inevitably indifferent to or ignorant of the existence of many of these spheres. Each person's activities only encompass a small fraction of actual and possible public interactions. Tolerance of multiple interactions allows for a rich public life that can reflect, stimulate, and serve the varied interests of the population. But it would be naïve to think that these mini-spheres do not (in at least some cases) strive to attain significance through claims to generality. Different communities will engage the polity as a whole through the insistence that their choices model the best way to live. Such communities often stress unanimity among members in these confrontations with outsiders. To model a way of life for others is a major form public speech takes in a democracy. Such modeling often calls forth hostility between groups and tighter internal policing within groups. The co-existence of mini-spheres that represent fundamentally different choices of how to live depends on respecting autonomy of choice for both insiders and outsiders of any particular sphere. The polity, in other words, is still recognizably one polity when crossings from one sphere to another are frequent and do not carry dire consequences. Nothing guarantees that such conditions will prevail. Secession and civil war are ever-present possibilities, as current events make all too clear. Yet employing strong measures to achieve political unity appears futile at best, counter-productive at worst. Thus, draconian attempts to sever groups from their inherited language rarely achieve the desired assimilation. Tolerance of religious, ethnic, linguistic, and other differences may degenerate into dissolution of the polity, but tolerance's track record in preserving polities is better than its opposite.

3. My thoughts here are strongly influenced by Nancy Fraser (1992), who is interested in locating "subaltern counter-publics" and thus stressing the possibilities for public action (and interaction) which exist for those who are not at the top levels of existing hierarchies. I want to register here my uneasiness with the metaphor of "spheres" and my embarrassment with the clunkiness of "mini-spheres." I am not committed to the image, only to the argument that there are many sites of interaction and that they are neither centralized nor coordinated.

Another way to phrase my form/content split for democracy, then, is to say that toleration of substantive disagreement actually increases the chances for lasting formal cohesion. Think of it like a marriage. All is well so long as arguments do not entail the possibility of divorce. And there is some reason to believe that arguments can be more vehement precisely when the marriage does not seem at stake. But, of course, divorce is always possible. Some substantive disagreements may just prove intolerable. Form and content cannot be totally insulated from one another and there is no recipe for insuring that one will not infect the other. But democratic polities appear dependent on an attempted disentanglement of the two.

This account of public disagreements is so simple that it ought to make us suspicious. For one thing, it smacks of the kind of "invisible hand" reasoning found in Adam Smith. Each of us just has to keep earnestly trying to persuade others and, behind our backs, our individual efforts will create the democratic public sphere we desire. How convenient! Intellectuals just need to do what they are paid to do—read books, then talk (with students) and write (for other intellectuals) about them—and they will be doing democracy's work.

What is missing if we simply celebrate existing public interactions (in the university or elsewhere) is any account of the risks, the costs, of dialogic involvement. For a start, the term democracy names a whole range of desires in the contemporary world; not all of those desires are inevitably compatible with the vision of enriching, transformative public interaction that I am gracing with the word democracy.. Furthermore, democracy (even in the most broad uses of the term) hardly names the only desirable things in the world—and it is not compatible with many of those other desirable things. Finally, even functioning public spheres that do operate in the way I am celebrating are almost always parochial, that is, shielded from the power and resource inequities that afflict all but the smallest and most exclusive communities in the contemporary world. It is a pretty safe guess that anyone who has been privileged enough to experience democratic interaction is privileged in more obvious material ways as well.

The specific name for the privilege enjoyed by academic intellectuals is professionalization. George Bernard Shaw says somewhere that every profession is a conspiracy against the lay person, a statement true enough to bear repeating. Professions manage to create public spaces of dialogic interaction by gaining almost exclusive right to govern who can join the dialogue and who cannot. Long apprenticeships, peer review, and self-policing are just three of the mechanisms a profession uses to control membership. Such control is only won when the profession manages to gain consent (most crucially from the government, but also from professionals in other defined fields and from the more general public that is the profession's clientele) to its right by virtue of expertise and competence to monopolize a certain service or labor. The profession's monopoly covers both its exclusive right to provide the service (or do the work) *and* its exclusive right to determine (through credentials or licenses) which individuals belong. Professions do not possess absolute autonomy; to varying degrees they do remain answerable to their clients and the government and the market. But they certainly enjoy a semi-autonomy that gives professionals a freedom in their work afforded no other laborers in today's economy.

That freedom, especially for academics, is intimately connected with job security. Tenure is a dinosaur. The kind of job security it provides has been lost by just about every other significant body of workers in contemporary society. When fighting to defend tenure, academics should recognize how privileged they are to still have that security. The argument for tenure should not rest on the uniqueness of what we do, but on the reasons that job security should be a basic right for all workers. The assault on tenure (especially the greatly expanded use of part-time or adjunct teachers where tenurable or tenured faculty previously were employed, but also various schemes to do away with tenure for full-time faculty) is, in some cases, connected to efforts to combat professional monopolies. But such assaults are much more frequently connected with the contemporary economy's maximizing of productivity through use of a modified piece-work system. Workers are only hired for the specific times and the specific tasks for which they are needed, and are not carried by the employer during slack times. This practice is not only cost-efficient and conducive to organizational "flexibility" in relation to demand and other economic fluctuations; it also drives down wages, since non-secure and temporary workers are much less able to hold out for decent pay. Contemporary assaults on tenure have very little to do with academic freedom, but are connected to new economic practices that have greatly lessened job security across the board in the United States (and elsewhere).

These questions of professional privilege and labor market practices are relevant to the left intellectual for reasons beyond the appalling job market for new PhDs in English and related fields. (I do not mean to suggest that job market questions are unimportant; quite the contrary. But the specific factors involved in our particular job market would require an analysis that would supplement the more general discussion of academic professionalism being offered here.) In regards to the professions, the leftist academic is in a bad spot, somewhat similar to his position vis-à-vis the welfare state. Welfare does not work very well, if only because dignity and self-worth are so completely connected to having a job in our society. (Just ask any of our unemployed PhDs how they are doing, before you sneer at the work ethic or bemoan the complicity with capitalism of reform programs that focus on employment.) To defend welfare against its current abolishers is to argue for a flawed program against outright cruelty. Similarly, remembering Shaw, a full-scale justification of professionalism seems (to me at least) hardly the democratic route. But we should recognize that, at the present time, the work conditions afforded academic professionals much more closely approximate the kinds of work conditions that would accord with various democratic ideals. In other words, it does not seem particularly productive to destroy professional privilege because it is enjoyed by so few, when many features of that professional privilege enact the very practices we want to see more fully available and practiced in our society.

In arguing that intellectual work in the contemporary academy models the democratic interactions I want my work to promote, I do not want to be hopelessly Pollyannish about academics' work. The academy is also riven by inequities that are systematically produced and maintained. But I do believe that we have more autonomy than afforded most workers; that we participate in an agonistic give-and-take that both constitutes a public space of interaction and serves to influence the on-going formation of opinion by individual participants; and that such transformative interactions are a crucial component of the kind of democracy I hope my work can foster and that I wish to inhabit. I certainly believe that I have the best job going and that my ability to have this job depends on the labor of many people who do not get to work in conditions even remotely comparable to mine. Therefore, it seems incumbent upon me to think about how the freedom and security accorded me can stand as an example of the way work can be, taking into account that the translation of freedom and security into other spheres of activity would result in very different institutional arrangements. (I am not aiming for a world transformed into so many campuses. God forbid.) In sum, I think our professional privileges are justified partly by the work we do, but much more importantly by the example we provide of a democratic existence.

To think of myself as an example is to think of myself as a teacher. Many intellectuals today, and almost all literary intellectuals, teach. If I influence my students, it is to a certain extent directly due to the things I say and the material I give them to read. But I also influence them indirectly by my way of being in the world of the classroom. To me the classroom is to be, as much as possible, a utopian space. It is to be that democratic public space of transformative interaction I want to occupy. Certainly, as both a student and a teacher, the classroom has been a magical space for me, a place where I am often most fully the person I would wish to be. That self—and, indeed, the social space it inhabits—is created through the give-and-take with the others in the room. The classroom probably acquires its magic in large part through its immunities. Nothing momentous, nothing on which life hinges, is at stake in most class meetings. But before we hasten to declare such immunity inevitably trivializing, let's think about security one last time. We can be open to change, to influence, to letting ourselves follow a thought or a whim where it goes, precisely when nothing absolutely vital is at stake. And nothing absolutely vital is at stake when employment or other forms of security are not in play. All of which is a way of arguing that a democratic public sphere looks like it is dependent on a minimal material security that cannot be jeopardized by one's activities in that sphere. If this is true, it is no longer surprising that classrooms and other academic sites are our society's closest approximations to such a democratic public sphere. Where else are the stakes so carefully separated from economic consequences?[4]

I appear committed to a very aestheticist notion of the classroom here, finding in its separation from the "real world" its ability to foster some freedom of imaginative play, , some fairly uncensored dialogic interactions. I might even go further and think of the models enacted in the classroom as "hypothetical," thus linking up to theories of art that stress its fictional, creative, or "as if" qualities. Northrop Frye (1957) offers a good example of this view for my purposes because he connects it to the "task" of the intellectual. "Literature," Frye writes, "in its descriptive content is a body of hypothetical verbal structures. The latter stand between the verbal structures that describe or arrange actual events, or histories, and those that describe or arrange actual ideas or represent physical objects, like the verbal structures of philosophy and science" (125). Freed from any constraining tie to

4. Thanks to Susan Bickford and Donald Hall for sharpening my thoughts here by strongly disagreeing with my notion that nothing vital is at stake in the classroom.

reality, poetry produces "the universal creative word which is all words" (125). Frye then links poetry to "the autonomy of culture, which may be provisionally defined as the total body of imaginative hypotheses in a society and its tradition. To defend the autonomy of culture in this sense seems to me the social task of the 'intellectual' in the modern world" (127).

On the level of practice, I fully admit that the classroom is hardly untainted by power inequities or by the economic pressures that send many students to college against their own inclinations. It is not autonomous in the way that Frye wishes to claim for the all-creating poetic word. But I do want (foolishly?) to believe that the practical concerns of jobs and credentials are not utterly determining in the final instance. (I tackle these issues more fully in chapters 2 and 4.)

On the level of theory, I am even more conflicted. To what extent am I committed to the positive effects of a semi-autonomy for the aesthetic or for the university? I don't know—and think that my indecision is pretty common among literary intellectuals of my generation and my (leftist) stripe. My unwillingness to simply abandon a hankering for separate spaces is grounded on my intuition that democratic interaction is crippled where basic necessities, like enough money to live, are at stake in all interactions. Without some job and income security, democracy is a nonstarter. But I think we lose much—way too much—if we make existing economic inequalities trump in every instance. Such radical reductionism recalls the original use of the term PC to refer to a joyless inability to affirm pleasure in the here and now. We need to lighten up somewhere, somehow, if only to model the world we hope will exist as a more generally available reality in the future. Yet we have to retain our awareness in 2001 that it's a privilege to have fun, to conduct thought experiments. That awareness and the freedom to slough off burdens sometimes have to find a way to co-exist productively. It's the brave aestheticist who goes the totally hedonistic route: all that matters is my pleasure and I will pursue it full bore. Almost all aestheticist versions of art's unique and separate identity offer a redeeming social value in the end. For Frye, nothing less than human freedom is at stake. I can't follow Frye, partly because of the grandiloquence of his claims for art, partly because the argument seems circular: define art as unconstrained by ties to either reality or any other human endeavor/need and then find that art is where humans experience freedom and so art must be preserved in order to preserve freedom. I prefer Kenneth Burke's (1973) view that literature lets us try out hypothetical attitudes and provides "equipment for living," an account that still needs to defend art's relative autonomy. Burke's view puts art into a more direct give-and-take with the world we inhabit everyday, but still insists on a crucial gap between art and that world.

We can approach this problem of the classroom as an experimental space from another angle: to what extent is the intellectual (or anyone else for that matter) required to "live" his ideas. "Intellectual" was a term of abuse when first used: it designated someone who was disconnected from daily realities and thus believed all sorts of foolish nonsense.[5] For Lionel Trilling (1955), "the characteristic error of the middle-class intellectual of modern times is his tendency to abstractness and absoluteness, his reluctance to connect idea with fact (163)"[6] This fear of abstraction, of an abiding unreality, finds its most extreme form in the assertion (which usually, but not always, comes from the right) that it was intellectuals, those with ideas and programs for the world's improvement, who did the most harm in the horribly bloody twentieth century.[7] According to Trilling, this suspicion led Orwell "to respect the old bourgeois virtues because they were stupid—that is, because they resisted the power of abstract ideas. . . . [H]e began to fear that the commitment to abstract ideas could be far more maleficent than the commitment to the gross materiality of property had ever been. The very stupidity of things has something human about it, something even liberating" (166). Floating free of material realities, the classroom can seem a dangerous space—and precisely the kind of space that intellectuals would create and cherish. All kinds of unreal ideas can be entertained and elaborated there.

5. Williams (1976) writes: "Until mC20 [middle twentieth-century] unfavourable uses of *intellectuals, intellectualism,* and *intelligentsia* were dominant in English, and it is clear that such uses persist. But *intellectuals,* at least, is now often used neutrally, and even at times favourably, to describe people who do certain kinds of *intellectual* work and especially the most general kinds" (142).

6. It is worth quoting more of the passage: "[T]he prototypical act of the modern intellectual is his abstracting himself from the life of the family. It is an act that has something about it of ritual thaumaturgy—at the beginning of our intellectual careers we are like nothing so much as those young members of Indian tribes who have a vision or a dream which gives them power on condition that they withdraw from the ordinary life of the tribe. By intellectuality we are freed from the thralldom to the familial commonplace, from the materiality and concreteness by which it exists, the hardness of cash and the hardness of getting it, the inelegance and intractability of family things" (163). Richard Rorty (1998) offers a similar critique of intellectuals' neglect of the material realities of most citizen's lives. Rorty, however, focuses on the abstraction from one's country (or nation), not family.

7. Paul Johnson (1988) provides a particularly expansive version of the right-wing scorn of intellectuals.

Such worries reflexively call forth solemn statements about the "responsibility" of intellectuals. I am tempted to see the residual tension between abstraction and commitment as constitutive in the case of intellectuals. The constant swing from celebrating the intellectual's critical distance and autonomy to exhibiting the intellectual's commitment to the welfare of others and the noblest ideals replays the same uneasiness that leads apologists for art's autonomy to find, at the very end, an explanation of that autonomy's social utility. I have stressed so far the intellectual's allegiance to an –ism, but Ralf Dahrendorf (1969) insists that "all intellectuals have the duty to doubt everything that is obvious, to make relative all authority, to ask all those questions that no one else dares to ask" (51).

Both Edward Said's career and his various pronouncements on intellectuals seem particularly locked into this recurrent *pas de deux* between commitment (responsibility) and skepticism. Said continually celebrates "exile," the "distance" of the intellectual from the prevailing idols of the tribe. "[I]t has often been the intellectual . . . who has stood for values, ideas, and activities that transcend and deliberately interfere with the collective weight imposed by the nation-state and the national culture" (1983, 10). For Said, the urge to belong must be fought at every step; it is the worst temptation to which an intellectual could succumb. Yet the very specter of irresponsibility that such non-belonging evokes requires repeated statements of fidelity to the most exalted ideals. Thus he must connect being an outsider with a privileged relation to salutary virtues. "The strength of the Canaanite, that is the exile position, is that being defeated and 'outside,' you can perhaps more easily feel compassion, more easily call injustice injustice, more easily speak directly and plainly of all oppression, and with less difficulty try to understand (rather than mystify or occlude) history and equality" (1988, 178).[8] Said takes here the polar opposite view from Orwell's. Abstraction from the blinding loyalties and compromised affiliations of daily life enable a less mystified vision of the grand ideals that daily realities continually travesty. I think neither position supportable. Nothing about the positioning of the intellectual in relation to others or social institutions proves a very reliable

8. Said (1996) makes essentially the same point, in even stronger and more sweeping terms. "Because the exile sees things both in terms of what has been left behind and what is actual here and now, there is a double perspective that never sees things in isolation . . . . Intellectually this means that an idea or experience is always counter-posed with another, therefore making them both appear in a sometimes new and unpredictable light: from that juxtaposition one gets a better, perhaps even more universal idea of how to think, say, about a human rights issue in one situation by comparison to another" (60).

predictor of his or her virtue or the trustworthiness of opinions. The romance of the exiled truth-teller is intimately connected to the romance of art's autonomy—with its claim of superiority to sullied bourgeois commercial culture. The varied views enunciated by high modernist aestheticists from Flaubert to T. S. Eliot should make it clear that "distance" can produce many opinions, some of which would hardly qualify as virtuous.

I do not mean to discredit Said, a figure I admire greatly. I just want to separate the merit of his positions from any causal link to a condition of exile. And I want to suggest that the absoluteness of his ban on belonging necessitates the absoluteness of his claims to virtue. "The attempt to hold to a universal and single standard as a theme plays an important role in my account of the intellectual," he writes. "Universality means taking a risk in order to go beyond the easy certainties provided us by our backgrounds, language, nationality, which so often shield us from the reality of others. It also means looking for and trying to uphold a single standard for human behavior when it comes to such matters as foreign and social policy" (1996, xiii–xiv). If he gave a little bit on the one front, he'd be less defensive and less self-righteous on the other. Thus it is not just coincidence that his call for an "oppositional" criticism, one that finds "its identity in its difference from other cultural activities," is immediately followed by the solemn assertion that "criticism must think of itself as life-enhancing and constitutively opposed to every form of tyranny, domination, and abuse" (1983, 29). Said misses the emptiness of this pronouncement—who would claim criticism should support tyranny?—because his extreme valorization of alienation from the culture the critic inhabits has put him on the defensive about the question of responsibility. I think John Michael (2000) gets it right when he says that "the transcendent, however contingent and conflicted it may be, remains a necessary part of, and grounding for, any politics and any political position at all. Universality and transcendence are not philosophical absolutes; they are contested terms in political disputes" (11). Neither exile nor an appeal to universal standards of justice or truth secures the intellectual's virtue. The intellectual is in the mix just like every one else; he or she does not occupy some privileged place called either exile or the dwelling of the universal, even as appeals to specific locations and to universal values are made—and will inevitably be made.

This brings me to the difficult topic of irony, a topic that recurs again and again in this book as the site of an anxiety I can never put to rest. Said writes: "'Ironic' is not a bad word to use along with 'oppositional' (1983, 29). Abstraction can be tied easily to persistent irony, and then such irony can be taken as a positive or a negative attribute. Understood in a Kierkegaardian way, irony signals dissociation, the intellectual's less than full endorsement of the words he or she speaks. Irony may result from the "as if" quality of the intellectual's pronouncements, divorced from the "worldly powers" that actually translate words into policies and deeds. Or irony can reflect a self-conscious recognition that the intellectual deals in universals that are, in fact, contestable. Richard Rorty (1989) has championed this kind of irony as one of two essential virtues (along with a hatred of cruelty) for a liberal polity. Said tackles it as a question of "how to keep a space in the mind open for doubt and for the part of an alert, skeptical irony (preferably also self-irony)" (1996, 120).

Such irony can function in the classroom in several ways. At times, the teacher will enunciate positions he or she does not endorse in order to inform students or to challenge them. Irony can also be a playful way to signal dissent from prevailing orthodoxies. Or the teacher may be ironic as a way of undercutting the authority of the institution within which both teachers and students are located. Crucial to my meditations here is the extent to which irony is enabled by the semi-autonomy, the tenuous irreality, of the classroom—and the extent to which irony is a major feature of intellectual work. Intellectual activity may require some play-acting, some trying on of ideas for size.

I have no firm conclusions to offer here. I am as uneasy with celebrations of irony as I am with claims for art's autonomy. What I am groping toward is some sense that irony and commitment are entangled in complicated ways in the intellectual, just as I sense that the classroom is both complicitous with and yet somehow distinct from an economic order that extracts work from one and all. Intellectuals, like artists, get to play, but are continually defensive about that play and therefore offer accounts of the important "work" that their play does. Yet they can also do that play in ways that signal a delight in getting away with something, in escaping the general drudgery. Similarly, the work done in a classroom can be exhilarating at times and seem to shadow forth a different way of existing with others. But the nagging worry is the issue of loyalty. Intellectuals can appear less consistently or reliably loyal than non-intellectuals because intellectuals occupy hypothetical spaces, are abstracted from concrete entanglements like home and country, and are adept at ironic dissociation. Since such abstraction can appear irresponsible and an outrageous privilege, intellectuals often compensate with pronouncements of allegiance (like mine to democracy).

Perhaps this analogy between the abstraction of art and the abstraction of the intellectuals explains the literary sensibility common to so many of the major intellectuals of the past two hundred years. Certainly Theodor Adorno (1978) thought so; he continually associates the "negativity" of art, its irreality in relation to empirical fact, with a similar "non-identity" (127) of thought with the material that it engages. There are nonliterary intellectuals to be sure. But a surprising number of intellectuals have a literary background before they begin to attend to other issues. From the Romantics on, literary intellectuals who have attempted to influence the polity have generally done so through the lens of "culture." As Raymond Williams (1983) has taught us to recognize, "culture" proves such a productive term because it accords (in one of its senses) a privilege to the arts, while (in another of its senses) its generality of reference enables discussion of the social whole. Finally, "culture" is both immanent to a society, but not directly identical to its political institutions or social relations. It provides a standpoint from which to criticize.

The cultural critic, almost always drawn from literary ranks, calls society to account. The evolution of this figure (which is the evolution of one prominent type of intellectual) can be tracked from Swift, Samuel Johnson, and Coleridge through to Carlyle, Ruskin, Arnold and beyond. This path is marked by uneven development, but the direct appeal to religion wanes (even as the prophetic style is retained), steadily replaced by standards drawn from national heritage and cultural traditions. This English line differs significantly from its nineteenth-century counterparts in France, Germany, and the United States. I cannot trace all those differences here. What I want to highlight is a certain style of intellectual activity in which the intellectual stands above or apart from the specific conflicts of day-to-day politics, but exhorts the polity as a whole to act in accordance with more general norms that the intellectual claims it is neglecting. Very often, the exact connection of allegiance to those norms and specification of the issues of the day is left unstated, either because the connection is deemed too obvious to spell out or because attention to the specific might blunt the focus on wider principles. There is a tendency to want to stay above the fray, along with a desire to be conciliatory, to articulate common allegiances that will bring contending parties together.

These intellectuals proceed by interpreting particular actions (political or social), artifacts (plays, novels, paintings, buildings), and institutions in light of the unspoken ideals and motives they reveal. (Carlyle's "Signs of the Times" and Ruskin's "The Nature of Gothic" are exemplary in this regard.) They then contrast these implicit ideals and motives with a set of explicit norms the society is called to honor. The aim is directly moral; the mode of discourse is analysis (or interpretation) followed by exhortation.

I believe that contemporary cultural politics is a direct descendant of this nineteenth-century practice (an argument made more fully in chapter 5). What justifies, then, my title's reference to "the rise of cultural politics"? I am playing a bit fast and loose here. Just as I link the emergence of intellectuals to democratization from 1750 on, so I believe that cultural politics can be recognized as a distinctive mode (not the sole mode, but a new and distinct one) of these emergent intellectuals. If we need to name founding figures, Diderot, Coleridge, and Schiller will serve.

But I also believe there has been a decided up-swing in cultural politics over the past forty years (roughly since 1965), an up-swing that explains the complaints of Richard Rorty (1998), Todd Gitlin (1997), and others against the current dominance of this one mode of intellectual activity. Cultural politics in its contemporary manifestation attempts to intervene in cultural processes of representation, categorization, reflexive understanding, ideological production, and creation of/adherence to values in such a way as to change current hierarchies, divisions of labor, prejudices, and (in general) the conscious and unconscious taken-for-granteds of a society that consistently mistreats various social groups. Because late nineteenth-century figures (most notably Marx, Nietzsche, and Freud) stress the unconscious elements of behavior so strongly, the diagnostic moment in cultural politics has expanded greatly since the days of Coleridge. Criticism or "critique" is required to uncover the bases of actions and social behaviors. But unconsciousness also makes it difficult to see to whom the cultural criticism is addressed or where the site of transformation is located.

Elizabeth Grosz's account of attitudes toward the body is emblematic; she calls for the transformation of the attitudes, but also places such transformation beyond the capacity of individuals. "The investments and significances attributed to the different regions of the body image . . . are never self-determined, voluntarily adopted, or easily shaken off, for they are to a large extent a function of socially shared significances. No matter how much the individual may wish or will it, male and female genitals have a particular meaning in Western patriarchal cultures that the individual alone—or even in groups—is unable to transform insofar as these meanings have been so deeply etched into and lived as part of the body image. The reinscription of sexual morphology in terms more conducive to women's corporeal and sexual autonomy . . . would entail a thoroughgoing transformation of the social meanings of sexual difference, and consequently of different body images for the two sexes" (1994, 82). We have here an appeal to a norm ("corporeal and sexual autonomy") and an analysis of society's failure to honor the norm; what we don't have is an account of how to effect the desired transformation. Hence interpretation of society's "deeply etched" practices occupies the lion's share of the critic's attention.

Why the contemporary rise of cultural politics? And is that rise to be lamented? A number of historical transitions are involved. Note that the nineteenth-century practitioners of cultural politics often wrote poetry or novels as well. True, Carlyle and Ruskin are already specialists in criticism. But the absolute divide between critic and "creative writers" dates from the 1920s at the earliest and, arguably, from the 1950s. Standard anthologies of literary criticism include very few non-creative writers prior to 1920 and very few creative writers after that date. The proliferation of criticism by specialists is partly caused by professionalization. But here we need to distinguish cultural criticism from other kinds—including philology, literary history, and close reading. In Germany and America especially, professionalization from 1870 to 1960 primarily worked to banish cultural criticism from the academy. The cultural critic—examples are T. S. Eliot, Edmund Wilson, and H. L. Mencken—was still seen as a "man of letters" and was not an academic. Professional criticism was scientific and apolitical, aimed at the production of knowledge, not the expression of opinion. Professionalism set its face against the cherished "amateurism" of the English tradition. The only real exceptions to the studied apoliticism of American academic literary criticism prior to 1965 were the humanists led by Irving Babbitt in the 1920s and the New York intellectuals of the 1940s and 50s. Things were rather different in England, where F. R. Leavis moved the cultural criticism of the literary tradition that Williams would later celebrate into the university in the 1930s. It took the upheavals of the 1960s, with the attack on notions of "objectivity" and the desire to make university work more "relevant" to social developments, to bring cultural criticism dramatically to the fore in American literary studies. Institutional coincidences, such as the arrival of French theory and the increased pressure to publish, then contributed to the forms that cultural criticism took (as I discuss in chapter 3).

It is commonly alleged that cultural politics, especially as practiced by "tenured radicals" is a reaction (despairing, cynical, resigned, or appropriate, depending on the commentator) to the "failures" of the sixties' more direct political goals. This argument relies on accepting that cultural politics is an indirect, torturously circuitous, route to social transformation as contrasted to direct political action. At the crudest level, this divide between direct and indirect action replays the sixties debate between changing the system through the available political means of voting, civil disobedience, and staged protests versus changing people's heads, a debate famously enacted by Herbert Marcuse and Norman O. Brown. Again, once the unconscious is invoked, changing people's heads becomes awfully complex, and an ongoing frustration with cultural politics is its continual vagueness about the means to be adopted and the pathway toward (or even the markers of) success. Another complaint is that adherents of cultural politics often claim direct and more traditional political action is ineffective at best and counter-productive at worst, which can make such adherents appear callous toward current suffering while dreaming of transformations to come.

But the political experiences of the sixties offer three more compelling ways to characterize the appeal of cultural politics. The first takes into account the student movement's inability to make a connection with a wider popular political base. In Richard Rorty's *Achieving Our Country* (1998), he calls for the revival of a "reformist left" (as opposed to the "cultural left") that works for "piecemeal reform within the framework of a market economy" (105). By making common cause with those whom that economy slights, the left "can forge a winning majority in national elections" (101). The left, in denigrating America as racist and capitalism as unredeemable evil, has alienated its potential allies among the less prosperous. "The public, sensibly, has no interest in getting rid of capitalism until it is offered details about the alternatives" (104) and the cultural left has no such details to offer. The problem with Rorty's prescription is that it ignores everything that has happened in American politics since 1964 (or since 1948, when Dixiecrat Strom Thurmond carried four Southern states in response to Truman's integration of the military).[9] Cultural divides—over race, religion, and lifestyles (for want of a better term)—have consistently trumped economic solidarity in the United States. The dif-

9. For a wonderful and extremely instructive history of the fortunes of the Democratic Party specifically and the left more generally in American electoral politics of the twentieth century, see George Packer (2000).

ference between intellectuals in the 1930s (including Rorty's hero, John Dewey, who had no truck with Roosevelt's Democratic Party) and intellectuals, coming out of the 1960s, is that there existed in the earlier period something like a mass movement of the Democrats to the left, a workers' movement with which many intellectuals were proud to align themselves. The sad story of how the Communist Party as well as racism and rabid anti-Communism combined to destroy that movement cannot detain us here. But the point is that the 1960s left was in the position of trying to create a mass movement from scratch; there wasn't one that it could connect to. And the traditional formulas of the "old Left" about how to create such a movement simply did not work. That no one has figured out what will work is one of the rationales for cultural politics—as exemplified in the work of Stuart Hall (1988).

Hall's project, framed in response to Margaret Thatcher's victories in Britain (which mirror Nixon's and Reagan's victories in America), emphasizes the rhetorical work required to forge social "blocs" in a political landscape in which allegiances and votes are in flux, depend on multiple factors, and often coalesce around powerful symbols. His claim that the right's success resulted in large part from the work of its ideologues makes cultural politics central, albeit not all-determining, in electoral politics. It is not enough to have a platform (who pays any attention to it?). There must be ways to articulate, to represent, to symbolize the party's goals that capture people's imaginations and create a sense of participation in the program and fellow-feeling with other adherents to it. Cultural politics, in other words, begins to look like, if not a necessary preliminary to successful direct political action, at least a crucial concomitant step. It is about casting around for the new formulas that will help create the popular base for a leftist politics. The intellectuals who practice leftist cultural politics are "out of touch" with the people; but, *pace* Rorty, there is not any group already existing out there, ready-made, for them to get into touch with. That group—or coalition of groups—needs to be made, to be forged, through the performatives of cultural politics. (I take up this notion of the performative in chapters 5 and 6.)

Second, I think cultural politics must be seen as a response to the civil rights movement, surely the most successful work of direct political action on the American left during the twentieth century. Its very success in ending legal segregation revealed the limits of political transformation unaccompanied by cultural changes. Of course, the movement also produced tremendous cultural changes. But its great promise has been thwarted by the intractable persistence of racism throughout the culture. Legal and institutional reform meets its limits when it runs up against deep-rooted cultural habits. A different kind of work seems called on to address these cultural obstacles to full racial equality and harmony. Again, it is not that cultural politics has solved this problem. But its efforts are driven by it. Direct political action, even where successful, is not enough.

Finally, there is the rise of the "new social movements." Coming out of the civil rights movement and the sixties, feminism, gay liberation groups, environmental groups and the like introduced a new set of political concerns, ones that, like racism, pointed toward economic inequities suffered by oppressed groups, but also highlighted noneconomic indignities and harms as well. When recognition and respect from one's fellow citizens is at stake along with more tangible goods and protection from more physical harms, direct political action cannot achieve all that is desired. Since what is left of the left as a popular mass movement resides in these "new social movements," it is no surprise that intellectuals have taken up their themes. More accurately—in all these feminist, racial, ethnic, gay and environmental groups—there has been an "organic" (to use Gramsci's metaphor) connection between the intellectual and these movements that is unprecedented in American politics and belies the claims about the decline of "public intellectuals." The interaction between academic work (including highly theoretical work) and the new social movements is obvious, from appeals to "difference," "identity," and "hybridity," to empirical work that documents the "feminization of poverty" and historical work that recovers the lost voices of various groups. Finally, we can see with the rise of the new social movements and the alliances of many intellectuals with them, the shift on the left from some version of socialism to some version of democracy as the most often stated political ideal.

In sum, there are good political and intellectual reasons for the rise of cultural politics over the past forty years. There were also identifiable institutional causes as well. Intellectuals, especially literary intellectuals, have been moving into the academy since the 1850s (I consider this history and some of its consequences in chapters 3 and 4). The American university in particular grew tremendously during the 1960s to accommodate the baby-boomers (many of whom were hiding out from the draft), among whom were some students who represented groups previously absent from American campuses: women especially, but also some non-whites and/or from poorer families. The new students often wanted different things from education than their predecessors. And the new professors hired to teach these students, working under new conditions as the boom sixties yielded to the economic hard times of the seventies, challenged prevailing intellectual paradigms, using "theory" in all its guises to disrupt settled assumptions.

A primary assumption, of course, had been that academic work was apolitical. The new style no doubt went overboard in declaring that *everything* was political. But I fully intend in this book to honor the aspirations that motivate that insistence. Intellectual work, it seems to me, is pretty pointless, a schoolboy exercise, if it does not aspire to address the polity. In this book, I explore the difficulties of acting on that aspiration in light of the various conflicting and incompatible pressures on intellectuals who are, for better and worse, placed by this society in academies. And I also explore the affinity of intellectuals, particularly literary intellectuals, for cultural politics, attempting to balance an appreciation for the questions and dilemmas that elicit that strategy with my persistent skepticism about the airs it assumes and the claims about its effects.

Sometimes I think my stance just reflects a sense that the cultural left is too subtle by half. Injustice and the indignities that attend it are just not that complex. In particular, I find any reliance on intricate accounts of psychological mechanisms implausible—and politically troubling when attached to claims about unconscious processes. Democratic interaction depends, I believe, on a faith that people generally know what they are about and that rhetorical efforts to shift their self-understandings can be direct. After all, the intellectual will resent attempts at indirect manipulation and will believe herself able to see through this. Why not accord the same ability to our audiences? Once we have to rely on strategies that by-pass conscious beliefs in order to transform those beliefs' unconscious underpinnings, we have entered a realm of discourse that renders autonomy, consent, and equality problematic. That this trinity cannot be assumed is an important truth; that the attempt to achieve it is to be abandoned is far less evident. Doubtless, the cultural left (of which I am indubitably a member) shares my political commitment to democracy, which is why I feel it important to indicate the undemocratic flavor of some work in cultural politics.

The most usual complaint, of course, is that this kind of intellectual work hardly addresses the polity because it is written in a vocabulary only accessible to academic initiates. I address this issue, which is more complicated than is often admitted, in chapter 3. For now, suffice it to say that such work is produced under multiple pressures, ones that its style reflects.

I want to conclude by considering how my own literary education may have contributed to the commitment to democracy I have articulated here. I take it as both necessary to my own democratic desires and as pedagogically required that I be as swayed by what happens in the classroom as I hope my students to be. That transformations occur over a semester is more important than any particular transformation or conversion occur. To take this open-ended position would be to get entirely off the hook of illegitimately influencing students' beliefs. And, to a certain extent, teaching literary texts goes well with such openness. What many English teachers want to convey to students about novels and poems is how they complicate the direct, simple, univocal notion of a message sent from speaker to hearer. The literary text works on its audience on a variety of levels and its messages cannot be easily unified or summarized. We want to make our students better able to become entangled in the miasma of emotions, thoughts, arguments, analogies, and associations that a literary work evokes.

But it would be ingenuous to claim that any and all transformations are equally prized. I do not see how the teacher committed to democracy can avoid a commitment to the cherishing of plurality. Liberality is a crucial virtue in democratic societies that include substantive disagreements.[10] The literary is prized for its expansiveness of vision. Does this mean that everyone who reads literature—and especially those who do it for a life's work—gains an expanded vision? Surely not. We don't want to smugly claim some moral superiority for ourselves. But the embarrassment of self-righteousness aside, don't we really believe, somewhere deep down, that a literary education is a moral education? I am uneasy with this thought, and don't fully know where or how to push it. But I think it leads toward the question of sensibility, toward considering whether democracy—insofar as it entails cherishing and enjoying the agonistic and potentially transformative interaction with those who think, feel, and believe differently from me—calls for a certain temperament. If a democratic

10. Amy Gutmann and Dennis Thompson (1996) explore, as their subtitle puts it, "why moral conflicts cannot be avoided in politics and what should be done about it." Their solution rests on "reciprocity," on the rational granting of liberty of opinion to others that I grant to myself. My comments about sensibility here and my appeal to liberality, which entails generosity of spirit rather than a calculation of what is fair, indicate my desire to beef up tolerance rather differently than Gutmann and Thompson do.

education includes the effort to nourish such a sensibility, do we believe that time spent reading, discussing, and responding to literature has a role to play in that nourishing? The presence of some such belief may explain why literature classes in both high schools and colleges are more likely to rely primarily on discussion than classes in other subjects.

My final thought will return us from the classroom to the written work of literary intellectuals. The combination of a commitment to democracy and to a vision of the literary as non-univocal has, I have suggested, made it likely that literary intellectuals will have a taste for and want to champion a taste for plurality, for difference. The blatant, obsessive, and by now boring display of that taste forms the stereotypical image of the politically correct literary academic of our day. I am as bored by politics worn on the sleeve and public stagings of virtue as the next guy. But I don't want to throw out the baby with the bathwater (at least not now and in this place. I think I have been guilty of such rash flingings in the past.) It is not surprising that literary intellectuals will, for the most part, practice cultural politics, by which I mean practices meant to intervene in the basic categories of thought and the basic repertoire of represen- tations circulating in the society. Such practitioners tend to fluctuate wildly between proclaiming that the only true and effective political ac- tion must take place in the cultural realm *and* bemoaning their endless marginality and ineffectiveness because real politics happens elsewhere (in the halls of power, or on the streets, or any place but the arts, the classroom, and the mind). In similar fashion, educators tend to either wildly overstate the impact of education or to proclaim the complete impotence of schools in face of the all-determining influence of families, peers, and the wider culture.

Cultural politics, like education, is one kind of work; it is neither triv- ial nor omnipotent. I happen to think it is more likely to have an impact when its real limitations are acknowledged from the start, when the other sites of political action/intervention are also named, if not (at this mo- ment) engaged. My point is that I do not think literary intellectuals should back down from their interest in how literary texts (in different instances) foreclose or enhance plurality in specific social realms. Similarly, images of and attempts to make the classroom a utopian space must continually be tested against categorical and representational exclusions. An obses- sion with difference is salutary and is likely to remain so for any foresee- able future. But preaching to the converted and the ritualistic displays of right belief are less useful, whereas to believe that an engagement with prevalent forms of thought and representation is the be-all and end-all of democratic activism is to leave far too much of the field to those indifferent or hostile to democracy. My ideal intellectual, then, may only work in the field of cultural politics, but he or she keeps open the lines of communication with what is happening in other fields, and always reminds himself or herself (and his or her readers and students) that important work is being done elsewhere, and that a richly plural democratic polity calls for these varieties of work. Finally, the intellectual's work would be pitched in such a way that not only does it allow dialogic interaction with those in one's own specific field, but also provides an opening for those in other fields who want to maintain a sense of that field. In our written work as in our classrooms, we can strive to model the very forms of interaction that we want to claim are vitally important and desirable in a democracy.

I

CLIMBING THE WALLS:
THE INTELLECTUAL
AS ACADEMIC

The next four chapters ponder the consequences of the almost universal location of contemporary American intellectuals on college campuses. Chapters 1 and 2 are frankly autobiographical and take up questions of "the profession" and teaching respectively. Institutional forms and dilemmas dominate my attention as I contemplate what I am doing, where, and with whom. The next two chapters are more wide-ranging. Chapter 3 offers a series of observations about the changed landscape in which intellectuals work now, as compared to thirty years ago. It surveys from above, if you will, the transformations that the previous two chapters view at ground level. The final chapter of this part considers the impact that intellectuals positioned within the academy wish to have as contrasted to the influence I think they can realistically expect to wield. The question of cultural authority taken up in chapter 4 calls forth the first intimations of the pluralism that is further developed throughout part 2.

CHAPTER 1

At the 1986 MLA Convention

I wrote this essay in January 1987. I was up for tenure that term and knew that I would get it. Six years earlier I had lost my first tenure-track job when the department had been folded in the recession during Reagan's first year in office. I had done adjunct teaching and worked for a university press for two years before finding my second tenure track job. Now tenure was imminent and I was feeling both survivor's guilt (of the twenty-five students who started graduate school with me at SUNY-Buffalo in 1974, thirteen received their PhDs, but only seven ever got tenure)—and something else that was harder to define. I was afraid of losing my irony, losing my perspective, of becoming one with this role of professor. In my first job, the department had responded to being under siege by sending around a "monthly activities report" that had "books published" as the first category. Churning out articles that were more often rejected than accepted for publication while also writing short stories that were always rejected, I swore that I would never write a word of literary criticism after (if) I got tenure. But now I knew that wasn't true. My apprenticeship had done its job; I now thought in the form and would continue to work in it. Like the dyer's hand, my nature was subdued. Or so I feared. This essay was to prove to myself that I could write in another, less academic, form—and to make a public pledge that I would maintain my integrity within the academic forms.

I didn't have the right connections at the time to get this essay into any hands that could print it while it was still timely. After one journal had turned it down, the next two said it was too late to be of use to them. Friends who read the essay liked it—and one regularly had his graduate students read it over the next four years. I include it in this book, despite the fact that I no longer agree with everything I wrote, because I still think it captures an ambivalence felt by many graduate students and junior professors, an ambivalence that is seldom publicly expressed. I have resisted the temptation to revise it, just as I will resist the temptation to explain here what in the essay I still believe, what I would now renounce.

This essay had a companion piece on the job market. But I can now locate neither a hard copy nor a computer file. In the jobs essay, I used some of the statistics now found in chapter 2 and some of the arguments. But the two main points of the jobs essays were that the MLA's reported statistics about the employment of PhDs were wildly inaccurate and that we were fast headed toward a two-tiered profession in which tenured professors teach majors while graduate students and adjuncts teach freshman and sophomore English. This is no longer news. And it should not have been news in 1987, but it was. The job market for English PhDs had been bad since the early 70s, but the mandarins of the MLA refused to see what was happening. When I was teaching composition for $900 a section in 1979 (the year after receiving my PhD), I ran into a Berkeley professor I knew in the supermarket. He asked me what I was doing. I told him I was teaching part-time at the University of San Francisco and still trying to find a tenure-track job. What kind of job would I like, he inquired. I was taken aback, but replied that a small liberal arts college would be my ideal. "Well," he said, "have you called Reed College? It's a fine school."

The MLA's job statistics at that time came from the reports of degree-granting departments. That is, each department told the MLA that it had awarded this many PhDs in the past year, and that this number of those PhDs had gotten teaching jobs. My anecdote suggests how much the professors in those departments knew about their students' experiences on the job market. The result was that the MLA statistics showed less than 20 percent of recent PhDs in non-tenure-track positions at a time when government statistics showed that over 40 percent of college instruction was being done by part-timers.

The story of my essay's fate sealed my sense of the MLA's willed blindness. I submitted it to Profession, which bounced it to the ADE Bulletin. I then negotiated with the editor of the Bulletin over the next 30 months. He finally accepted that my critique of the MLA's statistics was valid. (And the MLA subsequently changed the way it gathered its data and became somewhat more sensitive to the plight of PhDs.) But he would only print the first half of the essay. He would not accept the "over-passionate" sociological analyses of its second half, in which I had said that the differentiation occurring in our profession simply mirrored the similar differentiation occurring throughout the workplace as companies relied increasingly on part-time labor while executive salaries sky-rocketed. I wish I hadn't lost the essay because I remember it as passionate, cogent, and steely. (So maybe I should be glad I can't find it; it could hardly be better than my memory paints it.) In any case, I refused to let them publish a truncated version and withdrew the essay. I then submitted it to College English, which turned it down with the comment that they refrained from picking fights with the MLA. I threw it in a drawer after that—and, four moves later, maybe it's in some box up in my attic.

This story has one final grace note. Two years later my wife did a workshop with the editor of the ADE Bulletin. She told him of her connection to me. To which he replied: "Yes, it was a well-written essay. I was sorry that it didn't work out; I hated to deprive him of a publication."

THE SETTING

The Marriott Marquis was notorious before a girder had been slapped into place. They tore down the Helen Hays Theater to build this convention hotel. "Marquis," I take it, is a stab at the kind of cutesy pun that earns coffeehouses names like "Just Desserts" or "The Edible Complex." The new hotel contains a theater, with the accompanying marquee to announce the current offering. Even more spectacularly, the facade also sports a four-story high advertisement for Kodak, which currently features an idyllic snowscape of an unreality only achievable by Kodachrome, or by invocations of nature at the corner of Broadway and 45th Street. This Cyclops eye so completely deforms the building that you hope it is a joke, a joyous postmodern celebration of Times Square's vulgarity, an example of what we have learned from Las Vegas.

If we take the Marriott Marquis as paradigmatic, however, postmodernism provides neither joy nor light nor peace nor help for pain. The building's designers can only manage to play out the aristocratic implications of its name by offering the standard symbols of extravagance found in various Hyatt Regencies from coast to coast: glass elevators lined with chrome and glitter lights, the by-now inevitable emptied out center around which the rooms are arranged, and large plants meant to convey a lush tropical feel. The Marriott utterly lacks the various Hyatts' conviction of their grandeur. If the Marriott winked at us, asking us to revel in these banal and glitzy codes of sumptousness, we could bring our Venturi and Jencks to bear and talk about how the hotel successfully speaks both to the cognoscenti and to those who swallow it whole. And, if such were the case, the primary theatrical metaphor would work perfectly. The hotel would resemble any number of contemporary Broadway plays, especially the musicals, which thrive on a pumped-up energy that they also fully admit is contrived and unreal.

The Marriott doesn't even manage to pump up sufficient energy to start playing off its primary signals. One problem lies in the cheapness of the basic materials used: poured concrete, the deadly white wood that cheap bookcases are made from, thin carpeting of the type that surrounds swimming pools, and some unidentifiable fake leather substance to cover the benches (not chairs) of the lobby. All the glitter appears only a way to hide the building's essential mediocrity, and the glitter's lack of conviction suggests the designers' awareness that no true extravagance resides here. The hotel speaks most clearly about a corporation's desire to do something as cheaply as possible and of the architects' disgust with the limitations within which they had to work, and with the signals of aristocratic opulence they were required to supply. The true metaphor here is not that of the theater but of that other denizen of Times Square: the prostitute. The Marriott displays all the prostitute's self-hatred even as she or he works to keep up the appearances on which livelihood is dependent. The cynical disgust, both with the world and with oneself, that is indicated by the shoddy materials and workmanship suggests that no honorable work nor ennobling public identity is possible in this postmodern world.

Yet the rooms in this hotel are very nice. They are also recognizably postmodern, but are utterly relieved of the burdens of public appearance. Both Victorian clutter and harsh modernist asceticism have been banished. The furniture is modest, comfortable, and usually a bit on the small side, deliberately dwarfed. The colors are those muted greys, roses, and slate blues that have become postmodernism's hallmark, while the arrangement works to open large, usable spaces. These are rooms clearly designed with the idea always firmly in mind of the people who will use them. These warm, witty, and comfortable rooms affirm the coteries (beyond family, the individual firm or business or university) formed by professionals, who gather at conventions for good uplifting talk about the things that concern and interest them. These rooms bespeak a faith in certain kinds of conversation, certain kinds of quasi-public friendship, that somehow escape the deformities of both the larger public world and of overheated local intimacies. The dream lingers of a work world in which we can honorably pursue what interests us and strikes us as serious, as does the hope that we can find an appropriate community of peers with whom to work.

What is the overall message the Marriott sends us? The arts (and maybe this is true of many other pursuits) have been talking to themselves for quite some time now. And the conversation is damned good. Within the small worlds of the various disciplines, exciting, serious, and innovative work gets done. Only when the connection with the general culture is made does a certain embarrassment, even self-disgust, surface. The translation of the work into the marketplace inevitably changes it, if only because the fundamental motives for the work shift from intrinsic to extrinsic ones. "Trade mars everything it touches," claims Thoreau. Postmodernism is particularly vulnerable to self disgust because it has abandoned the heroic modernist adversarial stance toward commercial culture. Defeated by capitalism's endurance and the seeming decline of all political alternatives (both left and right) into barbarisms that make the West look benign, the postmodernist accepts the market's right to rule. Yet he can't quite lose his resentment at what the market makes him do and hangs on to an attenuated dream of an alternative space, a humanly scaled room of his own.

THE PLAYERS

Into the Marriott—and several surrounding hotels—last December came some twelve thousand college professors and graduate students to listen to over two thousand papers on various topics, to interview candidates for teaching jobs (or to be interviewed), to browse through book exhibits set up by over two hundred publishers, to gossip, to drink, to make contacts, and to see old friends. The gathering constitutes a large, but hardly representative, sampling of America's English and modern language teachers. Not representative because the MLA, for one thing, is largely a young woman's and man's convention, attracting those who are on the make. Prominent older scholars do make an appearance, and so do the older teachers shut up in hotel rooms most of the day, interviewing job candidates. But most of the papers are given by twenty-five- to forty-five-year-olds who are still in the process of constructing careers, either striving for tenure at their own universities or looking to move up the ladder by finding a job at a more prestigious school. Tenured professors who are content with their lot in life or, at least, have resigned themselves to their place in the profession's pecking order have little incentive to attend. Half the talk (easily) centers on summarizing your career's progress since the last time you met your fellow conversationalist; such talk can only embarrass if you have not published much recently or had job offers from other schools. Much better to stay home with the family for Christmas than to submit yourself to the humiliating comparison of your success with those of people you went to graduate school with. You'll go to the convention when that book you've been working on for eight years is finally finished and has been accepted by a publisher. Local success, prestige, and security must suffice the eighty percent of professors who regularly skip the convention.

I am an MLA junkie. Each year I tell myself I will not go the next year, that I will free myself from this bondage to my career and my ambitions; but I am helpless in front of this disease and have attended eleven of the last twelve conventions and the last ten in a row. I went to my first convention (in Chicago) despite having gotten no interviews and sat in a college friend's apartment in Hyde Park weeping in front of my best friend from graduate school (who had two interviews) and his wife, feeling utterly excluded from the world I wanted to join. I skipped the next year because I still had no interviews and was no longer naive enough to think that attending the convention could do me any good. I had no need to repeat the previous year's suffering; I was busy trying to imagine other careers for myself that I could stomach. The next year—after teaching composition part-time—I had three interviews and landed a job in a Humanities Department at a large state university. It was a fine job, except for one drawback. The department was under siege from various David Stockman types in the administration. So I simply continued to look for other jobs—albeit unsuccessfully—and attended each successive convention because I always had an interview or two. I began to acquire a group of MLA friends, people I never saw, talked to, or corresponded with except at or in relation to the convention. After a few years, I began to realize that I was actually enjoying myself, even if three quarters of what I witnessed outraged me. Love's dominance in this love-hate relationship became absolutely clear when I finally got myself a second job (after another year and a half of semi-employment following my first department's dismemberment) and continued to attend the convention despite any pressing need. The disease I am trying to anatomize is my own.

For years I attended the convention and never went to a single paper, too busy socializing and sightseeing in this year's city, too full of contempt for (and, doubtless envy of) these earnest and ambitious professors of literature whose closed shop I could not join. Three or four years ago I began to listen to various talks, at first those of friends or of people it was professionally prudent of me to meet, then (in the past two years) to papers on topics that interested me or by critics whose work I had reason to admire or to be curious about. I had crossed some crucial boundary; I was now one of those earnest and ambitious professors myself and went to the convention, in large part, to place my ear to the ground and make sure I was fully aware of what it is we are doing this year. As anyone even remotely connected to literary criticism knows, the past ten years have presented us with a dizzying number of movements, positions, and theories, many of which have the shelf life of a harlequin romance. The convention, presumably, allows you to recognize what's past, what's current, and what's to come.

Reflecting on my selection criterion now, I recognize the true test is whether I have read anything by the speakers featured in a given session. I almost invariably go to hear people that I have heard good things about but have never gotten around to reading. They get twenty minutes to convince me that I need to correct that omission. Similarly, the topics that draw me in are those in which I have some interest but have not investigated much. Far more than anyone could read is published, so the convention becomes a way of sampling what one is missing.

From my feelings of relief when someone is not impressive, I realize that I am mostly hunting for justification for my failure to read various work my conscience tells me I should. And I am always glad to find that some school of critics—the Freudians or the Marxists or the phenomenologists—are still asking the same questions and giving the same answers as when I last checked in on them, a year ago or three years ago. I can safely ignore them for a while longer.

Maybe I am not representative, but I cannot believe that. Certainly my ambitions, my interests, and my sensitivity to shifts in the wind mirror those of my MLA friends when we exchange notes at the evenings' cocktail parties. We go from session to session like drunks in search of that fabled drink that will quench all thirst. We are searching for a theme and searching in vain. One problem is that we don't know if our thirst is intellectual or professional. Are we searching for the truth, for that method or system that will allow us to take texts—and, tomorrow, the world—firmly in hand? Or are we just seeking out that niche that will give us a defined and recognizable stall within the professional stable? After all, even lacking a theme, we all continue to do our professional work, teaching those classes, writing those essays. We window shop, with the notion that maybe it's about time that we choose which window to display ourselves in, and, like most people without faith, we alternately envy and ridicule the easy life faith seems to afford. We would also like the window we choose—if choose we eventually must—to be the one that consistently attracts the largest crowds, while also being a place where we can stand without shame and with conviction.

This last desire has become institutionalized in the profession's current tender concern for political correctness. Forget post-structuralism, deconstruction, neo-Marxism, and reader response theory. The message of the 1986 convention was that you can do any one of these or a thousand other things and the activity alone will not determine if you are in or out. The only demand currently is that you self-consciously locate your critical practice within the political/cultural context and that you demonstrate how your political stance is holier than anyone else's. In this regard, feminism provides the paradigm for current literary studies in the way that Derrida did five years ago, Levi-Strauss ten years ago, Northrop Frye twenty years ago, and New Criticism thirty years ago. Every paradigm dictates what can and cannot be said. What characterizes the movement from New Criticism and Frye to Derrida and feminism is a shift from a ban on talking about matters extrinsic to the text to a contempt for intrinsic matters as trivial and uninteresting. The location of the art work within the larger framework of cultural discourse (or "practices" if you follow Foucault instead of Derrida) dominates critical talk today.

But—and I guess this development is inevitable once these cultural issues are raised—critics are not content to merely talk about these things. (Or, to put it better, they highly resent the suggestion that their talk is mere talk.) To examine literature in relation to cultural discourse is to consider the tension between literature's way of talking and the culture's way of talking. Invariably, literary critics value the times when and places where literature talks differently. Which is not to say that literature's difference from the general culture is secure. Much recent criticism reveals with great subtlety, using the hermeneutics of suspicion, various texts' implication in the general (or "dominant") culture, even texts that make seemingly radical gestures. But such criticism always works from the implicit viewpoint that union with prevailing cultural norms is to be avoided. What we are willing to champion and celebrate in texts focuses on the ways we believe they authentically challenge cultural orthodoxies; we look to literature and to criticism to offer new perspectives and new vocabularies within an all-too-familiar cultural scene.

This valorization of novelty is, itself, nothing new. But now we justify our praise of novelty for political reasons, not aesthetic (novelty's pleasure), perceptual (theories of "defamiliarization" or of attention), or epistemological (poetic insights poised against logical or scientific truths) ones. Our outlook assumes the dominant cultural discourse is oppressive and that the development of new idioms is liberating. The critic acts as the political correctness police person, indicating where a text reproduces the prevailing cultural norms of thought, organization, language, and power, while every once and a while bestowing a smile on texts that disrupt such norms. Other critical positions are subjected to the same test. The primary defense of any critical theory today takes place on the grounds of its political consequences, not in terms of its logical consistency, its faithfulness to the text, or to its reproduction of a certain audience's experience of the text.

I must pause here momentarily to mention that it is indicative of the current situation that to describe that situation in the way I am doing is to be labeled a conservative. Yet I feel myself a full participant in the current obsessions. I am not advocating a return to earlier justifications for criticism, only trying to describe our current biases toward a particular set of justifications, to the exclusion of other possible sets. My sensitivity to the apparent conservatism of my own position clearly marks the extent to which I also wish to be politically correct. I am sympathetic to the claim that ordinary language embodies social and political arrangements that are repressive and that we value literature and criticism to the extent that it imagines alternatives. What I wish to distance myself from, however, is the way in which current criticism has itself developed into a repetitive orthodoxy; surely I am not alone in experiencing its implicit censorship of certain positions that violate its fundamental axioms. But my desire to distance myself makes me yet another instance of a critic who tries to become holier than the rest by occupying the position of most radical difference, while the charge of conservatism would stem from the insistence that my attempted differences only smuggle back in the despicable cultural contents that the radical critics want to escape. I cannot resolve this issue, but can only note that I am fully implicated (emotionally as well as by virtue of my argument) in this continual effort to occupy the political high ground. I am, to repeat, anatomizing my own disease.

Current criticism's political content can only be assured if we believe in a "talking cure." The primary axiom of the whole edifice must be that the way we talk makes a difference—and that the more different the talk, the bigger the difference. As someone rather attracted both to vulgar Marxism and to populism, the idealism (strictly speaking) and elitism of this position bothers me, especially since so many of its adherents apparently believe that they are Marxists. (I am not playing St. Karl games here, just asking for truth in labeling.) To put the point vulgarly, the history of twentieth-century Western capitalism attests to its thus far unthreatened capacity to endure all and any kinds of deviant talk without its essential economic and political structures being in the least altered. Furthermore, to bring in the populist element, highly deviant talk (as in modernist poetry and various experimental novels) has proved itself of interest only to very small audiences of specialists. At the very least, I think the neo-Marxists need to formulate some theory of how deviant talk works its political miracles if we are to accept their attachment to it. Marx's materialism and his reliance on the numerical superiority of the proletariat are intuitively convincing (at least to me); I am fully ready to admit that our century has proved such intuitions completely unfounded. But idealist and elitist positions have not even begun to address the fact that they need a theory of change. The most profound representatives of this position, Adorno and Marcuse, gave us pessimistic theories of capitalism's all-but-invincible power in lieu of some model of change.

I phrased this objection rather differently when I asked a friend over breakfast in the Marriott's coffee shop why anyone who truly wanted to promote a feminist or Marxist revolution would ever make the decision to become an English professor. Surely there are more direct avenues to such an end. I suspect that most of us got into the literature business first and acquired our political commitments later; now we were rather sloppily trying to make the two fit.

My friend replied that we all had modernist adolescences; modernism habitually portrayed itself as revolutionary and liberating, and to some extent it was those things. After all, he and I had read Joyce, Lawrence, Eliot, and Conrad as teen-agers and had used them, like we used rock music, to escape the suburbs in which we grew up. Only now, with postmodernism's assault on such modernist certainties, did the gap between art and radical politics yawn so wide, and the current theatrics were a response to the horrible suspicion that art was as completely co-opted as everything else. Besides, he added, look around. What other alternatives are there for the political radical; where else can you imagine a tolerable life for yourself? We may have—we certainly seem to have—uneasy consciences about our political correctness, but what other sphere offers a better opportunity for integrity? I had to admit that he had described my bind perfectly—and with a kindness that put my impatient hostilities to shame.

The convention highlights one further blindness inherent in current critical practices. Speaker after speaker stages his or her call for distancing ourselves from the dominant culture within a setting that calls attention to the persistent desire to belong. (I know that my years on the outside looking in have made me hypersensitive to needs for recognition and membership, but surely the convention exists precisely for people to whom such needs are central.) I am not claiming that we are hypocrites, just the contrary. If we are guilty of any sin, it is an overly non-ironic earnestness. Our lack of irony blinds us to the gap between our talk and the influence it might have on the world, and our lack of irony makes us inattentive to the unconscious needs communicated by our talk. For students of the word and its duplicities, we are remarkably deaf to the resonances of our own conversations among ourselves. These manifestos of high liberationist discourse, based on a celebration of difference, are presented in a forum where our audience listens in hopes of keeping up with the latest developments, and where extra-literary discussion is all about who gets what job and joins this department or that university. We may experience this urge for success, recognition, and membership within a professional elite as oppressive insofar as it deforms our personal lives, governs our waking and sleeping thoughts, and dictates how we spend most of our time, even our supposed leisure time. But we testify to that urge by attending the convention, and to deny the power of our aspirations to positions of cultural prestige and influence is to alienate ourselves from a vitally important constituent element of the arts we study, the profession to which we belong, and the audiences of students to whom we present works of arts and our beliefs about them.

A dialectic of identity and difference comes much closer to describing the arts and their relation to culture than some model of absolute negation. Which is not just to say that any work necessarily contains some elements of the culture that it struggles against, but also to say that every work contains the desire to be a recognized and even celebrated part of the culture even as it struggles to differentiate itself from some aspects of the culture. (An added complication, of course, stems from the culture's valuation, since the romantic period, of difference, so that you gain acclaim and membership by being distinctive.) Such a dialectic more richly describes our own practice as critics also. And, I would insist, only within this dialectic does it make any sense at all to believe in talk's effectiveness. The irony of simultaneous urges for separation and belonging might seem a formula for impotence, but in fact provides the necessary elements of engagement, commitment, connection, and evaluation that a purified, absolute separation can never provide.

Let me repeat that we are not hypocrites. But we are also not entitled to beliefs in our own purity, and I do not think we are well served by dreams of purity. We do not have unmixed motives. Our allegiances are both to intrinsic and extrinsic values. We believe and delight in the intricacies of our work; we could not do it so well and so abundantly otherwise. We also cherish and desire the external rewards offered for good work: recognition, salary raises, better jobs. This second fact often embarrasses us and, like the Marriott, we often display that shame at the points where we connect to the wider world. Meanwhile, overcompensating perhaps, we take the high road in talk among ourselves, preaching a critical practice exemplary in its purity. Such preaching has become more vociferous as the external temptations become stronger. (We all know that the job market for "big names' and "rising stars" has heated up, with sweet deals offered that begin to resemble—on our own small scale—free agency in baseball.) Our sense of ourselves—and our critical practices—could benefit from a more flexible sense of and overt acknowledgement of our mixed motives.

OUR IDENTITY

I entered the room a little late for the session on criticism and social change. The first speaker, a woman, was already telling the audience of about sixty that "structuration" was the sociologists' term for what she wanted to describe, but that she would avoid using such hideous jargon. She was here to talk about her experiences working for change as a woman within the profession. Examples of prejudice were multiple: a department decides to hire a Renaissance scholar instead of someone in women's studies; two new assistant professors are hired, the man with degree in hand, the woman ABD, so that he has a head start toward tenure; a woman is given onerous committee assignments, thus hurting her chances to publish. The speaker began to explain university bureaucracies and methods of negotiating with them in the vocabulary supplied by personnel management theories and organizational psychology. Her examples of prejudice had made me uneasy; now her valorization of the stuff MBAs are made on and her use of their horrendous neologisms positively offended me.

Academic audiences are hardly demonstrative. I was feeling puzzled, wondering if I was showing my curmudgeonly colors by finding her so distasteful. She was perfectly politically correct, a warrior for women's rights, and there was every reason to believe that an audience gathered to hear her, a well-known critic of criticism and a prominent neo-Marxist, talk about criticism's ability to effect social change would be sympathetic to her goals and achievements. In any case, I sensed something was wrong, but thought it might just be me.

The speaker obviously felt totally in control as she rounded the final corner and gave personal testimony about her career in "implementing change." A veteran of the sixties and of the New Left, she had refused to be discouraged by the movement's collapse, going off instead to take a workshop that taught her how to become a "change agent." At the first university where she was employed, she had put together a coalition of women who presented the administration with one hundred demands, some of them substantial, some of them fluff that was meant to be bargained away in negotiations. They got the administration to accede to all the demands they had agreed among themselves were essential. Subsequently, she had acted as a liaison between women scholars and various publishers as part of a concerted effort to overcome the long-standing tendency of women academics to publish less than their male counterparts. In conclusion, as someone "who had implemented much change in universities," she could tell us that change is possible if you work for it.

She thanked us and sat down. In silence. The moderator of the panel stood up and introduced the second speaker.

My first thought was, so much for our commitment to political change. Here is an audience that fondly believes itself radical, but when presented with an energetic and effective political activist, turns up its nose. The speaker might very well have interpreted our failure to applaud as further proof that aggressive women offend in this society. If so, she misread her audience. Our response was more fundamental, less a matter of prejudice against her activities or her manner, than a complete failure to recognize her relationship to what we do and believe. Some class snobbery was present. She was dressed and talked like an in-house corporate lawyer—someone with a law degree from Notre Dame or a state university; but she was on our side. More crucial was our intellectual snobbery. Her analysis of the issues was crude and simple-minded. Worse, perhaps, was her straightforward pursuit of economic goods within the world we inhabit; academic radicals prefer their politics more refined: abstract visions of justice for all in some utterly transformed social order. Her attachment to the pseudo-academic disciplines developed for bureaucrats by the nation's business schools violated our allegiance to our more humane, subtle, complex, and elegant literary vocabulary. Finally, the tin ear that allowed her to use the word "change" in such inappropriate ways and a phrase like "change agent" without the slightest tinge of irony proclaimed that she was not one of us.

I am not defending our failure to applaud. I have never witnessed or even heard of a similar occurrence at an academic conference. It was certainly not premeditated and had all the feel of a cowardly group action; no one started the applause and thus it never began. Then, as the second speaker started in, we realized what had happened. We applauded the second speaker rather timidly, retrospectively embarrassed, and perhaps awed, by our discourtesy to the first speaker.

I do believe, however, that our impoliteness did dramatically reveal what we English and modern language professors, despite our various internecine quarrels, share in common. For better or for worse, this is who we are: a group that values complex political analyses over crude, if effective, political action. We are skeptics who find it difficult to credit direct accusations of sexual discrimination, even while developing theoretical models that designate a whole culture and all its linguistic usages "patriarchal"; habitual pessimists who have become so comfortable with our ritual denunciations of contemporary culture and all its works that any intimations of possible change offends us; political activists who fully intend to leave the dirty political work to others; and, most crucially, writers and teachers whose most firm allegiance is to language. You can say anything at the MLA convention and receive applause so long as you do not abuse our highly developed sense of linguistic decorum. To know, practice, and defend the intricate, unwritten, rules of that decorum makes you a full-fledged member of our group.

OVERSTIMULATION

My nephew, two weeks before his fourth birthday, announced to his parents that he wanted a party on the momentous occasion. His parents tried to head him off, but to no avail. They knew all too well what would happen. Matthew would spend two days in overwrought suspense, run around manically for the first hour or so of the party, and then throw some kind of tantrum, which might last anywhere from two hours to three days. His circuits get overloaded and he blows a fuse.

I cannot help but compare myself to Matthew when I'm at the MLA. I talk non-stop, hurriedly and mostly incoherently, from dawn until the early hours of the morning. I leave parties at one-thirty in the morning, knowing that I am exhausted, only to lie awake in bed until seven replaying all the day's conversations in my head. I am overwhelmed with anxiety about my career and my work. I feel alternately incredibly energized—ready to work at a pace previously unknown to me and with a new found strength and clarity—and utterly paralyzed, overwhelmed by how much good work is being done and the futility of thinking that any particular work could make a difference or find its way to attention and acclaim.

Does the tantrum come? In some form or another. Some one thing slips out of control in the frenzied rush, and the self's hold on the world feels threatened. One year the brief case with all my money and my hotel reservation got left in a cab. This year I was stuck with nine other people in an elevator made for seven; we spent a relatively calm hour—starting a little after midnight—together, but it was a supreme effort. More usually, I can displace the shakes onto travel anxiety. There is nothing worse than the plane ride home from the MLA convention. Unless it is sitting at my desk the next free morning and realizing that normalcy has returned; I can't remember all those things that seemed so clear to me four days ago; I have the same talents, the same work capacities, and the same stubborn slow mind that I had before immersing myself in the profession's cyclotron.

RESOLVE

The convention ends just in time for new year's resolutions. I make the contradictory promises to myself that I will publish more essays this year, in more prestigious journals, and that I will start extricating myself from the obsessional and endless preoccupation with my career. Surely some kind of separate peace is possible, some more sane relation to my work, some way to accomplish it at a pace that does not banish pleasure (in the work itself or in outside activities) nor remain tyrannically dictated by anxiety. I resolve not to attend the 1987 convention as a symbol of my embracing sanity. I do not believe myself for a moment.

I also decide to write more honestly. I think I know what I mean by saying this. Over the past eight years I have published a number of essays and a book, and I have carefully kept most people I know personally from reading any of it. I have worked in deep isolation, writing my pieces, sending them off to editors I don't know and who don't know me, and seeing them appear in various journals, never read by anyone. Their primary existence is as lines on my vita. Such anonymity should promote freedom, but in fact does just the opposite. I have pursued the aesthetic course, adopting any line of argument that helped to shape a coherent, elegant, publishable essay since I was never held accountable for what I said, never made to defend as my own convictions the positions that I took. Like all disciplines, literary criticism has any number of ready-made arguments lying about and I used the tools at hand as the need arose. My teaching felt much different; in the classroom I faced a challenging (in the best classes) audience and felt called upon to stage myself as an engaged respondent to literary works and various cultural and political facts. But in my essays I only needed to stage arguments, and the rules for such staging were relatively clear and could be routinely mimicked.

My professional contribution to this convention was a paper on Matthew Arnold delivered the very first night to a small audience of thirty people, twenty of whom were various friends of mine. When I agreed to give the paper last spring, I had planned a fairly straightforward Foucauldian reading of Arnold's poetry. Working on the paper this summer, I discovered that such readings were rampant; Arnold's poetry, lots of people had noticed, is tailor-made for discussing issues of power, discipline, and socialization. After reading three or four such accounts, I began to react against what seemed to me the unexamined and really implausible model of power that informed these critics' work, and I ended up writing a paper that attacked certain Foucaultian orthodoxies by way of proposing that Arnold's various essays on education offered a better schema for understanding the individual's relation to culture and to the state. I knew my paper was bad, not because Foucault is right, but because it is preposterous to attack Foucault by way of Arnold. I was groping toward issues I did think were of some real importance, but, constrained by my announced topic (Matthew Arnold), settled for a defense of Arnold's thought that had the sole virtue of being novel. But I let myself off too easily if I merely blame the topic. I also knew exactly how MLA papers work. You speak your piece for twenty minutes or so to an audience that applauds at the conclusion and that's it. All sessions always run overtime, so there is never time for questions. And the paper is not even in print, the ultimate in non-accountability. True, I was concerned about the impression I would make on my fellow panelists, whom I respected. But I consoled myself with the thought that I only managed to listen intermittently to papers given in a session where I also had to speak and the same must be true for others.

What I had not counted on were so many friends being in the audience, most of whom had never actually read anything of mine. They took my paper seriously and wanted to discuss it with me when we all went out for drinks afterward. I found myself in the awkward position of trying to sort out for them—and for myself—what things in the paper I believed and which were there only to solve the logistical problem of having to talk about Matthew Arnold and say something new. I felt myself a hack, a whore.

And I found myself attuned, throughout the rest of the convention, to the distinction between the wares we sell, the lines we take, and our deeper convictions, anxieties, and desires. The cynic can easily say that all those deeper motives are ones of professional ambition, which is why the surface texts are so arbitrary. Plenty of evidence exists to support such a view. But there also exists a truly felt uneasiness that exhibits itself in a continual struggle to find adequate forms for our convictions about the subjects we love and discuss, about the issue of art's and our place in this culture. I resolved to join this struggle.

That edged silence after the "change agent's" talk had been more honest, truer to our beliefs, than most of the words I had heard spoken at the convention. Eloquent silences, however, can hardly serve our needs or satisfy our ambitions, not for us who live in language. We have prostituted ourselves to the exigencies of academic advancement and the perks of academic success, yes, and experience the resultant self-hatred and ironic distrust of appearances.

But the situation is more complex. We have also become the prisoners of forms not supple enough to express our relation to our work or that work's relation to the world. All this postmodernist anxiety—focused on those thresholds where representative strains to reach the represented and art connects to that elusive cheat, life—cannot be reduced to some primal act of bad faith. Within their own terms, artists and critics are doing good, honorable work. But we have lost a way to bring such work to an audience in any way that does not belie the very aspirations that inform its creation. We stand, represented in the books we write and read, slightly askew, captured in words that refuse to ring quite true. We repeat endlessly to ourselves formulas and beliefs that we know anyone outside our discipline finds difficult to credit, and can never really rest quietly in the easy conviction that we simply are right and they are wrong. Our forms are inadequate because they cannot wrest assent from the general culture and our talk rings false because we cannot fully believe in ourselves when such assent is consistently withheld.

This, for us, is our greatest indignity, the cross the times make us bear. No doubt, it is a rarefied complaint to bewail that the age does not afford us forms or words which seem adequate to our purposes. No doubt, we should recognize how persistently we currently say "political" when we mean "linguistic." Without a doubt, we need to be more skeptical about the extent to which forging acceptable forms and linguistic usages for ourselves (the endless task of writers) entails political changes. First, before we can even consider the true relation of language, the material we work in, to the political, the arena we claim we wish to transform, we must acknowledge the primarily linguistic nature of our endeavors, as a modest initial step toward honesty.

CHAPTER 2

Teaching Literature:
Where, How, and Why?

Teaching literature is fraught with so many perplexities that I have come to feel like Buridan's ass as I walk from my office to the classroom. I am of so many minds about what I am doing and about what possible impact it might have on students that I am not sure I am in fact doing anything at all. Surely sending this array of mixed signals to my students must result in everything canceling out, just noise. On the one hand, on the other nine fingers . . . .

Whenever I hear or read others on what they accomplish in the classroom, I am filled with envy and overcome with a sense of unreality. The second response, my incredulity, is no doubt a defense against the first, my sense of inadequacy. Still, no matter where on the political spectrum the speaker/writer locates himself, a simple-minded model of education's impact on students prevails. The conservative who wants to transmit traditional values, the liberal who wants to inculcate habits of disinterested inquiry into truth, and the radical who would foster oppositional views all assume that the classroom is distanced enough from everyday life for a different set of values and procedures to prevail for fifty minutes three times a week—and for those values to then "stick" when students leave the room. It makes me wonder if any of these supposed teachers have ever read a set of student papers. All the commentators display a touchingly naive sense that what gets overtly taught in a classroom is what students learn. Only a much more dialectical account of the university's relation to other cultural spheres, to the economic imperatives of finding a job, and to the political allocation of resources could hope to do justice to the complexities of the social field within which the teacher works.[1]

So the first question is where. Where in our culture is the university located? Where within the university is the teaching of literature located? Amid what others—and in what relation to them—does the university make its pitch, its effort to shape the minds and hearts of the students who pass, so fleetingly, through its classrooms? No general answer to the questions can be completely satisfactory, because the "university" is not a singular entity. Not only is it divided among disciplines guided by very different canons of inquiry and knowledge, but those disciplines themselves are also the site of various conflicts over those canons. Furthermore, not all universities are created equal. Ivy League schools occupy a markedly different social niche from open admission, commuter-student state schools and community colleges. The gap between having a college degree and not having one is no wider than the gap between a degree from Oklahoma Panhandle University and Princeton. These gaps can be measured in the market value of the degrees and in the kinds of access (to graduate programs, to various cultural, political, and/or corporate circles) the degrees can provide. "Where" a university is can partly be specified by seeing where its students can go next after attending it. What social and cultural terrain is adjacent to this or that university?

We should also ask to what social and cultural arenas do university faculty and other functionaries have access? Some academics—although far less than a majority—are asked to bring their expertise to bear on issues confronting the government or industry. Scientific research is regularly underwritten by funds which come from outside the university. A "partnership" (the word usually used) between the university and other segments of society is formed, a division of labor in which the university supplies a certain product to an external consumer. To a lesser extent, social scientists are also involved in providing direct services to government agencies and private organizations which come asking (and paying) for advice. And, increasingly, corporations contract with the university for particular services, especially research in the health sciences. Locating the

1. Watkins (1989) and Guillory (1993) offer two important attempts to think about the work done by American university professors, especially teachers of English, in such nuanced ways. My general point derives from my reading of Bourdieu's (1993) work on the "social field" within which academic and artistic work takes place.

university involves, then, considering its affiliations, the movement of people, resources, and information into and out of this or that particular university.[2]

English departments are oddly situated. Like most of the humanities, English finds its product of little interest to anyone outside the university. English professors do not have clients who underwrite their research or pay them consultant fees. Beyond a few private foundations and the continually endangered NEH, both support for and consumption of the work done in English departments comes entirely from within universities. Although humanities professors often think that their work is of crucial moment to other segments of society, those other segments do not evidence a reciprocal conviction and, for the most part, pay scant attention to that work. Degrees in the humanities (classics, English, philosophy, history, and the foreign languages) have no market value apart from the school system itself, although they are not an absolute detriment to securing certain jobs or admission to certain professional schools. The humanities are, by and large, sealed within education itself, with very few avenues of access to other segments of society.

In a United States where the economic security of the middle class has been severely undermined over the past thirty years, the place of the humanities has also eroded. Those portions of the curriculum that teach skills primarily relevant to work within the university have steadily yielded ground to fields of study that provide (or purport to provide) skills more readily marketable outside the university. Bachelor degrees conferred in English topped out at 64,439 in 1970–71, hit a low (32,254) just ten years later (1980–81), started climbing again in the mid-eighties, and stood at 50,698 in 1995–6. This last figure, despite the reversal of the downward trend, still represents a fifteen percent decline in absolute numbers. The proportional decline is even greater, since 839,730 undergraduate degrees in all were conferred in 1970–71, compared to 1,164,792 in 1995–96 (Digest 266). Over roughly the same time period, BAs in business and management grew from 105,580 in 1969–70 to 227,102 in 1995–96.[3]

2. My use of the word "affiliation" follows that of Said (1983, 16–25). Generally, Said's work, along with that of Robbins (1993) and Gouldner (1979), has greatly influenced the thoughts I present here.

3. Statistics on degrees come from *Digest of Education Statistics* (1998, 292–93). The most MAs in English were awarded in 1970–71 (10,689), the most PhDs in 1975–76 (1,672). Master's degrees in English hit a low in 1983–84 (5,010) and had climbed back to 7,893 in 1995–96. PhDs in English hit a low (961) in 1986–87, but had returned to almost historic highs by 1995–96, when 1,535 PhDs were awarded.

English departments are unique among the humanities, however, in that their position within the general university curriculum has not suffered greatly over this same time period. While the trend has been to remove required courses in the humanities (history and foreign languages have suffered most in this regard), most universities still require two years of English of all students. In other words, English, while sharing in the general decline of the humanities as attractive majors for students, has managed to retain its time-honored status as the most required academic subject. For multiple and none-too-obvious reasons worth pondering, English remains the subject our culture deems most necessary for students from the first grade to the sophomore year of college to study.

I'll consider some of these possible reasons when I get to "why." Still on "where," I want to worry a bit about the impact of requirements on the teaching of literature. (As I hope is obvious by now, this essay is about teaching literature to undergraduates and, a bit, to high school students. The dynamics and difficulties of graduate education in literature are very different.) For starters, the decline in numbers of majors (matched by a similar decline in the numbers of graduate degrees awarded) means that more university English teachers spend more of their time teaching required courses to non-majors. This change in the basic working conditions of most English professors—and its relation to the job market for PhDs—is rarely noted. Professors eager to avoid teaching lower level courses have countenanced the hiring of part-timers and the maintenance of large graduate programs (even when there are no jobs for the students). The growth of the creative writing MFA is also linked to the need for cheap labor in freshman and sophomore English. Put most bluntly, by the time most graduate students receive a PhD, they have been taught to despise the work many of them will be actually employed to do. Most English professors (i.e., those who do not teach at the thirty or so schools with the top graduate programs) now teach in conditions fairly similar to those facing any high school English teacher. The fact that English classes are compulsory, that they take place within an authoritative setting, establishes an adversarial relationship between teachers and students which fosters a wide range of policing tactics on the part of the former and resistant practices among the latter. The surveillance and record keeping of teaching—from grading to taking attendance to giving quizzes—are repugnant, but the alternative (students not doing the reading or other assigned work) is equally bad. Embrace either horn of the dilemma and the possibility of conveying to students the love of literature and the conviction of its crucial importance (which made me become an English teacher in the first place) vanishes. "Trade mars everything it touches," wrote Thoreau, a sentiment often in my mind as I slog through a text I love in order to teach it, dreading what it will become tomorrow in my class of bored and often sullen sophomores. In twenty years of teaching, I haven't even come close to a solution I can endure to this dilemma, especially since my despair is complicated by a respect for my students' resistance to force feeding. Anyone with any gumption should resist this regime. The classroom comes to seem an utterly tainted locale.

If, ignoring the various complications I take up in chapters 5 and 6, we take literature as a form of culture, then the location of literature within the university classroom places it at a severe disadvantage, provided the goal is to win the allegiance of an audience of potential consumers (readers). Literature has so negligible a presence at cultural sites other than schools that the educational system is in the position of always trying to lay another culture alongside of or on top of or in place of (the metaphor one chooses is significant here) the various other cultures to which students already belong. Almost inevitably, students will experience the school culture as forced upon them or, at least, presented to them by authorities (in every sense of that word) whereas the other cultures (street culture, ethnic culture, popular culture, and—to a lesser extent—religious and family culture) will seem freely chosen in many cases, and acquired more simply and painlessly (more "naturally") in all cases. Other forms of culture are assumed in the course of living and are experienced as affirmations/creations of one's identity. School culture is experienced as the attempt of outside forces to mold one's identity, to force identity to take a new course, even to abandon some of its already formed allegiances.

Bruce Springsteen sings, "We learned more in a three-minute record than we ever learned in school," and that rings true to me. So I am always amazed at the hyperbolic claims made about the impact of schools on students and by the over-the-top responses of parents and newspaper columnists to curriculum proposals ranging from sex education to reading *The Autobiography of Malcolm X.* I think it more accurate to see such public battles as much more about the conflict between different social forces than about what is actually happening to the kids.[4] I take it that

4. Gouldner (1979, 43–7) reads these conflicts as triangulated among the "new class" of intellectuals who staff the educational system at all its levels, the state which mandates and funds educational institutions, and other nonintellectual classes who must hand their children over to these institutions. What Goudner highlights is that schooling is perceived by many parents and students as the intervention of a very different social group, with very

much of the impetus of "cultural studies" comes from a conviction that the most significant formation of values, attitudes, and beliefs in today's world does not center in someone's relation to *Oliver Twist* but in their relation to the culture available outside of school in the marketplace. Cultural studies aims to intervene at the sites of cultural production that have the most impact. On a theoretical level, cultural studies asks the kind of question I am asking here: what are the significant differences among various cultural sites as places where identities are formed? My point thus far is that schools—especially in their introduction of students to the cultural form of "literature"—will, under the sign of compulsion, establish a very different relationship between students and literary works than their relationship to most other cultural forms.

But let me not be too hasty to dismiss schools—and serious engagement by students with what goes on there—as irrelevant, even quaint. After all, school culture does become some people's primary culture. It is exactly that for most teachers. The joy of the profession is to be promulgating something in which one utterly believes, even if the pain is to be promulgating it to nonbelievers under circumstances not exactly well-suited to winning converts. (If these metaphors make us out to be missionaries to the savages, blame the very terms within which we do our work, not me. Salesman metaphors could also work, but are hardly any more appealing.) There is nothing particularly shameful in striving to maintain and secure the continued existence of institutions that allow a cherished cultural activity to continue. The problem, of course, is that school doesn't really pay its own way, and that its continuance depends on selling to the society at large the notion that doses of literature that it doesn't really want are nonetheless salubrious. In this way, we true lovers of literature get to have our cultural institution at the not inconsiderable, but still very tolerable, price of peddling our wares to an unappreciative audience. I remember thinking it quite a scam when I realized (as an undergraduate) that someone might pay me to read books and talk about them. Nice work if you can get it. (I entered graduate school just as the market for English PhDs took what has since come to seem its permanent downward plunge.) Twenty years later it still seems a pretty cushy and privileged sinecure.

---

different values, into the processes of value and identity formation. See Rorty (1995) for a convincing argument that debates about the university and its curriculum are better understood as symptomatic of other social conflicts rather than about the feared ill effects of education.

There is a market for school culture, then, just not a market that makes its way only by selling to those who would voluntarily shell out for its goods. In other words, this a screwy and subsidized market. Where else within capitalism do people pay top dollar for something they don't want? Of course, they want the degree. But many of them don't particularly want to read *Oliver Twist*, yet still pay to have us try to force them to read it, all the time figuring out ways to evade that forcing. (I understand that I am overstating the case here. Much of our students' resistance is passive; they actually also "kind of believe" that reading novels is good for them—although they couldn't articulate why—and they enter our courses with good intentions of doing the assigned work; it's just that there is so much to do, much of it more appealing, and so they get around to doing only some portion of what is required. The percentage of that portion differs according to individual calculations of what can be squared with conscience, of what can be neglected, without drastic consequences to one's grade or self-esteem.) Add to this odd relation between seller (the university) and consumer (the student) the fact that some students (or, more usually, some parents) pay upwards of $80,00 for the degree, and are subsequently expected to be so grateful for the privilege that they should (and in some cases will) voluntarily continue to send more money to the school for nothing in return every year for the rest of their lives, and it becomes clear that this is no ordinary market. Imagine the movies operating in such a fashion and the canyon between school culture and popular culture becomes apparent.

In sum, the teaching of literature takes place within a particular location in two cultural institutions: the high school and the university. The transfer of information, the purveying of culture, which takes place at these locations, is marked by its being compulsory. That educators themselves have come to adopt that originally compulsory culture as their own primary culture should not lead them to expect that school will influence all, or even the majority of, students as it did them. We need a much more nuanced view of authority if we are to assess how much a teacher's overt values influence students. Authority does possess some advantages in winning consent from underlings, but it carries distinct disadvantages as well. In other words, our students possess more autonomy in their responses to education than most accounts of education and its results admit.

At the same time, because American schools are far from "total institutions" (in Foucault's chilling sense), but are instead permeable to outside influences, teachers are far less autonomous than usually acknowledged.

The impact of the teacher's enthusiasms and values will be greatly influenced by the reinforcement or denigration of what happens in the classroom by parents, peers, and other cultural messengers. It won't do to paint teachers as completely active and students as completely passive when, in fact, both groups are some of each. The messages flow in all directions, as any halfway sensitive teacher knows. There are things a teacher cannot simply do—such as assigning *Moby-Dick* over a three-week time span—because the class as a whole will resist. I find myself feeling a class out for the first three to four weeks of a term, trying to discover just how far I can push them without losing 60 percent compliance. Then I ease back and work at a level where I sense that 70 percent are with me. I assume other teachers make similar pragmatic adjustments, not just in assignments but in the difficulty of the material they present during class meetings. But you would never know about these compromises by reading the claims about what people are doing and achieving in their classrooms. I also suspect that teachers continually mistake their own epiphanies (another great reward of teaching) for revelations successfully imparted to students.

Which brings me to "how." Admittedly, one presumably has to know "why" the activity of teaching literature is being undertaken before considering "how" to do it. But my considerations of the "why" are going to be so convoluted that it seems best to say my brief piece on "how" first. Besides, like the young person who knows she wants to be a writer before she has a theme or a voice, I think that we English teachers adhere to a method—discussion classes—that comes with the job and is rarely explicitly justified. Of course, many literature teachers talk most of the fifty minutes of the class hour. But few literature teachers—as distinct from more than a few history, philosophy, or chemistry professors—walk into the classroom with prepared lecture notes, fully intending to talk the full time even if a discussion threatens to break out.

At a state university like mine, English is also (along with being the most required course of study) unique because its class sizes are so small, twenty for freshmen and sophomores, forty in upper-division undergraduate classes. Apart from their English classes, few students (outside the honors program) will take a class with fewer than fifty students their first two years. And unless they major in philosophy, classics, the foreign languages, or in certain "programs" (i.e., not traditional departmental disciplines), students are likely never to take a small class except freshmen and sophomore English.

How does English merit this special exemption from the teaching conditions that prevail throughout the university? Certainly one explanation is that English professors are expected to assign and to grade a substantial amount of student writing, a task that can only be done conscientiously when working with a limited number of students a term. (Just what that number is becomes a bone of contention when, in tight times, university administrators try to increase class sizes. Often the English department's best line of defense is to argue that undergraduates would barely be required to write at all—aside from essay exams—if there were not some small classes in the humanities.)

Apart from such practical considerations, there remains the dominant pedagogical bias toward discussion within English as a discipline—and the success English has had selling the university as an institution on this intimate connection between teaching literature and discussion. That connection is more than a little mysterious. Discussion as the primary classroom *modus operandi* only surfaces in the 1950s, just as the New Criticism was beginning its reign as the dominant critical methodology. It has often been remarked that the New Criticism was especially appropriate to American higher education as it tried, following the Second World and Korean Wars, to absorb the increase of students produced by the GI Bill.[5] Since it requires no "cultural literacy," no knowledge beyond or outside a familiarity with the text, New Criticism is well suited to classrooms in which the instructor cannot assume any shared information apart from that offered here and now. "Close reading," with its attention to a text that every student can have open in front of him or her, would seem to lend itself to discussion. Yet as Gerald Graff (1987, 174–77) indicates in his account of the work of I. A. Richards, and as every teacher who has ever led a discussion of a difficult poem (by Donne or Stevens or Ashbery) knows, the suitability of discussion for reaching an understanding of the poem is far from self-evident. Viewed as a gesture toward the equal authority accorded to every participant in the conversation, discussion classes appear typically American. (Certainly, discussion is not the primary mode for the teaching of literature in France, Germany, or England.) Viewed positively, discussion looks democratic, egalitarian; viewed negatively, it looks like American know-nothingism, the blind leading the blind, a way of watering down education and pandering to students as mass education took

5. See Graff (1987, 173–79 and 226–32) for an excellent account of the institutional impact of New Criticism.

hold. In my own most suspicious moments, I link discussion to an American dis-ease with authority, which leads to managerial styles that dissimulate the realities of power. But my own disease on this score keeps me running my classes in discussion mode.

Speculations about national identity (a dubious notion in itself) aside, discussion runs counter to the dignity of the discipline as a profession— and suggests not a link to, but a working at cross purposes with, the New Criticism. Discussion promotes not only the anti-professional theorem that any opinion is as good as any other (or, at least, the notion that knowledge is not possessed by the expert but can only emerge through a collective process), but also the conviction that there is no truth in the matter. Here we are probably dealing with the overdetermined and unintentional effects of a New Criticism that wanted to establish the objective, even scientific, character of literary interpretation. Such objectivity entailed that there was a truth in literary studies, that English classes have a substantial knowledge to convey, and that certain opinions are worth more than others. But since that knowledge is no longer facts of the sort that the old historicists had presented, but now the readings produced by the literary critic, the profession began to crank out readings, the very proliferation of which undermined the truth and knowledge claims that motivated their production. Thus, professional developments tended toward the same conclusion—there is no discernible or determinate truth in matters of literary interpretation—that discussion takes as a justification for its mode of operation. This still does not explain why discussion was adopted as the preferred teaching mode in the first place or why it went on to dominate the whole profession's approach to teaching, as it still does today. A Deweyean and hence American bias toward active learning could underlie this preference for discussion. But that would still leave open the question of why English departments adopted that Deweyean position which, while immensely influential in primary and secondary schools, had very little impact on the teaching practices of most university disciplines.

Nor does a loss of a notion of truth and knowledge explain how the field of English convinced universities that it needed small classes for the reason that it needed to run discussions. Certainly, at least until the seventies, discussion was countenanced in English for precisely the same reasons that it was forsworn in history and philosophy, not to mention chemistry and biology. The lecture courses imparted information, whereas if you learned something in English, it was because you learned something other than facts. Just what students actually did learn in English was unclear. In those days, prior to worries about a fragmenting culture ("anomie" was not seen as resulting from a knowledge deficit), familiarity with the Western tradition was hardly ever offered as a justification for English studies, while teaching students how to read and write was too pedestrian a justification for a society not yet alarmed by a literacy problem. Probably most English professors who felt called upon to give the matter much thought would have fallen back on the Johnsonian notion that literature offered insights into "general" human nature or on the New Critical sense that English studied texts whose richness, ambiguity, and texture amply rewarded close attention. Given this vagueness of aims almost never articulated, and the fact that English departments had in their dominant professional and classroom practices mostly renounced the claim to be imparting knowledge, it is surprising that universities supported the discipline's allegiance to discussion by allowing it to teach much smaller classes than everyone else.

How has this bias toward discussion worked in the classroom itself? The results have, I think, been mixed. Too often English teachers fish for answers/comments from students when it would be far more efficient (and honest) for the teacher simply to state his point. I think I am representative of most English professors when I recognize that I have mindlessly adopted the conviction that perhaps the major sign of a good class is how many students spoke. I also know that my devotion to discussion has made it a continuing problem over the years to get my classes beyond character analysis when reading novels. And now that the New Criticism is dead and "context" almost all, there is less support than ever for the pretense that all the voices in the classroom are equal. Given even a minimum of sensitivity to issues of authority and power, discussion seems disingenuous at best and downright manipulative at worst, much more suited to helping the teacher like himself than to aiding the students. It's a way of making the students look like they are voluntarily subscribing to the compulsory, a pretense more likely to fool the teacher than the student, especially when backed up by the common practice of including "participation" as a factor in determining the final grade. However, I have no intention of abandoning discussion as my primary classroom method, even as I find myself hard pressed to justify it beyond the lame excuse that this old dog is uncomfortable, and hence even more than usually ineffective, when resorting to new tricks.

But let me offer my feeble efforts at more respectable justifications. I would like to think that discussion does make the average English teacher far more aware than his colleagues around campus of just how capable our students are, just how much they are "getting" from their classroom education. (This also follows from the fact that we read far more student-produced work than most of our colleagues.) Because we hear student voices, we have a much better view of how overwhelmed by, how under-prepared for, college-level material many of those students are. Lectures and hundred-page reading assignments in difficult books may work fine for the top fifteen percent of our students (the group to which professors themselves belonged when they were students), but the other eighty-five percent spend much of their time being lost. More interactive, less passive modes of instruction are essential for reaching these students—and discussion is a step in that direction, albeit only a step and one that requires thoughtful supplementation.

It is no accident that most of the exciting new work on college teaching—work on collaborative learning, group discussions, holistic grading, the use of computers, of Web forums, and the like which have revolutionized teaching practices in many English departments—has come from those in our profession in the trenches, teaching freshmen and sophomore English. It will be a shame if this wonderful work remains ghettoized in the lower parts of the English department curriculum, or in English departments apart from the rest of the university, since these new methods are relevant to all the teaching work done at colleges.[6] Armed with a bias toward discussion, English teachers experienced the inability of many college freshmen to process information presented to them solely through lectures and reading assignments and, in response, devised various classroom and study techniques that get students using information and developing academic skills in ways the traditional format does not encourage. In short, I am with Dewey when it comes to education, but think that simply relying on discussion will not do the trick. A carefully planned out mixture of classroom activities, each designed with a specific purpose, is

6. No grand synthetic overview of the "new pedagogy" is yet available. I hope that someone is writing that book even as I write this. In the meantime, Zemelman and Daniels (1988) cover a lot of ground. Tate, Corbett, and Myers (1994) is also helpful and provides a sensible (i.e. not overwhelming) bibliography. That such pedagogical work, even when done in their own departments, is unknown to many teachers of literature is underlined by the absence of any consideration of the teaching of writing in Graff's history of the profession. As for the university as a whole, the scandal of how biology, organic chemistry, and calculus are taught should be enough to convince anyone that the lecture course and a complete disregard of pedagogical strategies neither serve our students well nor promote the long-term health of the disciplines imparted in such a fashion.

needed; moreover, the intended purposes should be revealed to students as they undertake the activities, both to let them see what they (and you) are aiming to achieve and to keep to a minimum misunderstandings about the sources of direction, authority, and power in the classroom. Sugar-coating the pill of the compulsory does no good.

If I keep returning to that compulsory pill, it is because it lurks even more menacingly beneath the question "why." What is it I aim to accomplish in teaching literature? Why do this at all? Remembering that the study of literature is compulsory in this society decenters that "I" immediately. At stake is not what I want to accomplish but what society wants to accomplish so fervently that it makes every citizen submit to the attempt to impart the intended lesson. (Of course, university education is not compulsory in the way lower levels of education are. But, as I have argued, once within the university, the study of English is compulsory at most schools.) I am, to some extent, the means for an end not of my own devising. I am society's conduit. No wonder my students want to evade my charms, my cajolings, my blandishments, my jollity, my enthusiasm (all of which at times disgust me as forced or faked). I shouldn't take it personally. Very, very few of them do. It has little enough to do with either them or me.

Except, of course, insofar as it has everything to do with us, everything to do with how we are positioned in this highly differentiated society with its highly stratified allocation of rewards, prestige, and work (or lack of it). Maybe politics has become so hard because we so consistently dissociate personal interactions (in the classroom, at the workplace, in the marketplace) from what seem the impersonal (unreachable) social mechanisms that grind us each into place. That smiling English teacher who loved Yeats and urged me to do the same and my current unemployment seem utterly disconnected, the one absurd and harmless, the other implacable and death-dealing. How could they be connected? How would we ever begin the work of connecting them?

Along with many of my generation, my haunting by the compulsory, my asking of questions like those above, comes from the innocence lost when I read Foucault, Bourdieu, and other theorists of social power. It is to these writers that I now feel answerable when I ask myself why I do what I do and what effects I imagine that it has. Yet, inevitably perhaps, I cannot accept a total social determination and so try to smuggle the "I" back in, identifying at least some small room for it, for me, to maneuver. Here again, I find myself of (at least) two minds, suspecting such smuggling as just an attempt to evade the harsh truth, yet convicting the theorists of reductively missing the rarely unidirectional effects of the astonishingly multiple forms that human action takes. In the name of that multiplicity, I want to put some flesh on the bones of what has thus far been a very general discussion, and will use autobiography as the source for those details. Since I, problematically I admit, take my life as not unsimilar to others of my generation who went on to teach English, I enter now some nebulous middle place—the place of emblematic or representative detail. But since almost all of the arguments I have advanced thus far rely, it seems to me, on my reader's feeling that my account of what it means and feels like to teach fits with his or her own sense of that activity, the rhetorical leap is not that great.

At first, like the girl in the Lou Reed song, my "life was saved by rock-n-roll." Sequestered in my room under the eaves, rock promised me that there existed other worlds beyond this suburban desert I was desperate to escape. From Dylan and the Byrds to Dostoyevsky, Conrad, Lawrence, Joyce, and Camus was a short step. I prepared myself for the escape to college by imbibing a strange brew of aestheticist disdain for mundane suburban life and existentialist heroism, which entailed casting a cold eye on this essentially tragic life and death. (I taught *The Myth of Sisyphus* to a group of bright undergraduates a few years ago. Not only did they not get it, but I also found myself unable to explain to them or to myself what about the book made it my Bible when I was a sophomore in high school.) An anti-war, pro–civil rights politics that put me at odds with my parents came along with my immersion in the giants of early modernism, but mostly politics bored me. I walked the slums of Baltimore for McGovern, but secretly found him insipid and had no faith in political solutions. America's problem was not bad government, but bad style: the wrong desires generated by the softness that comes from endlessly lying to oneself along Pollyanna-like lines. The self-love and self-approval of those Pharisees whose reaction to the poor missed Phil Ochs's Biblical point that "there but for fortune go you or I" disgusted me, but the religion of high art that I pursued got little further than disgust. (Bourdieu [1984, 485–91] offers a wonderful account of "disgust" as a repudiation of the "vulgar" on aesthetic grounds.) Politics, like most other activities, was finally guilty of diverting attention from the deep and eternal, which the great artists opposed to the transient and shallow. With Dostoyevsky, Conrad, and Lawrence I would gaze into the primal heart of darkness that "civilization" tries to paper over; with Joyce, I would exile myself from the stultifying life of my pious and patriotic parents. Handed Sartre and Nietzsche by my college professors, I became in all things existentialist.

Looking back, I can see that my resolute aestheticism—the insistence that art cannot be compromised by ties to anything else, that art be true to and owe allegiance to only itself—and my belief that art offered the only avenue of insight into the deepest truths were bound to come into conflict sooner or later. Mine was not the playful aestheticism of Wilde, delighting in art's uselessness, but an aestheticism determined to protect the utterly separate world of art from any sullying contact with non-art. Just how this escapist aestheticism yielded finally to a view of art as totally immersed in and incapable of transcending the social worlds in which it is produced and consumed is my story and the story of many of my generation—a story that leads through French theory and feminism to the various social constructivist positions that seem most convincing to us today. I think that an interesting story, but one far too complicated to relate here. One key turning point for me was the recognition that arguments against the immunity of art extended to my immersion in it. After reading Bourdieu, how could I deny that my adherence to the religion of art had been the means for moving myself from one social/cultural level to another?—a point driven home most forcefully by my parents' utter incomprehension of what I do, an ignorance somewhat willed, since partly fueled by resentment of my being paid so much to do so little. I was not just moving from one place (the suburbs) to another (an urban university, the republic of letters), but from one social stratum (the middle middle class) to another (the professional middle class).

If one narrative about the movement away from aestheticism invokes the encounter with theory, another narrative must needs consider the institutional setting of studying literature. "Teaching literature" is, to some extent, a misnomer. What is taught are ways of talking about, of explaining, of interpreting, the literary text. In a wonderful essay, that last aestheticist William Gass (1985, 277) describes what he calls the "six regularly scheduled trains out of the text." They are historical/biographical background, the world as referent (truths about life), reader response, literary tradition/influences, the construction of the text (formalism), and "hermeneutical heaven: replacement of the text with its interpretation." Whether there are only six trains or actually sixty-six, Gass's point is well taken: each way of talking about the text carries us away from it and toward either a paraphrase (in close reading or impressionist criticism) or toward explanatory, extrinsic materials (social context, psychological subtext, traditional and generic conventions, intertextual influences, etc.). My high school immersion in the early modernists was almost entirely extracurricular; I threw myself into the experience of these novels with all the infatuation of those model novels readers, Don Quixote and Emma Bovary. I was Paul Morel and Stephen Dedalus for months at a time, and my aspiration was, of course, to write novels myself. I talked of these things to no one and wrote of them only in a journal meant for no one's eyes but my own.

It was not novels I was asked to write in college. And my experience of reading those novels so dear to me proved highly resistant to being put into words or being offered up in classroom discussions. The language of criticism, of explanation and explication, worked along very different lines—and I was slowly converted to this new language. I was good at it, which helped, but it was also what was required of me, and like the dyer's hand, my nature was subdued. I don't want to be overly nostalgic or wistful about this; I don't really think my "nature" was subdued, since I think my talents clearly weighed more heavily on the side of criticism than of artistic creation. (I wrote fiction for another four or five years after getting my PhD; most of it was bad, some of it decent, none excellent.) And certainly I more than gave my intellectual assent to the kinds of explanations that criticism has to offer; I came to believe that achieving such explanations was vital as well as interesting work. Still, there remains a tension between the experience of reading literature and the paths followed in studying it, a tension that critic/scholars/teachers all too often fail to see (one wonders if they ever read for pleasure any more or love some books that they could never imagine teaching) and which makes the hostility of poets and novelists (even those who teach in university English departments) to academic purveyors of literature not only understandable but also to some extent justified. To give one's allegiance to the academic forms through which literature is discussed and taught is to withdraw (at least partly) allegiance to literature itself. One language displaces another. We can, of course, be bilingual. But we cannot speak two languages at once.

I know that to phrase the tension in this way, especially to use the phrase "literature itself," is to grant to the aestheticists precisely what is being contested. And it is precisely the sign that I locate myself on the academic side of the ledger that I want to delineate this contest as a struggle for mastery, a struggle both within the university as an institution and within the culture at various sites. Once this move is made—the inscription of any defended conviction within the dynamics of a larger social conflict—any category (like "literature itself") that claims autonomy will be discredited. When Roland Barthes defines literature as what gets taught; when Michel Foucault describes the school as an exemplary institution within a disciplinary society; when Pierre Bourdieu identifies one's tastes, one's choices of what to read, as moves to secure social distinction and cultural capital, the very possibility of "literature itself" is shattered. Once having accepted the legitimacy, even the truth, of these locations of literature as one player within a larger social game, as institutionally supported and enforced by its particular interested partisans, the teacher of literature cannot teach literature itself, cannot present the heroic modernists or even the ironic postmodernists on their own terms. Irony is endless and uncontrollable, linked as Kenneth Burke (1969, 51–17) discusses, to the "humility" of recognizing that no text or self can ever fully account for itself, but can always be placed in another context that makes it speak quite differently. The decentering of the "I" of the teacher which accompanies thinking about the compulsory goes hand-in-hand with the decentering of the "I" of the author when thinking about how the literary work is produced from a certain social site and is articulated within a certain set of social relations. In other words, the language of "literature itself" is as much a social language as criticism is, and has no claim to be more authentic or primal. But it is a different language and we might mourn its being totally displaced by other languages.

Why, then, teach literature? To shatter the innocence of immediate experience (and love), replacing that first encounter with a more adequate understanding of the various forces that impinge upon the reader as the pages get turned?[7] Pondering such issues leads to various plausible answers to why society requires the teaching of literature. The discipline of learning to read, including the forms of reason modeled by the organization of texts and the need to pay attention to detail, reinforces other micro-disciplines, which produce docile, disciplined bodies (Foucault [1979]). The infinite grades of distinction established among students on the basis of their ability to stomach Twain or Wordsworth or Flaubert inculcates the notion of a natural elite marked by their refined taste and superior intellect (Bourdieu [1984]). The presentation of a glorified national identity through the masterpieces of its culture works to negate the cul-

---

7. Feminism, more than literary or pedagogical theory, has agonized over the status of "experience," since it often both wants to honor the experience of various women and to avoid being naïve about experience's apparent transparency. See Scott (1992).

ture of others and to justify subordination of the foreigner without and the barbarian within (Viswanathan [1989]).

Even armed with these answers, and often highly suspicious of these social goals, we teachers still forward them in spite of ourselves. Everything in our training leads us to reward attention to detail and logical, orderly presentation when we grade papers. Our own profession continually reinforces patterns of distinction in which working on various authors or various issues brings greater respect—not to mention the greater acclaim granted accomplishments on paper as contrasted to accomplishments in the classroom. And our discipline continues to organize courses and academic specialties mostly along national lines and still searches for the cultural characteristics that texts grouped along these lines share. In other words, if one reason to teach literature is to gain a greater self-consciousness about why society requires students to learn about and read literature, such self-consciousness does not automatically bring with it practices that disrupt what society sets out to accomplish.

It is far from clear how one could teach literature in such a way as to disrupt the normalizing and socializing aims of the institution that supplies the resources, the site, and the students who enable the would-be oppositional teacher the opportunity to do anything at all. The dilemmas proliferate to the point of making me dizzy, of throwing up my hands in despair. It all seems such a muddle, starting with the odd status of these things—novels, poems, plays—which we are called upon or actually desire to teach. At least since 1800, most literary writers have stood in some form of opposition to the dominant economic, cultural, and social tendencies of their time.[8] This opposition is as true of conservatives (who hate modern democracy, mass society, mass media, the modern metropolis, the "new" woman, and large bureaucracies) as it is of writers on the left. All sides are equally convinced that something is radically wrong with modern society. As Lionel Trilling (1965) pointed out years ago, these writers' very rage against the way things are makes the institutionalization of their work within the curriculum unexpected (almost inexplicable), while the overall effect seems to be the taming of the literature, not the radicalization of the academy. On the other hand, for those suckers who actually buy into the values of the texts they read rather than simply dutifully going through the paces (in other words, those most likely

8. See Williams (1981, 72–75) for a succinct account of the multiple factors which converge to place most artists since 1800 at odds with modernity.

to go on to become teachers of literature) oppositional stances are like mother's milk to them.

Thus it comes as a shock of seismic proportions when theorists like Foucault and Bourdieu suggest that literature is one of the cornerstones of the dominant social order and that in teaching literature we serve that order. To maintain our own oppositional credentials, we have either to recuperate the literary works by explaining how they were bent out of shape to become the bulwarks of orthodoxy or we have to devote our teaching and scholarly activity to exposing the literary work's complicity with the dominant order. Needless to say, both strategies have been pursued over the past fifteen years. Since it has proved pretty difficult to brand particular authors, or even particular works, as purely orthodox or purely oppositional, the results have, quite literally, been mixed.

Not surprisingly, there has recently come to be a reaction against this kind of score-keeping—here Blake is radical, here he is not—but without any clear indication of where we are to go next. The profession seems to be suffering a kind of identity crisis. No longer satisfied with indicating where works resist prevailing identities, we have become interested in how works contribute positively to the formation of identities; yet we retain a deep mistrust of all identities as imposed and as repressing some kind of primal heterogeneity.[9] Once you start calling identity formation "subjectification," the deck is stacked. Few will embrace the job description: "subjectifier." Only the negative work of undoing identities becomes acceptable. At present we seem left with a wishy-washy conclusion that all texts, like all selves, are variegated mixtures. But unless we decide to celebrate any and all mixtures for diversity's sake, we still are left with the work of deciding which elements of the mixture seem helpful in empowering us to achieve our goals and which unhelpful.

I will return, all too briefly and inadequately, to what seem to me the essentially ethical issues just raised. Right now, I want to suggest that attention to the mixed nature of texts and selves leaves us with an unexamined and poorly understood problem: how do texts shape or influence the values, attitudes, and actions of the selves who read them? It is hardly obvious that, if I desire to create oppositional attitudes in my students, the indirect road of reading literature is to be preferred to the direct road of proselytizing. (Of course, critics of "tenured radicals" believe teachers

9. Butler (1990) remains the most powerful and influential rendering of the current suspicion of identity.

like me have already given up the first for the second.) When I consider my own experience, I guess I would conclude that I was softened up by my earlier immersion in literature (which was, after all, premised on a hostility to the life my immediate world seemed to offer), but that the hardening of my political attitudes, the replacement of various vague sympathies with substantive positions and arguments, came from my experience of the job market and of work, and from reading theory, that is, academic discourses about literature and other social forms/institutions. In short, it was in learning to ask "what cultural and social work does the literary text do?" and "what work am I being required to do in order to get a job as a professor and then keep it?" that I came to articulate the criticisms of the contemporary world which literary texts had suggested and thus (paradoxically) to question the separateness of the literary texts from the world I had originally hoped to escape by reading those texts.

Does the reader recognize that we are back to where this essay began, to the question of what effect do we have on our students, either through the indirection of what we require them to read or the direction of what we say to them in the classroom (or elicit from them in discussion)? What my education of the past twenty-five years seems to have taught me is that it is all tremendously complicated, that my input as a teacher or *Frankenstein's* input as a reading experience interact with the individual student in mostly unpredictable ways.[10] This should not surprise us. Raise two children as strict Catholics and one might become a priest, one an atheist. The unintended happens again and again—and that thought is consoling when I think of the more sinister social goals my work as a teacher abets. Thank goodness this process of indoctrination is so inefficient, so regularly circumvented.

But if the unintended happens again and again, so does the intended. And we have no feasible alternative to continuing to act with intention; we all contribute our mite toward trying to push the world in one direction or another; we all find it disturbing to think that our intentions may be subsumed within larger social forms that use our actions to further quite different intentions. The very gap between personal intentions and social intentions that I have been worrying for much of this essay leads

10. The tension between theory's attempt to generalize (here an account of the text's impact on readers) and the differences introduced by particulars, differences which theory can never fully encompass, has become a commonplace in postmodern considerations of intellectual work. Sedgwick (1990, 22–27) on theory's responsibility to the individual seems exemplary.

some to try to steal a march on consequences by devising strategies, methods, and techniques deemed more surely effective than just contributing one's mite. Institutional analyses or psychological models both suggest that conscious and individual intention is only a minor player in the game. Psychological models, for example, whether focusing on dynamics of transference/identification/ambivalence or on accounts of how best to package material for cognitive comprehension and retention, rely on uncovering hidden dynamics and parameters, an understanding of which will grant us greater influence over those we teach, a more sure imparting of information and (presumably) values.

I find that I have a deep-seated (and no doubt liberal humanist) distrust of anything smacking of manipulation, a distrust tied obviously to some desire to respect my students' autonomy even as the theories most convincing to me deny the very possibility of autonomy. What delights me most in students is when they are aglow with things they have figured out or discovered for themselves. Unhappy the generation that does not have its own novels, ones never taught in any classroom anywhere. And, along with my residual liberal humanism, I retain a deep-rooted suspicion (adopted from the early high modernists) of all talk of values. I hate all this claptrap about how our schools should be teaching values, in part no doubt because forming one's values for oneself should be a key hallmark of the autonomy which I try to respect (and, if it is not oxymoronic to say so, foster) in my students.

But lately this whole take has come to seem untenable to me. I don't see how education can be anything other than value-laden. To teach literature represents a choice, a choice that is staged for my students every time I walk into the classroom. I am saying that this pursuit—reading books and talking about them—is so valuable that I have chosen to devote my life to it, and what I model in the classroom is what it looks like to live that choice. Like any true believer, I am racked by doubts, and I model those as well. But there is no way to duck the fact that I (alone among those in my classroom of twenty year olds) have made a choice based on what I deemed was worthy of my time and energy, and that my students, who will soon have to make choices of their own, look to their teachers to gauge the consequences, the possibilities afforded, by this choice or that. Just like the novels I read, by turning their backs on a certain mundane existence, were value-laden despite their claims to be beyond good and evil, so my pursuit of this activity—teaching literature—conveys a judgment even if I strain for even-handedness on every topic raised in class.

All of which is to say that, even after the shocks administered by Foucault and Bourdieu, teaching literature is haunted not only by the compulsory but also by Matthew Arnold. For it is Arnold who insists that the connection of culture to identity formation necessarily raises the question of the "best self." What Arnold dramatizes is that once you accept that culture shapes selves, then it becomes a matter of crucial importance just what bits of culture get to do that shaping. No one is ever (or ever could possibly be) brought into contact with or under the sway of an entire culture (all its accumulated knowledge, traditions, texts, superstitions, practices, rituals, self-understandings, and self-delusions). So those who undertake the task of education will always be choosing what they deem the crucial bits to present to those under their charge. And what could possibly serve as the principle of selection except the goal of creating the best selves? Just what will constitute that "best self' will be a matter of contention. Best for what purposes? Classic debates ensue. Is education in a democratic society aimed primarily at preparing students for the labor market or at preparing them to be fully competent citizens? Can education achieve both of these goals (and others) at the same time? Details aside, however, what Arnold makes clear is that the formation of selves becomes an ethical matter the moment one begins to intervene purposively in that process.

Where Arnold gets scary, of course, is in taking it for granted that "the best" is easy to discern (at least for those who read their Homer correctly) and that the power of the State should guarantee that the best prevail. The State, he claims, can be "the organ of our collective best self, of our natural right reason" (Arnold, 1965a, 136). We at the end of the twentieth century can hardly share Arnold's sanguine vision of the state. But we should not think that we can push the state off the stage just because it's an embarrassment or worse. If Arnold is right to see that education inevitably involves the ethical, he is also right to see that, from his time on, education also inevitably involves the state. (As a school inspector, Arnold was a functionary of the growing state involvement in education in England; meanwhile, he argued ceaselessly and vehemently in his essays for the establishment of schools run directly by the state.[11])

Connecting *Culture and Anarchy* to the mid-nineteenth-century origins of compulsory public education suggests that the compulsory and the ethical in this case entail one another. So long as culture is encountered hap-

11. See Arnold (1965b) for one instance of his advocacy of public education.

hazardly or through the self's personal interactions with family and other intimates, the process of acculturation appears "natural," unshaped by deliberate human planning. But once education becomes compulsory and its course, its curriculum, is planned (and, most likely, standardized so that many students follow the same course), then the question of what kinds of selves the educator is aiming to create must arise. (To claim that I as teacher will merely undo identities already formed elsewhere seems to me to let us too easily off the hook.) Because this education is going to be required of students, a justification is also required. Why teach this rather than that? I think that these justifications will always, in the final analysis, come down to moral claims about this line of study producing the best self for this good purpose. To be in education is to be in the business of shaping selves and thus, no matter how uneasy the talk of "best selves" makes us, to become involved in trying to shape one kind of self as opposed to another kind.

Now it is possible, I suppose, to be a cynical or ironic teacher, one who walks into the classroom and dissociates oneself from the purposes that the powers that be are aiming to achieve there. The difficulty of such a stance is that, although various details about what goes on in my classroom are out of my control (and the impact my class might have on students depends heavily on what else they are experiencing in other classrooms and the culture as a whole), no one held a gun to my head and made me become a teacher. The ironic teacher, the one who indicates by his behavior that a socialization over which he has no control and which he personally disavows is using him as a conduit against his personal will, is most likely going to strike his students as a whiner. Of course, power is omnipresent in our society, but I must say that, especially at the level of university teaching (but even lower down in the school system as well), the choice to become a teacher is, I think, rather unconstrained. Power, in fact, seems to be working just the opposite way: to prevent people from being able to actualize that choice. More people want this job than can get it. It will not only strain most students' sense of things to convince them that you, a functionary of the compulsory in their eyes, are actually a victim of the same power that compels their presence in the classroom, but also violate their sense that teaching is a pretty cushy job.

These difficulties do not render ironical teaching impossible. But I believe that its opposite is much more frequent, which adds another sense to Arnold's talk of the "best self." When I walk into the classroom and model the choice I have made to be a teacher of literature, I am also getting a chance to be the self that, in many ways, I am most proud of. I am acting upon a fiction that is more mine than the students' in my modeling. The classroom becomes a utopian space of purity where I live my choices and convictions utterly, where shorn of the messy complexities and contradictions of my ordinary self, I actually get to have (for fifty minutes) an identity, a oneness that very few other activities (playing basketball, some precious moments with my wife, children, and dear friends) afford me. (Interestingly enough, the other intense experiences of my existence—writing and reading—do not provide that unity. Writing instead generates multiplicity as I, like Mr. Dick in *David Copperfield*, try to keep my thoughts from running to King Charles's head. Reading allows my self to fall away utterly.) I think that the tendency of teachers to enthuse over what they are accomplishing in their classrooms often comes from mistaking their own delight at the self they get to be in this pure devotion to the intellect with whatever it is that students might be getting.

For, as I keep trying to emphasize, if the classroom is a utopian space for us as teachers, there is no reason to think many students experience it as such. (True, I found the classroom a delightful space during much of college and graduate school; but I was also heartily sick of being a student by the end of three years in grad school, by that point uninterested in entering another classroom unless I was the teacher.) The striving for purity in this utopian space manifests itself in the profession as a whole, it seems to me, in the search for the truly oppositional. This striving I would characterize as the modernist moment in our teaching and writing, the moment in which we attempt to create an "other" to the messy and often despicable world and selves we inhabit. Literature offers a privileged vehicle for such a pursuit, since it is itself so often animated by a similar purpose. But this modernist moment is dogged by our postmodernist lives, by the impurity and multiplicities of our convictions and cravings. The classroom is no utopian space, once we think of the lines of power that traverse it, or even the fraudulence of our staged best self. So some of us strive to deconstruct that self almost as soon as we present it—only to realize that this act of deconstruction reinstates a best self, now understood as a self alert to the temptation (to be resisted) to posit unity, autonomy, and integrity/purity.

I do not see any way of wriggling out from under this modeling of a self. We as teachers are performers and the rush comes not just from the audience's appreciation, but also when the momentum of the performance carries us to new selves that feel, despite their novelty, so utterly, so perfectly, what we have always wished to be. In awakening and some-times fulfilling these wishes about identity, teaching literature does a cultural work that remains mysterious yet powerful—the joining of desire to ideals, of identities with public, cultural forms—and, as we maneuver within this terrain, that work is done on ourselves as well as on our students. Why do that work? Because this is who we want to be. I, as a teacher, want to be involved in the cultural shaping of selves, acting and acted upon as the process unfolds, never completely dictating its outcomes, but trying my damnedest to negotiate its surprises in ways that produce what I deem the best outcome. Doing that work, I have found myself located, fleetingly but more than rarely, at spots of time where a convergence of all the factors has produced a self in relation to its world and to others that I can utterly endorse. I only hope that participating in such moments offers my students some comparable serendipity or, at least, some inkling of its possibility. And I hope that I can continue to insist that we hold the world up to the standard of that possibility.

CHAPTER 3

An ABCs of
Post-Theoretical Academic Style

AUDIENCE

Postmodern architecture, Charles Jencks (1984) tells us, is "double-voiced." It addresses two audiences at once: the public who uses and sees the building, and the professional cadre of architects. For many (although not all) academics, the work would not seem worth doing if not for the (admittedly strained) pretense of its potential impact beyond the university and the national professional organizations. The nonacademic audience is a necessary fiction, a shaping presence upon the work.

Broadly speaking, social scientists imagine their work reaching policy wonks, whereas humanities professors dream of the general reading public. Only scientists get to be single-voiced; they write for the fifty or so other people in the world who are working on and could possibly understand their corner of the universe. (Scientists have their own necessary fictions, but they dream of impacts that don't depend specifically on audience.)

The styles of different academic work are shaped in relation to the imagined audience. The topics, the modes of argumentation, the authorities cited or argued against, and the amount and kinds of documentation are mandated by the protocols of the discipline or profession. But the discursive style—telegraphic almost to the point of bulleted speaking points on the one extreme, *belles-lettres* at the other—indicates the non-academic reader that the writer dreams of swaying.

Theory—taken in the all-encompassing sense of a quasi-philosophical discourse that questions the assumptions of the various disciplines— makes the problem of audience more acute. Theory is more abstract, more abstruse, and more self-reflexive, hence more "academic" in every sense of the term. (By "post-theoretical" I mean work undertaken in an academic landscape permanently altered by theory, not some presumed "death of theory" followed by a restoration of the pre-theoretical universe. And my observations here pertain only to the "American scene.") Yet theory usually comes with a social and political agenda born of a suspicion of the academy and the way it organizes knowledge in disciplines and aids power through the institutional regulation of knowledge. So theory hardly relinquishes the hope of having extra-academic effects. And theory, insofar as it is successful, unsettles the unanimity of the professional audience, while also inviting academics outside any one discipline to eavesdrop on and even criticize the work within that discipline. Academic work is potentially addressed to even more audiences now, and those audiences are less likely to be homogeneous within themselves.

BOURDIEU

Academics take pride in the work they do. They believe it is necessary work and that its necessity justifies the honors and salaries attached to it. But they also know that ambition drives much of their efforts and that professional advancement rather than an impact on the world is the most likely fruit of any particular piece of work. How to avoid cynicism under such circumstances?

Teaching helps. Most academic writers regularly face non-academic audiences in the classroom, and much academic prose is shaped by pedagogic purposes. Making one's knowledge and expertise available to the noninitiated takes some of the sting out of participation in the kind of professional maneuvering that harps on ownership of ideas, exclusivity of innovative work, and competitive assessments of others' work.

Some kind of belief in progress is also necessary. In one way or another, the academic thinks that the production and acquisition of knowledge is connected to making the world better. Just as the teacher aims to leave her students better off at the end of the term, academic writers want to better the world, not harm it. Even where they think their chances of a positive contribution are nil (because from their marginal position they have no lever with which to move history), they usually believe their efforts, while pathetic, are harmless.

Where the belief in the work's salutary effects joins the pedagogic impulse in essays addressed to the professional audience, we get the weird effects characteristic of a contemporary academic style that is also cognizant of the rising status of the professional middle class at the expense of the non-professional middle class. The stakes in professionalization are so much higher now because the economic and social gap between professionals and non-professionals is wider. While the long economic boom has made entrance into certain professions easier, there has emerged a more clearly marked hierarchical system in higher education. Graduating from a "good" school is more important than ever before. The job market for academics is generally much tighter than that in almost all the other professions, although conditions vary from one academic specialty to another. And despite the fact that almost every school now requires some professional publication by its faculty, the gap between the working conditions, salary, and privileges of faculty at "research universities" and their colleagues at lower-rung state universities and community colleges has never been wider. That gap is also institutionalized at many of the research universities themselves, where untenured and nontenurable adjuncts teach the lower level courses for miserable pay while the "research faculty" writes its essays and books. That written work becomes more professional (more specialized, more technical, more oriented to disciplinary disputes, more footnoted) corresponds to this greater differentiation of professionals. Yet the same work, when done by academics who are teachers, often implies an ethos of providing the author's knowledge to all comers and often makes explicit claims about the social good the author's knowledge or arguments could serve. Increased professionalization, in other words, is accompanied by more fulsome claims about the wide-ranging benefits of professional work. The writer often appears to be trying to convince himself.

I suppose innocence about such matters prevails in some quarters. Not every academic has read Bourdieu and thus has not had to face the challenge of cynicism directly. But in America the academic professions have offered such a standard way to escape the middle middle class for its upper reaches (with the resultant—and inevitable—alienation from one's family and origins), that the split between the professional and the non-professional is a lived reality for many academics. Top-echelon research professors do not have to have read Bourdieu to understand that their jobs and privileges look like a scam to the folks back home—and to the adjuncts and graduate students on their own campuses. And so their work, even at its most academic, also addresses that skeptical audience (lodged within as well as back home) to affirm the benefits and nobility of the pursuit of knowledge.

CRITIQUE

The folks back home are also troubled by how "negative" academics are. Academics are so critical of everything; nothing ever meets their standards. Marx's call for "a relentless critique of everything existing" might be written over the lintel of the modern university. Colleges as the repositories of received knowledge, with professors as the custodians of the tradition, have yielded to the multiversity, with its emphasis on the production of new knowledge (the sciences and the quantitative half of the social sciences) or on the critique of existing knowledge (the qualitative social sciences and the humanities).

Critique, of course, has tried to undermine the faith in progress attached to the production of new knowledge. The relentless critique of everything has now reached to the efficacy of critique itself. Another form of cynicism lurks here. Does critical reflection, lucidity about the social and intellectual processes by which habits and values are formed, gain us anything?

The watchword of critique has always been that the truth will set you free. And that faith has proven marvelously resistant to attack over the past thirty years. Much work in the humanities and social sciences still follows the path of demystification, revealing the true motives, actual causes, hidden structures, and processes behind appearances that are consistently misunderstood by the majority of social actors. If only we can replace such mistaken beliefs (that gender is natural, that our hierarchies reflect merit) with recognitions of the true state of affairs, we will be better off.

The arrogance of this position is among the least reasons that it has come under increasing attack. More prominent have been worries about truth claims. Why believe reflection superior to first impressions? What could stand as independent criteria for reflection's being correct? Humans lie to themselves all the time. What exempts critique's reflections from being "rationalizations" (in Freud's sense of that term)? The "critical distance" and "cool, hard-headed" style for which critique congratulates itself runs athwart recent arguments about the situated character of all thought and the complete interpenetration of thought and emotion.

Furthermore, the translation of knowledge and understanding into action is problematic. What moves someone to act? I know that funding for public schools is grossly unequal across the various school districts in my state, and I believe this is wrong. What am I doing in relation to this knowledge and this belief? Not as much as I am doing to write this essay. There are many options for action in relation to our multiple convictions, and there is no simple path from conviction to action. We can know that capitalism is corrupt and exploitative, believe (and the temptation here is to add an emphatic like "strongly" or "truly") that capitalism's practices are wrong, and yet not change our behavior very much from the ways we acted prior to acquiring that knowledge and those convictions.

Such considerations make the rhetorical as opposed to the informational component of critical writing more salient. If "engaged" academic writing has become more "performative," it is because critique has come to the point where it questions its own simplistic faith in the power of knowledge. Of course, rhetoric and knowledge are not opposites. Facts, arguments, anecdotes (stories true or false), examples, and moral principles are always presented in a particularistic style in relation to a projected audience. But contemporary work is much less likely to believe that "the facts will speak for themselves." Even if the writer has no grander design than to convince the readers of an academic journal to publish his or her essay, the contestation within theory of just about every possible position means that assertions must be carefully constructed and buttressed.

Where the aim is grander, we might say that "critique" of the Frankfurt School variety had yielded to the kind of hegemonic work described by Laclau and Mouffe (1985) or Stuart Hall (1988). It is not enough to lay bare the bones of our social reality. The writer must also, like Mr. Venus in *Our Mutual Friend*, articulate the bones. The writer must create the skeletal frame out of the scattered facts and values lying to hand in the current moment and strive through words to breathe life into that body.

DIFFICULTY

What happens when you cross the godfather with a poststructuralist? You get an offer you can't understand.

Theory is difficult. That statement is almost always a complaint. Most pointedly, the difficulty of theory appears in direct contradiction to its ostensible political goals. If these theorists want to have an impact on society, it seems absurd to write essays and books that less than one percent of the population can read. Manifestos with footnotes capture the laughable plight of today's would-be radical intellectual, a careerist in the university who believes himself a threat to the status quo. Luckily, he has Roger Kimball to bolster his self-esteem.

The situation is more complex, more difficult, than the common complaint allows. Note that what might be called the literacy gap parallels the economic gap that has opened up between the professional-managerial class and the rest since 1965. Graduate students must master much more difficult material and write in a more difficult style to get jobs teaching students who will be less literate than the students of forty years ago. While the university (especially in graduate studies) have become hyper-literate, the school system (from community colleges on down) has become less literate.

But let's not get sidetracked by nostalgia. Fifteen percent of the population reads eighty-five percent of the books that get read in the United States. There is no reason to believe that these numbers have changed significantly over the years. The vast majority of adults read very little at all, so it is ingenuous to blame an academic for reaching less than one percent of the population when the best-selling novelist reaches three percent. Any argument about the impact of books must take a trickle-down form because no book can compete with the mass media for direct contact with audiences. Books, for better or worse, are directed to a small minority, and what no one wants to face (in the democratic context of the United States) is that we cannot assess books' impact without considering the power of elites to influence society out of all proportion to their numbers.

The real issue of difficulty, then, is what audience among book readers the author hopes to reach. Difficulty is rewarded if one seeks acclaim as original or as being a major thinker. (Of course, just being difficult insures neither of these rewards.) But difficulty can jar with populist aspirations, the desire to imagine (or even achieve) contact with an audience beyond the academy. Richard Rorty offers an instructive example here. He quite deliberately abandoned the technical style of his early work on the philosophy of mind for the breezy, synthetic, and dramatically binarized (public vs. private, solidarity vs. irony) style of the later work. As a result, he became the philosopher most likely to be read by non-philosophers and occupies the public place once held by John Dewey and Bertrand Russell, a place that had been vacant for many years because no philosopher chose to break with discipline-specific notions of rigor, care, and difficulty.

The word "chose" in the previous sentence makes me nervous. Rorty obviously did make some choices. But style is not infinitely malleable, not a simple matter of choice. The difficulty of writing stems partly from this resistance—of what to what? To say the words resist one's ideas doesn't seem quite right. In any case, it is difficult to express what one wants to say in writing. Writing is an endlessly frustrating—and perhaps for that reason endlessly fascinating—enterprise.

This brings me to my last two thoughts on difficulty. Pre-existing models and forms create worn grooves that can make writing less difficult—both for the writer and the audience. Formal experimentation is, of course, a hallmark of modernism in the arts. Where the thought aims to be new, a new form must be invented for its expression. Theory, in general, partakes of this commitment to novelty and the concomitant attraction to new forms. So it sets itself as well as its reader a difficult task.

But difficulty also seems an outgrowth of temperamental imperatives. A writer is driven to worry a point and the reader is, finally, willing or not to follow the writer down that path. Proust manages to get me (but hardly every reader) enchanted by his two hundred page consideration of the difficulties of getting to sleep. I find Stanley Cavell's idiosyncratic self-indulgences charming, because his explorations of his obsessions strike me as productive. But my love of Derrida as a close reader is tested by my impatience with his starting so many essays with a meditation on the difficulties of getting started. In my own writing, I find the question of where to cut short, of where to stop complicating the issue, continually troubling. How much of my audience am I losing at each new turn of the screw?

EXEMPLARY

The divide between quantitative and qualitative work is as deep as the divide between the "hard" sciences and all the other disciplines. Qualitative work is burdened and blessed by the perils of exemplification.

The example is synecdochic; it is the part that represents the whole. The problems raised by claims to typicality are endless—and thus serve to generate lots of revisionist work for academics. Victorian culture looks like one thing if my sample comes from its novels and poems, quite another if I take newspaper articles and court cases as exemplary. More intriguing than the endless disputes about what the Victorians believed *tout court* is the question of whether such holistic claims must underlie our attention to and interpretation of particulars. It is the rare academic work that does not justify its attention to particulars with some gesture toward what that attention reveals about the wider social reality (as if it is self-evident that the audience is more interested in and the work more justified by claims about Victorian culture than the story of Tennyson's invalid wife). The handling of examples, in other words, indicates where academics believe significance lies. What the example is taken to be an example of names the target of the work.

From the left (as it were), Derrida and others have questioned the ability of the example to do this work, while the quantoids (from the right) have always scoffed at using examples to make general claims. The example is both never enough and always too much. It is never enough to secure the general claim while, in all its wonderful detail, it always provides too much material. How does the investigator decide which details are exemplary, which supererogatory? The suspicion deepens that he finds what he came to seek, unless (happily?) he manages to let the example's particularities distract him.

There is a hermeneutic circle here. The writer chooses the example(s) for his study guided by what he wishes to emphasize. Underneath or alongside the use of the example to make holistic claims is the commitment to certain holistic claims, a commitment connected to what the writer wants his work *to do*. The example, then, is moral insofar as it unites purposes both enacted (by the writer) and urged (by the writer upon himself and/or audience). So, for example, Mary Poovey (1988) takes Dickens's *David Copperfield* as her example of the gendered professionalization of the literary author. Her choice is invested by her desire to tell a cautionary tale about what she claims is our culture's dominant image of authorship, an image derived from historical developments during the Victorian era. Her own work strives to be an example of how to question that dominant image.

For the professional audience, the work is also an example of how to do work. Even in the quantitative and hard sciences, work is important not just in terms of *what* is studied or concluded, but also in terms of *how* the study is conducted. The illustration and implementation of methodologies is important—and is considered the "theoretical" part of the work in some disciplines. This attention to methodology is both messier and more central in qualitative work. With the questioning of all assumptions that has characterized theory, every work in the humanities exemplifies as well as argues for a certain way of doing work. The writer must position herself amidst competing models even as the method is modeled. Formal experimentation goes hand-in-hand with methodological exemplification when a consensus about the correct way to proceed does not exist.

FIELD

I want to write that in qualitative work there used to be disciplines, but now there are fields. Unfortunately, I do not believe that is true. Disciplines have proved awfully resilient. The inertia of academic institutions should never be underestimated. The structural force of institutional arrangements (especially departments and the organization of under-graduate majors and graduate degrees along departmental lines) carries much before it even after the intellectual rationale and/or unity of the disciplines has been lost.

A field is defined by whom one reads and to whom one addresses one's work. We can take this in a Bakhtinian way: my field is shaped by myself and my interlocutors. It is not a question of whom I agree with, but of whom I *must* engage. The "must" indicates that these choices are primarily not personal ones. If I want to publish in a certain place, to become a participant in a certain field, I must engage the prevailing voices in the field as currently constituted. In my field of literary theory, for example, I cannot talk about examples without at least mentioning Derrida or about intellectuals without considering Bourdieu. But I can ignore Nelson Goodman on examples completely, and Shils and Gouldner on intellectuals.

The point is that many topics are shared by different fields. The difference resides not in the object studied, but in the constellation of positions about the object that the writer takes into account. Thus queer theorists have to consider psychoanalytic theories about human sexuality but can ignore with complete impunity biomedical work on the same topic. To some extent, biologists are beneath their notice; they have other people they want to engage, impress, convince. Fields rely on quick dismissals, founded almost entirely on ignorance. "There is nothing of value and interest being said by those people." Contempt circulates promiscuously between and among academic fields.

Much of this is a life-saving strategy. Theory has brought the injunction that one should read everything. It looks with suspicion on the traditional academic disclaimer: "That's not my field." But theory has had to develop its own forms of dismissal, since there is simply too much out there. We all need some way to account for our choices, to explain our ignorances. But I am discouraged that fields—which seemed to offer such interdisciplinary promise—have often been as bad as the disciplines. I hate the close-minded disciplinary attack on "theory" as the misguided attempt of literary critics or historians to be "philosophers" or "sociologists," as if all these enterprises cannot overlap or as if only strictly disciplinary training enables productive, instructive, and excellent work. Theory's interdisciplinarity, its construction of a field across the boundaries of disciplinary homes, is one of its great strengths. But I am equally distressed when I see theorists dismiss Anglo-American philosophy or liberal political theory wholesale, reading such work (when they do at all) with the foreknowledge that their job is to disagree with every word they read.

Fields, then, are both smaller than disciplines (which often encompass several fields) and potentially larger (because attuned to work in numerous disciplines). The trick is to try to import a new voice or new perspective into the current constellation. Success is very dependent on authority—starting with the establishment of one's own authority within the field (a laborious process). As Stanley Fish (1999) has argued, in most cases only an author possessed of such authority can succeed in introducing new material into the field. This suggests that innovation comes from established practitioners who first gained an audience by doing more conventional work.

Fields, like disciplines, are fluid, and are scenes for professional ambition. Fields even have their professional organizations and journals. But fields cut across the institutions structured according to disciplines and challenge the codifications of disciplinary training, disciplinary methodologies, and disciplinary right of access to particular object domains. The disciplines are far from dead, but they now have to co-exist (uneasily) with fields that refuse to simply function as sub-areas within the disciplines.

GRAND GESTURES

The most obvious impact of "theory" on American academic style has been the adoption of grand gestures in matters intellectual and political. American academics prior to 1965 generally followed the middle way advocated by Robert Merton, eschewing grand theorizing or all-encompassing projects. True, literary critics believed in epochal unities called Romanticism, Modernism, and the like, while also crediting (as did historians) notions of national identity. But they used terms like capitalism and imperialism rarely, and patriarchy, Western metaphysics, disciplinary society, and phallologocentrism were unknown.

There were, of course, engaged intellectuals, especially in New York City. But their style was rarely denunciatory on the grand scale, and even before 1950 the words "socialism" and "communism" were used tentatively in most cases. This was more a matter of decorum, of an intellectual antipathy to the unsubtle, than a matter of politics. Grand denunciations of Western civilization as rotten to the core did not enter American intellectual or academic life (these two overlap, but are not everywhere the same) until the Frankfurt School and French poststructuralism joined large-scale analyses with overt political commitment. The style caught on in America and is still around, although in decline. A certain diffidence, which was also a certain kind of irony, almost disappeared for twenty years (1970–1990), replaced by earnest declarations of political purposes and the ability of academic work to further those purposes.

For a skeptic like myself, who wants finer-grained analyses and a more tempered view of the connection between academic work and political effects, the decline of the grand gesture is still to be mourned. Ambitious, provocative, energetic, and idealistic work is always in short supply, even when (as is very rarely the case) academic fashion favors such work. And there is the suspicion that the current decline was largely the result of the constant sniping, inside the academy and out, about "political correctness." While I, too, cringed at the excesses of much leftist work, I'd rather take my stand with the leftists—both politically and stylistically—than with their enemies. I feel answerable to (because I share many of) the political aspirations of the left, while leftists constitute one of the audiences I want to read and be influenced by my work.

The recent decline of the grand gesture, the return of academic modesty, has also influenced the shape of academic careers. The babyboomers' attraction to grand theorists made various academics born between 1925 and 1950 attain prominence within the academy in their forties. Many of these magisterial figures—Harold Bloom, J. Hillis Miller, Edward Said, Sandra M. Gilbert, and Fredric Jameson in literary studies—are still active, but very few critics born after 1950 (Judith Butler, Henry Louis Gates, Jr., bell hooks, and Eve Kosofsky Sedgwick are the prime exceptions) have written books that everyone in literary studies feels they must read. After a period when "theory" served as a *lingua franca*, literary criticism has fragmented again, and reputations have become more localized even in those cases where the ambitions are larger.

HERMENEUTICS

Hermeneutics, the art of interpretation, as contrasted to the gathering of fact (historical investigation) or the presentation of causal explanations has irrevocably, it seems to me, upset the apple-cart of positivism. Even in the quantitative social sciences, "interpreting the data" now includes a heightened sensitivity to the categories that underlie statistical groupings, while the "hard" sciences will never again enjoy the unquestioned epistemological prestige they possessed prior to the advent of theory. Outside the quantitative fields, interpretation has won out over biography, editorial and other kinds of recovery work, and straightforward historical narrative; it is more prestigious and more universally required of students.

To the extent that the most prestige attaches to "theory," we should recognize how much of theory is interpretation of large-scale social structures and patterns. Literature departments were the first to embrace theory because they were already much involved in interpretation. But the locus of interpretation shifted from the single text to that text as symptom or representative of larger cultural forces. Just as theory was refracted through the interpretive practices of close reading in literature departments, it is refracted through specific interpretive traditions in anthropology, sociology, history, and the like when it makes an impact in those fields.

The increased emphasis on interpretation coincides with the loss of methodological consensus. When there is a proliferation of ways to do the work in any particular discipline or field, facts are more obviously byproducts of interpretive strategies, and those strategies must be more self-consciously deployed amidst competing possibilities. If the arrival of theory is experienced as a fall, that's because the serenity of self-evidence now has departed, presumably never to be regained.

IDENTITY

The perplexities of identity are endless. I'll start with a minor puzzle: How did the poststructuralist focus on difference (Derrida's *différance*) transmute into the obsession with identity?

There are two prominent images of modernity. The first is generally conservative and emphasizes how a rampant individualism has destroyed communal values, external checks on selfish behavior, and social order. Modernity is the chaos of all against all in the unbridled competition of a world shorn of all transcendent meaning. This vision can look radical when it inveighs against a godless capitalism. It invariably pits a nostalgia for community, imagined as a vague noncoercive fellowship with like-minded others, against experiences of *anomie*. The hallmark of this conservative vision is a willingness to trade in some individual freedom for order, authority, consensus, and fellowship. (That this vision co-exists with a nostalgic attachment to an individualistic entrepreneurial capitalism is just one of the internal contradictions of contemporary conservatism.)

The other account of modernity declares the notion of increasing individualism to be a myth. The modern world according to Weber, Adorno, and Foucault features increasingly powerful bureaucracies (both state and corporate) which manage individual lives down to the smallest detail. All modern societies tend toward totalitarianism, either of the overt type or of the more insidious forms that produce "mass society" through cultural institutions (schools, mass media, sports, the arts) and corporate capitalism. Centralized government, vast business enterprises, and the large-scale production of cultural meaning/value prevails. Differences are steamrolled into sameness, or, worse, recalcitrant differences are ruthlessly eliminated. (In Foucault's more diabolical version, differences are produced in order to make domination more effective.) Modern societies are less, not more, free than premodern ones. Under such circumstances, the Frankfurt School concluded that struggling to retain autonomous individuality (despite the fact that autonomy is the keystone of Kantian liberalism) is a radical response—and about the only one available in dark times.

An obsession with difference, then, coincides with the claim that modernity works to eliminate differences. But where is difference to be located? Poststructuralism, generally, does not locate difference at the level of the self. Derrida is not talking about the difference between one self and another. Mostly he seems to locate difference in units even smaller than selves. Individuals are fragmented, constituted of conflicting elements that threaten the very coherence of the idea of, the claim to, a self. Difference understood this way deconstructs identity.

But Derrida also, at times, locates difference in entities much larger than the self. He often writes as if "Western metaphysics" has an identity, while pointing toward the "Other" of metaphysics. The Other's difference functions rather differently than *différance*.

On the one hand, the Other is located in cultural formations or traditions that are distinct from or resistant to Western metaphysics. Here poststructuralism links up with what might be called "culturalism," defined as the poising of local, cultural differences against the universalizing juggernaut of modernization that is resisted through loyalty to and defense of specific "ways of life." One's identity stems from culture, not from soulless, uprooted modernity. Thus "identity" (as a source of meanings and motivations) names what is at stake in joining battle with modernity.

On the other hand, it is very hard to document modernity's crimes against the Other without, in the end, dealing with the individual. Walter Benn Michaels (1996) is interesting on this topic. How, he asks, do we characterize the crime of the Holocaust? Is it the attempted extermination of an entire culture or is it the murder of six million people? If we define genocide as the extermination of a culture, we seem to be valuing the culture over the lives, especially if we are aiming to say that murder is bad, but genocide is worse. Even if we do think there is a significant difference between genocide and mass murder, it remains the fact that mass murder is a crucial means to genocide. My point is that harm to otherness is almost always going to be measured, at some point, in terms of harm done to individual bodies. Thus it is difficult to have a discourse of otherness that does not locate otherness in individuality at least some of the time (where individuality is understood as marked off by the physical separateness of one body from another.) Identity is conferred by being the one subject to this harm, this injury. To the extent that poststructuralism focuses on the violence done to the other out of intolerance of difference, that other is going to be located, to some extent, at the level of the individual (the victim) who suffers that violence. And here poststructuralism comes very close (despite all its protests to the contrary) to espousing liberal notions of individual rights and pluralism.

The result has been a general confounding of poststructuralist thought with identity politics. Since the crudities and excesses of identity politics provide an easy target, both conservatives and anti-theory leftists have been quick to castigate theory for unleashing the multiculturalist hordes. To a large extent, the theoretical left has caved into this attack. Judith Butler (1990), Wendy Brown (1995), and a slew of collections with titles like *After Identity* (Danielsen and Engle, 1995) and *The Identity in Question*

(Rajchman, 1995) have marked high academic theory's abandonment of its erstwhile allies in the trenches of identity politics. The identity folks were an embarrassment. When it came to a choice between political alliances across differences in sensibility that reached in some instances (especially in feminism) beyond the academy and respect from their academic peers, the theoretical left only hesitated briefly before choosing their peers.

I will not defend identity politics from incoherence. How assertions and celebrations of differences fit in with notions of determination by group membership remains a mystery. But the emotional force of appeals to identity and the ability of such appeals to move people to action is worth a longer look. Here, surprisingly, I think Derrida rather than Foucault is closer to the impulses behind identity politics than one might at first suspect. The difference (dare I say) is between religious and secular outlooks, between piety and impiety. Modernity, generally, is secular. It understands identity as the self-creation of the self through action. Identity is out in front of me, in the future, to be made. The past is not a determinant. I can transcend my origins as I pursue a career open to talents. Here we have the quintessential American myth of the self-made man with the concomitant American impiety toward origins (and parents) and indifference toward the past. This rootlessness, this resting of identity on achievement rather than ethnicity, religion, gender, or region is characteristic of the professional class, of those who have benefited from and feel at home in modern society. They have used their careers precisely to escape their pasts.

But there is a whole different emotional relation to identity, and it is no surprise (careerist that I am) that I don't get it. Highly significant is the fact that this other sensibility now inhabits the professional world, instead of being checked at the door as the price of admission to it. Moreover, there is a generational divide here between those born before 1960 and those born after. For this later generation, there is a piety toward roots, toward the places from which one comes, toward the social markers of identity which is primary. Identity is not out in front of me, but back there from whence I came, and my goal is to express that identity in a world hostile to it (because of its differences). Identity is to be defended against the world's onslaughts against it, not abandoned and continually remade within the worldly structures of a career. Crucially, identity is not located within the self, not something the self makes and remakes as it proceeds. Rather, identity is lodged elsewhere, beyond and outside the self, and the issue is how to align the self with that elsewhere, to be true to its demands despite the world's attempts to seduce me away. Derrida would use very different terms than my students, but pious references to that elsewhere, and to the responsibilities it enjoins to the self, pervade his work. The primacy of the Other is what both gives the self an identity and the responsibility to protect it (as an otherness) against the stripping away of identity toward sameness characteristic of modernity.

JUSTICE

The old left focused on justice, especially economic justice. But the emphasis of the social movements of the 1950s through the 1980s was more on "rights" and "liberation." Academic theory followed suit. Freedom, not justice, was the major concern. This shift reflected the fact that issues of liberation (respect for identity differences, the end to legal discrimination against various stigmatized groups, struggles to expand the franchise and citizen participation, resistance to state compulsion in non-economic matters such as the draft, abortion, and sexual practices) proved more powerful than economic issues in provoking popular political action. There was also a need to reject a moribund Marxist tradition, to invent a "new left."

Now, in the 1990s, there has been an attempt to revive concepts of justice, especially in the environmental justice movement, but also in relation to welfare reform, and to the on-going widening of the gap between the haves and have-nots. Despite some gestures toward justice in theory circles (notably Derrida's wonderful and frustrating essay "Force of Law" [1992]), matters of justice still remain under-discussed. Political concern in academic work still centers in a cultural politics of representation, resignification, and liberation from the limits of received thought. Such cultural politics often looks therapeutic, focused on exposing and combating social pathologies like sexism and racism as psychological rather than institutional matters.

It is no surprise that academics who locate the most effective point of intervention at the cultural level are prone to use psychoanalytic terms and theory.

I know, intellectually, that this is a time worn and fruitless internal political squabble on the left. Do we most effectively promote change by reforming social institutions or by transforming people's heads? The answer is that work on both fronts is necessary, and that nothing guarantees the effectiveness of either strategy. You do the work you can where you are, without knowing how or if it will make any difference in the short or the long run. "Pessimism of the intellect, optimism of the will." And the experiences of the past fifty years, especially of the civil rights' movement and its aftermath, do seem to indicate the crucial importance, if not priority, of cultural politics. Ending legal discrimination hardly ended racism; fundamental shifts in belief, attitude, the taken-for-granted, and the habitual appear necessary to any progress in race relations.

So why do I still find cultural politics suspect, suspicious both of its analyses of the problems and its proposed solutions? Recognizing that I am probably being unfair, I still cannot help finding the characteristic discourses of cultural politics arrogant. The vast social majority is presented as benighted, unaware of how they actually think, how they process their experiences and make their decisions, unlike the enlightened writer, who holds the interpretive key to society's unconscious. Moreover, I cannot help seeing the displacement of economic and political inequality by an ideological terrain of beliefs, values, and attitudes serving to distract us from the relatively privileged position from which the authors of ideological critique always write. My response is shot through and through with intellectual and class *ressentiment*, and it is worth saying that Martha Nussbaum's high-toned moralism elicits the same response in me as Slavoj Žižek's bombastic psychologism. In part, I am a vulgar Marxist—and a vulgar liberal of the J. S. Mill and John Rawls variety—who insists that provision of the economic means for a good life (substantially beyond subsistence) is the sine non qua of a just society. Since our society hardly meets this standard, the first political duty is to point out that shortfall, and the second duty is to work to eliminate it. I understand that cultural politics pursues its indirect method because it believes that direct efforts have failed through the social psyche's inability to apprehend the problem of unequal distribution. But 65 percent of me believes cultural politics is too subtle by half. The people on the bottom know they are being screwed and the people on top know they are screwing them. The resistance to change isn't psychological, a matter of false consciousness or subject formation; it is simply the power of the powerful to maintain arrangements that suit them. No sooner do I write this, however, then my other 35 percent thinks of the convenient lies the powerful tell themselves (about effort, and merit, and opportunity) to get off the hook for the purposeful perpetuation of injustice, and of the "hidden injuries of class," of the ways the poor believe that they deserve their fate.

KNOWLEDGE AND TRANSFORMATION

Are interpretations knowledge? What exactly is produced when we "read" a text or an event? The hankering after knowledge, defined as the delineation of fact, of truths about a mind-independent reality, is still strongly present after three hundred plus years of epistemological battering. Even though more and more post-theoretical writers are trying to kick the habit, prevailing practices run against anti-realist principles. Canons of evidence (quoting from the text; offering statistics; referring to historical events and dates) assume a world out there and discernible facts pertaining to it. A pure anti-realism is probably unattainable, so we are not going to bypass the epistemological woes attending claims to knowledge by simply declaring that we make no such claims. But we can try to decenter knowledge claims, shifting the emphasis from what our work tells us about the world that existed before we wrote to how our work acts to shape the world that will exist tomorrow.

Writers are engaged in a species of magic. Freud discovered in the "talking cure" that to name a past that had been unnamed (unremembered) enabled the patient to project a new future. It hardly mattered if this act of naming was accurate in any traditional sense. What matters is that the patient has taken charge of his or her own life, has assumed the ability and the right to name the past and thus to name and own the future. This naming will not acquire reality, will not actually create a future, unless it is endorsed by others. Efficacious magic is a social, not a solipsistic, act. Others, however, do not have to endorse the truth of my naming; they may even vehemently object that I have gotten it totally wrong. The important thing is that they recognize my action and respond to it. I have already done something in that case. My action is an action because it provokes a response, puts me into new relations with those who respond, as well as to those things I have newly named. If we re-imagine our academic work as transformative action upon and within the world, its status as knowledge becomes secondary. Or, we might say, its status as knowledge is more about the intersubjective relations of addressing others (i.e., rhetoric) than about the lineaments of reality.

Let's, following Hannah Arendt, be fancy about it. This understanding of intellectual activity as the public enunciation of interpretive namings demotes epistemology (knowledge of the world) and promotes ontology (the creation of the world through dialogic interaction with others and objects).

KNOWLEDGE AND MONEY

While humanists pursue sweet dreams of creating the world through dialogic work, the university might be stolen out from under us. We live, as the pundits never fail to tell us, in an information age, in the knowledge economy. Universities have two functions: to educate students and to produce knowledge. The old idea was that the knowledge was disseminated in the classroom and through publication. It was placed in the public sphere, labeled as to origin (author), but underwritten financially by tuition dollars and general public investment (via taxes and philanthropy) in the university. Of course, there was some specifically commissioned research, especially that done for the government within the context of the Cold War. But foundations and donors generally took a hands-off approach to research topics and, more importantly, didn't claim proprietary rights to the research results.

All that has changed drastically in the past ten to fifteen years. While government funding has leveled off, the corporate world has increasingly turned to universities for specific research needs. And the recognition that the knowledge produced in (especially) scientific research has (sometimes) immense economic value has led to a sea-change in how research is commissioned and what happens to its results. Increasingly, new knowledge is licensed or patented, with the researcher, the university, and the corporate sponsor receiving designated shares in the product. Publication, even public discussion, of research results is delayed until licensing or a patent is secured. Professors in the fields effected are now as much entrepreneurs as academics, moving between the university laboratory and the business world.

Universities have gone down this path because they are money pits. Tuition—even with rises that greatly exceed the inflation rate—has never covered the costs of maintaining a university, especially a research university. The federal government underwrote much of that cost during the Cold War, and the humanities existed on the overspill of the federal largesse. But the corporate dollars that have stepped into the vacuum left by the shrinking of federal dollars are more directed than federal dollars, less tolerant of massive "indirect cost" rates. As a result, the humanities are in danger of withering away. Their only resource in the competition for dollars are alumni donors who retain a sentimental attachment to undergraduate liberal arts programs. Since the wealthiest donors, however, come from the same corporate world that is forging this new relation to the university, even individual donations are becoming more and more specifically targeted. The humanities increasingly have to "market" themselves and have to develop specific programs in response to donor demands or in the attempt to attract donor dollars. If the science professor is half entrepreneur, half academic, the humanities professor is on the way to becoming half fund-raiser and PR man. Universities are engaged in an endless search for money, and various units of the university are in competition for limited access to identified donors. Not having a product to sell to corporations places the humanities at a distinct disadvantage.

Of course, licensing is going to come to the humanities as well. There was always the opportunity to make a little money on the side by writing a textbook or editing an anthology. Such work was looked down upon, and you could only get away with it if you didn't do it to the exclusion of more prestigious (less remunerative) work, or if you simply brazened out your colleagues' disapproval. But the Internet may change this game by dramatically changing the sums of money in question. Right now, of course, copyright and its relation to the Internet is in flux. But humanists, while sometimes obsessed with intellectual property rights in ideas, have not had economic reasons for that obsession. Whether or not work in the humanities will actually attain any great economic value, we should fully expect speculative action based on that possibility. Licensing arrangements are going to become more prevalent—and will undoubtedly effect how some humanities professors view their work and their careers.

Beyond the sentimental value of the alma mater, all that remains to the liberal arts is prestige value. "Culture" of the highbrow sort still retains some value, although less and less all the time. But the prestige or "brand" value of the top universities has never been higher. University and college presidents rise and fall on the basis on the annual *U.S. News and World Report* ratings—and lower administrators have the squeeze put on them to pull their units up in the rankings. So the humanities do have some leverage on the general finances of the university because the humanities disproportionately (in relation to research dollars generated and numbers of majors) influence an institution's prestige. The humanities are a luxury item (for students as well as for universities) and, like most luxury goods, play a major role in both determining and representing status. For those of us who are foolish enough to take the humanities seriously, to believe in their transformative potential, the funding offered by bemused functionaries who find a little culture adds luster is just about worse than no funding at all.

LOVE

Critics of ideological readings of literature often complain that the "love of literature" has all but disappeared from today's English departments. What has love got to do with it? Consider the following statements:

> "I teach physics because I love electrons."
> "I teach the history of slavery because I love slavery."
> "I teach Shakespeare because I love Shakespeare."

Professionals, as opposed to businessmen, are supposed to love their work, to have other than mercenary motives for their undertakings. That is why, as Stanley Fish (1994) points out, professionals (with the exception of doctors and lawyers) desire handsome but not extravagant salaries (unlike corporate executives, who apparently have no qualms), and have elaborate non-flaunty ways to spend their earnings.

But to love your work does not necessarily translate into loving the object you work upon. The additional demand on English, music, classics, and art history professors has to do with aesthetics, not professionalism or education. English and other aesthetic departments often feel on the defensive in universities that seem increasingly driven to justify their work on utilitarian grounds. Especially in research universities, such departments are expected to publish, to make their contribution to knowledge. Yet sentimentality about the arts, about "culture" as something to be appreciated, generates a hostility toward the probing and questioning of Shakespeare even more than toward the demythologizing of George Washington or Thomas Jefferson. The on-going ambivalence of commercial society toward the arts—are they meaningless drivel of no worth or products of a social (spiritual?) superiority to be respected even where not understood?—phrases itself in this petulant demand that the professors love these non-utilitarian objects that they make their students study.

METHOD

Method, like amazon.com, is vastly overvalued. Methodology is an even bigger boondoggle. Rigor resembles nothing so much as *rigor mortis.*

As heuristics, methods, like disciplinary training, can open minds to new ways of thinking, to new angles of analysis. And methodology as the self-conscious consideration of the kinds of arguments being made and warrants being offered can help make the practitioner more aware of what he or she is doing. To believe, however, that methods or methodologies can either assure truth or conviction is to grossly underestimate the plurality of sources, connections, intuitions, prejudices, evidential conditions, and reasonings that play a role in any judgment of facts or values. Rigid adherents of method want to train (discipline) wayward minds and/or contain the messiness of thought and belief. The energy devoted to the enterprise suggests its similarity to efforts to hold back the sea. The leaks spring up daily and everywhere. I am not arguing that the effort has no benefits, only that the benefits are consistently exaggerated, the costs persistently under-reported.

One cost is dullness. How are you going to convince anyone if your careful, methodical work is too deadly to read? Methodological work is slow and predictable. It is "academic" in the sense of that word when applied to paintings. It keeps us going over the same ground again and again, never daring to assume anything, always required to spell out everything in excruciating detail.

Since you cannot, via care or method, guarantee your audience's acquiescence, why not step boldly into the dialogic arena? "Often wrong, but never in doubt," says Kenneth Burke. Let's make that our mantra for suggestive work painted in broad strokes, aiming to provoke as much as to convince. Let's be realistic about the various and unpredictable ways that an assertion strikes its auditors not merely as true or false, but as interesting, unsettling, inspiring, infuriating, depressing, exhilarating, boring, enlightening. When it comes to writing, energy is almost everything, method just about nothing. The goal, the trick, the difficulty is to get the spark down onto the page in such a way that it will then leap across the gap between writer and reader.

NIHILISM

It's always the other guy who is a nihilist. The modern imagination is haunted by two recurrent figures: the hubristic man who tries to step into the power vacuum created by the death of god (from Faust and Dr. Frankenstein to various criminals in Superman comics and James Bond novels) and the depressive who can't get out of bed because god is dead (from the Byronic hero to Camus's Mersault and John Barth's Jake Horner). Dostoyevsky brilliantly recognizes the two figures' essential affinity by combining them in Stavrogin in *The Possessed*.

Despite our being the Prozac nation, I am more impressed (as is Bruce Springsteen) by the regularity with which "at the end of every hard-earned day," we all once again "find some reason to believe." Bound by the networks of daily life with its persistent demands, its structures of involvement, and its worn paths of routine, the remarkable thing is how few people fall through the cracks and can no longer go through the motions. As a way of life, modern society has felt no less self-evident, no less solid, no less necessary to humans than any other historical way of life—at least if we go by the evidence of its relentless going-on. It seems less and less like modernity is built on sand, more and more like it is an implacable, unchangeable fact. And that implacability comes as much from its apparent ability to provide humans with all the meaning they need to keep functioning as from any other factor. Reports of nihilism are greatly exaggerated.

OBSCURITY

Modernity has its winners and its losers. On the most brutal economic level, this means the starvation of the "undeveloped." If modernity supplies them with any meaning, it is the meaning that rests in a desperate struggle for life itself. The obscurity of their suffering to the more fortunate relies, to some extent, on the geographical separations characteristic of the modern economic order. The prosperous are shielded from knowing on whom their prosperity rests. Consumers are carefully protected from suffering or even realizing the consequences (economic, environmental) of their consumption. Partly it is a matter of scale. It is hard to think through the consequences of my eating this hamburger when conjoined with 200 million other Americans also eating beef today. But there is also a concerted effort made to keep such information unavailable. Much is actively done to protect the sensibility of the consumer. The processes of manufacture are, like the poor, kept as far out of sight as possible. The complicity here is fairly complete: we (the consumers) don't want to know, and they (the producers) don't want us to know.

But this obscurity of consequences does not obscure the fact that there are winners and losers, and that the fate of the losers is precisely obscurity, to be shunted out of sight and left to fend for themselves. We should not underestimate the extent to which a clear vision of the consequences of losing keeps our noses to the grindstone. The "reason to believe" we find at the end of the day may often be little more than a vision of the cost of not getting out of bed to do it all again tomorrow. Nihilism is a luxury item.

All of this suggests that in the microcosm of the academy, where there are fewer jobs that those who want them and even fewer "good" jobs (the kinds of jobs which actually provide some chances of having the sort of intellectual life one got a PhD to obtain), the threat of obscurity looms large. Strategic decisions about the kind of work most likely to insure visibility must be made all along the line, and theory has made those decisions more difficult. Much evidence suggests that theoretical work is sexy. That's what students want to study; that's what the readers of academic books want to read. But to do theoretical work before tenure, and especially before having a job, can prove disastrous. There is some expectation in some quarters that people should do "traditional" or discipline-specific work first. But there is no consensus on this or any other topic of training or appropriate first projects. The job markets and prestige hierarchies, even within disciplines and fields, are fragmented, and thus every decision about what work to do has consequences, some of which cannot be calculated in advance. Obscurity always threatens, and the rules by which to avoid it are more obscure than ever.

POWER

After one hundred and fifty years of theoretical and all-too-real battles, four remnants of Marxism are left standing in American academic discourse (which came to Marxism very late): a certain sentimentality about class; a proclivity for analyses that locate causes at the structural or systemic level; a hopelessly confused reliance on concepts of ideology and hegemony; and a stubborn focus on power relations. Lenin's question of "Who is doing what to whom?" may not be asked in that form, especially since our notions of power have been depersonalized, but the centrality of power to any social analysis remains one hallmark of leftist thought.

A promiscuous understanding of power dominates the current scene. Power is doing it to someone at every conceivable site in every conceivable way—and "conceive" is the right word, because power is "productive." Foucault, of course, reigns supreme here, and I don't think it entirely coincidental that he was fascinated by the French tradition (from de Sade through the decadents to Bataille, Genet, and Artaud) that explores the erotics of inflicted pain.

Attention to power, whatever its genesis, seems essential to me, as does the insight that power operates in many different modes and, therefore, is contested in many different ways. No single key will unlock relations of domination. So there is nothing wrong with intellectuals in the human sciences focusing primarily on power's discursive forms and operations. We humanists are in the symbol business, so we should consider the symbolics of power. And the past eighty years (at least) offer ample evidence of the capacity of symbols to move people to action.

But I feel compelled to articulate two further worries about discursive, symbolic analyses. The first concerns judgments of harm. Some part of me wants to insist that sticks and stones may hurt my bones, but words will never hurt me. To collapse physical and/or material harm into discursive harm creates an undifferentiated mass exactly where the ability to make distinctions is crucial. Despicable as hate speech is, it is important to differentiate responses to it from appropriate responses to physical violence. At the "deeper" level of the discursive organization of thought, it is important conceptually to recognize that some acts of violence and exploitation are not accompanied by discursive categorization of the victim as "other." Greed, anger, and hate can be directed against my brother, even against my self. There has been a tendency to assert that discursive forms of violence, of categorization, underwrite all acts of physical and material harm.

My second worry is that a focus on the discursive too often leads to the naïve assumption that action on the discursive front will be transformative. Again, let me hasten to say that I am convinced that power functions discursively and that cultural politics has been demonstrably important on many fronts over the past fifty years. But I think we should be equally suspicious when intellectuals bemoan their impotence through marginalization and when they proclaim their corner of the universe—symbols—as the spot where the most fundamental action takes place. In other words, I accept, even insist, that power works discursively, but resist a unifying vision of power that places this discursive functioning at the ground level. Power works in myriad ways—and these ways stand in no necessary relation to one another. Not all of the ways have to be at work in any one instance, and the inter-relation among the ways will be different in different instances. Altering discursive practices has no necessary effects, and the political efficacy of centering our efforts on the discursive is never assured. There are decisions to be made every step of the way, decisions not only about what would be the most effective intervention in this case, but also decisions about what available resources make feasible in the way of action at the present moment, and what to devote attention to. There is no template that can substitute for or guide specific judgments made in relation to fallible assessments of the particulars.

QUEER

The most common assertion about discursive power is that it relies on strict categorization, on a place for everything and everything in its place. Thus the would-be challengers of this power favor the hybrid, the shape-changing trickster, the queer. That which confounds categories and crosses boundaries is thereby disruptive, if not transformative. Queer, then, stands strongly against the identity politics of homosexuality, eschewing the respectability and responsibility of a stable (albeit outlawed) desire for a mobile desire that cannot be pinned down by one name.

Queer importantly reminds us that sexual practices and desires are more various and fluid than our vocabulary for these matters admits. There may be nothing new under the sun when it comes to sex, but our language has yet to acknowledge what people are doing. Queer's disadvantage as a politics is akin to the flaw of all anarchisms. There is no discernible or imposable direction to the fluidities queer theory wants to celebrate. Beyond the liberatory hope that people will be left in peace as regards their sexual activities, a queer politics finds itself hard-pressed to think through issues of responsibility and harm in sexual relationships, not to mention even wider issues of human togetherness in society.

RACE

The lightness of queer theory, its failure to think past the lifting of social sanctions against non-standard sexual practices, is evident once we turn our attention to race. What could be heavier, more depressing? At century's end, the dream of integration is in shambles. The nation's schools are more segregated in 2000 than they were in 1960, and the actions of neither whites nor blacks show a deep commitment to fighting what has proved the path of least resistance. The benefits of integration have proved so elusive—hard to specify and even harder to achieve—that the constant effort required has come to seem not worth the trouble. Workplace integration has created a black middle-class, but with disastrous effects on the black community as a whole, both for the poor blacks left behind and for the successful blacks who suffer under the misconceptions and hatred generated by affirmative action. Society as a whole seems to have settled on peaceful co-existence; whites cede blacks certain spaces and a small slice of the pie, while coming down hard on every perceived threat (i.e., angry young black men) to the uneasy peace. The real achievements of the civil rights movement—the end of legal discrimination prime among them—begin to dim when contrasted with the woes attendant upon the continuing existence of blacks as a caste apart. A minimal legal tolerance of racial difference is no substitute for the interweaving of destinies which comes only from daily interaction.

Post-theoretical work should be honored to the extent that it has been obsessed with race. (Yes, white intellectuals have to be continually prodded by black intellectuals to keep race in view. But that blacks in the academy have such moral and intellectual authority already suggests a difference from how matters are arranged in other institutions.) Such work has refused to turn its face from a topic most of the country wishes would go away. Because of that wish, the obsession is more than justified. It is a responsibility. This effort to keep the intricate difficulties of race in America a continuing and continual topic of investigation, analysis, articulation, and debate exemplifies what a functioning intellectual class can—and cannot—do. Intellectuals cannot, on their own, make the nation face up to its persistent racial divides, but they can refuse to partake of the nation's desperate attempt to ignore the whole topic.

STYLE

The last entry wavers between intellectuals and academics. No surprise: most intellectuals in America are now, perforce, academics. The opportunities for a "man of letters" (with a partial exception for novelists) to make a living outside the university have shrunk to just about zero. So many academics are willing to write for a pittance (their monetary reward will come in pay raises) that newspapers and journals do not have to pay a living wage in order to fill their pages.

The much-lamented demise of the public intellectual stems from this stern economic fact. (In any case, Britain had true public intellectuals and, to some extent, still has. America did not. Every twentieth-century American you could nominate for the role was either in Europe or spent a lot of time on campus.) Once the universities began to subsidize publication, the economic burden of supporting intellectuals was lifted from the publishing firms. Of course, the existence of a "public"—especially a paying public—for the intellectual to address has always been a problem in America. *Partisan Review*'s influence and prestige had nothing to do with the number of readers it reached. *The New Yorker* has been losing money for over ten years now. So it is disingenuous —especially for writers funded by conservative think-tanks, the only extant economic alternative to taking an academic job—to blame academics for not addressing a non-existent public and for hiding out in universities which offer them the sole chance to have the money and free time needed to write anything at all.

The sting of the public intellectual debate comes in when one assumes that a narrowing of style is the real issue. The anti-theory crew takes the Wordsworthian position of calling for the plain language of "a man speaking to other men." Such a commonsense language has a broad appeal and rests on broadly applicable principles of logic, reason, evidence, and non-technical diction. Contemporary academic discourse, the claim goes, is too specialized, too exclusive.

The charge is close enough to the truth to score a palpable hit. Students both undergraduate and graduate have to be fairly carefully initiated into the mysteries of the craft before much academic prose becomes accessible to them. However, the common-sense language is hardly as broad as its apologists believe. Its standards of reasonableness and the like are no less limiting for going unnoticed.

The faults of contemporary academic style, however, have little to do with the triumph of theory and much to do with heightened publication requirements for securing, keeping, and advancing in academic jobs. The more that publication functions as *the* means for institutional evaluation of professors, the more such writing adopts professionally sanctioned forms. Hiring (via job markets organized by the professional associations), tenure (via the requirement of "outside letters"), and publication (via the reliance on "referees") decisions are increasingly centralized, with authority vested in national, not local, figures and institutions. (In practice, the local is often disvalued, with publications and/or presentations addressed to local audiences at best neutral and at worst harmful to one's professional standing.) The centralization of evaluation in the national professional community leads to increasing uniformity within fields. Departments with distinctive styles (the Chicago neo-Aristotelians) become more rare (only second-tier universities are now willing to risk oddness) as each department strives to be a microcosm of the discipline. Similarly, eccentric professors are an endangered species, since you can only publish if tuned into the prevailing questions and modes of argument in your field. Even the breaking open of the canon and the penchant of theorists to bring new texts into play have not worked very strongly against this move toward standardization. Nonstandard sources must almost always be bundled with more familiar materials, while the terms of the arguments made must be recognizable even if the text is not.

The issue, then, is not so much the difficulty of any particular academic's writing as the pressures of professionalization. It isn't that academic prose lacks a common-sense style, but that professional standardization works against having any style (defined as a distinctive angle of vision accompanied by a characteristic tone) at all. Apart from Derrida, Harold Bloom, and Stanley Cavell, who among the major figures of theory and post-theory could be called a great stylist, or even be said to have a distinctive style? Foucault is a great writer, but he has no particular style. Lacan had a style, but an awful one. Lyotard, Habermas, Deleuze, de Man, and Spivak are not even good writers. But lest I sound like a neo-conservative, let me hasten to remind you that the issue isn't good writing, but a distinctive style. The neo-cons' image of public discourse is equally flat, equally the enemy of style, although for different reasons. The academic audience doesn't miss style, because it wants the ideas, the engagement with the on-going debates in the field. In large part, the academic reads in order to fuel his or her own writing, and thus extracts the juice and throws the squeezed fruit away. The neo-conservative dislikes style because it is excessive, ungovernable, non-deferential (to common sense or any other extrinsic standard), unreasonable, apt to rock the boat. Just think of the wide range of nineteenth-century prose styles—vatic Coleridge; dyspeptic Carlyle; the jeremiads of Marx; the lay sermons of Arnold and George Eliot; Ruskin, magisterial one moment, whining the next; pompous, sentimental, and humorous Dickens; avuncular Trollope; cynical Thackeray; accusatory Zola; ironic Flaubert; playful Wilde—and you realize how shrunken our current palette is. Who today is a great personality in our public world by virtue of what he or she writes?

One contemporary response to this vacuum stresses autobiographical writing, with an accompanying interest in "voice." Where institutions flatten out the idiosyncratic, these academics (many of whom are women) want to recover the different through the personal. (We have another example here of an unexpected alliance between poststructural accounts of difference and an emphasis on differences located at the level of the self.) I am in favor of anything that works against the standardization of prose within or outside of the academy.

THEORY AND TRADITION

That the rise in theory coincided with a new aggression toward the tradition is contingent, albeit overdetermined. The increased demand for publication, with its insistence on novelty, makes the tradition feel like a burden while also disallowing the repetition of received truths. A publishing professoriate cannot just be the custodian of tradition. Scholar-teachers must use the tradition to generate new work. Negation of old chestnuts is the quickest path to novelty and notoriety, as Wilde and Shaw demonstrated one hundred years ago.

But we should also recognize that theory is an indispensable tool for the contemporary *arriviste*. Those who are to the manner born are steeped in the tradition; their sensibilities rise out of their immersion in a thousand books. As Matthew Arnold noted of the aristocrats he called barbarians and T. S. Eliot admiringly said of Henry James, such minds never rise to the level of ideas. General categories, codifications, and maps of the territory are instruments developed to aid those who are playing catch-up. Theory is a by-product of democratic pedagogy. It gives the student a handle on vast amounts of material he or she has never read nor experienced. The old-timers bemoan the ignorance of the theoretical, while the theoretical are amazed by the parochialism and complacency of the old-timers. We theorists read everything *and* have to publish, says my generation. But our elders point to all the things we have not read, all those minor poets who (because white males) have not benefited from the opening of the canon. Reading everything, they say, just means skimming the surface of more fields—with the resultant addiction to generalizations.

The fundamental shift, it seems to me, lies in the very goal of the whole enterprise. Formerly, the aim was cultivation, the development of a sensibility, and thus even the academic social climber had to bury any resentment he or she felt against the tradition and its institutions beneath an acquired and studied reverence. The Anglophilia of two generations of academics—pipes, sherry, and tweeds—marks this effort to become more lordly than the lords.

A more confrontational, irreverent, casual, and "authentic" style came in with the 1960s. Baby-boomer American male academics never feel quite comfortable in a tie and are never quite sure when they can get away without wearing one. Academics from this generation are no less *arriviste*, but are bound by a youthful oath never to "sell out." (This sensibility and its *pathos* are captured perfectly in Bruce Springsteen's "No Retreat, No Surrender," with its suggestion that the ultimate source is the kind of World War II movie that has now been revived by Steven Spielberg after the twenty-five-year lapse caused by the Vietnam War.) Certain notions of integrity, solidarity, and authenticity now had to be reconciled with going through the institutional hoops. Politically motivated work offered one possibility, a more critical and adversarial relation to the tradition another. (Don't get me wrong. That political work has personal motives is, for me, not a reductive dismissal of that work's significance or potential benefits.) In sum, the heightened demand for publication, the cultural and political sea-changes of the 1960s, the increased use of theoretical mappings to substitute for particularist immersion, the idea-oriented analyses of received bodies of knowledge, and the influx of women and non-white students with various reasons to be suspicious of the canon, all combined to change the status of tradition at approximately the same time (1970–75) that French theory hit these shores.

UNHEARD AND UNSEEN

Poststructuralism's interest in the "other" (dramatically evident in Foucault's work on madness, hospitals, and prisons) combined with the civil rights and feminist movements in this country to focus academic attention on neglected or forgotten voices. Much of the early emphasis in African-American Studies and Women's Studies was on "recovery work," bringing into the curriculum and the scholarly universe texts and other materials produced by or related to nondominant social groups. In literature departments, especially, it seems that the one thing we now succeed in conveying to all PhDs is a sensitivity to what has been or is potentially "excluded" in any syllabus or academic study. An ethic of all-inclusiveness, accompanied by a scrupulous attempt to search out the unheard and unseen, rules the roost, with some ludicrous, but many laudatory, results.

Theory's role here, to my mind, has been less positive. The problem is that much poststructuralist theory takes a strongly deterministic line, one that insists that thought and perception are products of conceptual systems that necessarily fall short of all-inclusiveness. To the Hegelian truism that something is defined in relation to what it is not, poststructuralism (in some versions) adds that we are necessarily unconscious of that thing which lies outside the borders of the defined. The "unthought" or the "unthinkable" constitutes all we are conscious of, but itself lies beyond the reach of consciousness. Yet we have an ethical responsibility to this unheard and unseen other. A hyper-scrupulosity accompanies this mysterious call of the other. We can't (because of the necessary limits of perception) hear the sound of the tree falling in the forest, but have an absolute responsibility to respond to it. And then we get one further scruple: if we do hear the tree, that hearing will be a translation of the tree's sound into our representational system, a translation that violates the tree's "irreducible alterity" and thus is precisely the opposite of a truly ethical response. "The violence of metaphysics" names this will to appropriation, this persistent drive to understand things on our terms.

Frankly, the appeal of this ethics (most fully developed in Levinas and Derrida, but also evident in Lyotard, Nancy, and others) baffles me. It is not that I am firmly in the "ought implies can" school, although I do think, given all the evil in the world, that focusing on achievable ethical goals would do more good. My chief response is that this ethics seems awfully thin when confronted by the textured thickness of our interactions with actual others. Levinas has written thousands of pages on an idea that seems exhausted to me after a few paragraphs—since any specification of what the call to responsibility might actually mean in the context of lived relations to others would violate the alterity that underwrites the absolute unrefusability of this ethical demand. This ethics goes on and on about "the other," but almost never talks of others, in what seems to me, finally, a very solipsistic or religious focus on the relationship between self and God (now renamed the other), instead of a social focus on the many relations in which we stand to numerous other people. As a result, too much of what is ethically relevant in human existence is just passed over. Since humans continually mistreat, in very specifiable ways, others who are not absolutely beyond the pale of our modes of thought and representation, I'll gladly settle for an ethics that starts closer to home and has concrete things to say and judgments to make about particular courses of human action. To be worrying about some other of whose existence I am unaware because of the inbuilt limits of thought seems quite a luxury when there are millions of others I can see and hear who are suffering from the ills "man does to man."

I want to lodge a theoretical, as well as this practical, protest against poststructuralist ethics. I talk of "obscurity" above, which indicates that I am greatly moved by the general concern of academics over the past thirty years for the neglected and overlooked. For that very reason, it seems crucial to me to insist that nothing and no other is *necessarily* beyond our capacity to apprehend or *necessarily* harmed by the modes of that apprehension. Poststructuralism, surprisingly, remains addicted to transcendental arguments of the Kantian sort, the identifying of necessary (usually formal) conditions underlying an activity. The notion that form is determinative has gotten way too much credence. For example, a parliamentary form of government will tend to certain effects as opposed to an absolute monarchy. But what effects will actually ensue depends (contingently) on the interaction of the form of government with countless other factors in the actual society and time of the interaction. Similarities of form are no guarantee of similarity of outcomes. Thus, to claim that the form in which an other is described can be judged "violent" and "unethical" in every single case, with no attentions to the particulars of cases, seems to me simply wrong. Such an approach also takes the easy way out, enunciating a general principle to avoid precisely what makes ethics so troublesome: the need to make differentiated judgments on a case by case basis.

Transcendental arguments also violate the rule of symmetry, or what might be called the anti-arrogance rule. The philosopher (or social critic) should not arrogate to himself an ability to discern harm not allowed to others. If we are necessarily blind to certain harms or necessarily unable to articulate certain harms, then how does the philosopher know that some harm, some violence, is occurring? If the other who we say is harmed is unconscious of the harm, then where does the harm reside?

The basic principle here is that harm is a human concept, that contestation over what constitutes harm is the very stuff of ethics, and it abrogates the very enterprise by trumping that contestation in the name of a harm no one but the philosopher (and he only dimly) can perceive.

But what about the harm done to non-human others? Poststructuralist ethics, with its effort to get beyond the limits of human articulations of harm, is often seen as particularly useful for environmental ethics or animals' rights efforts. I don't see how an escape from the human is possible here. Ethical claims are claims made by humans upon other humans, sometimes in relation to non-human entities (the earth, the gods, animals). But until the claim has been articulated in human language, addressed to specific humans, and acknowledged in human practices, it does not take up residence in human societies.

And I, at least, would not want it any other way. Ethical claims can only be contested if they are made within the same kinds of dialogic space that enable social interactions. Poststructuralist ethics, oddly enough, aims at creating a primordial, absolute, uncontestable ethical demand (the unrefusable call of the other) below or prior to dialogic contestation. Somehow, the general claim that we are all guilty of harms we cannot even apprehend and all responsible for others we will never (and should never presume to) know is seen as guaranteeing that we will, at least, have an ethics. But I take it that the twentieth century teaches that there is no such guarantee. When the claims of actual others are so persistently ignored, the notion that the claim of unheard and unseen others will save ethics appears quixotic to say the least. Humans do evil things, just as humans construct ethical principles and make ethical claims upon one another in an effort to prevent evil. The contest between evil and ethics gives neither side an inevitable leg up—and no philosophical legerdemain can tilt this balance of power. Ethics rests on the multiple decisions made one at a time by the multiple human agents who live amidst others and their competing claims for recognition, love, care, resources, justice, freedom and the various other goods (material and non-material) that remain in all too scarce supply. There are various ways that these claims can be silenced or ignored, but no necessity that some can never be heard, and no remedy other than the persistent effort to gain a hearing in spite of the forces striving to maintain obscurity. That this conclusion will sound harsh to many of my readers only suggests to me that they still believe in some philosophical solution to, some transcendent substitute for, the endless human effort to restrain human evil.

Not only Republicans are worried about values. There has been a general outpouring of academic books, within theory and without, on ethics, morality, and values over the past fifteen years. Professional ethics in business and especially medical schools is a growth field, even as philosophers of all stripes have returned to issues and questions that lay long dormant in the wake of logical positivism's assault on moral statements as "noncognitive indications of preferences."

I have already suggested that poststructuralist ethics seems concerned to combat the ethical skeptic—and takes a surprisingly traditional route (the identification of an inescapable grounding necessity) to do the trick. My view of ethical skepticism (i.e. the denial of any or all ethical claims upon behavior) is akin to my view of nihilism. It is a phantom more than a reality. I take my cue from C. S. Peirce's critique of Cartesian doubt. It's a parlor game (as Hume also noticed) to discard one's commitments totally—and has no relation to how selves actually function in the world. Each person always already has beliefs and values. Those beliefs and values may change (although even that is a laborious process and probably fairly rare), but they are not shed altogether. Beliefs and values orient us in the world; they are what allow us to pick out the salient features (from the angle of vision they form) in any situation and to make decisions, register impressions, and act. A person without values would be a person without qualities.

Philosophical ethics has been far too preoccupied with trying to answer the hypothetical question: "Why have any values at all?" The more pressing question is: "How do we live in a world with multiple and conflicting values?" I believe that, as history bears out, we cannot achieve unanimity about values. Furthermore, as a matter of principle or theory, despite the dreams of some philosophers and many cultural conservatives, achieved unanimity around unquestionable absolutes seems much more dystopic than utopian. How could we wish for a world in which independent thought, a questioning attitude, and behavior that went against received opinion completely disappeared?

Yet, perpetual disagreement can only be desired when constrained within codes of civility that allow basic life-world activities to continue unimpeded. Civil war is not a condition to be wished on anyone. Some middle-ground between absolute agreement and absolute discord is the goal—which is why ethics as an enterprise must always resist simplistic solutions. We need two opposite poles—contestation and agreement—and in a proper balance that is contingently related to various other factors (such as degrees of economic inequality) in any particular situation.

I want to note two complications in prevailing attitudes toward values among contemporary academics. A significant plank of any liberal *ethos*, and the central plank of Kantian ethics, is the value placed upon individual autonomy. Contemporary theory usually takes umbrage at all things liberal, and has significantly and convincingly argued that selves are not as autonomous in their values and their decisions as liberal accounts imagine. Even if we adopt a fairly integrated view of the self as a bundle of beliefs, values, memories, and habits carried through time, that self is constructed through social processes that shape its most fundamental commitments. (In fact, many contemporary theoretical accounts make it hard to account for differences among the products of these social processes.) Yet even as autonomy is critiqued as a fact and as an ideology, almost all academics honor it as an ideal in their practice as teachers. Most of us believe it is an outrageous abuse of our power to insist (for grading purposes) that students agree with our opinions or values. More generally, most of us scrupulously strive to give our students the tools to think for themselves, rather than supply them with certain content as unquestionable truth. And in even the most radical and anti-liberal theoretical work, a bottom-line autonomy of selves is almost always assumed as among the ethical and political goods being sought. My point is not to claim that such work is hopelessly confused, nor that liberal values hold a universal allegiance even among those who claim to dispute them (Habermas seems to believe something like this), but to suggest that the ethical good we seek (that balance between absolute unanimity and dysfunctional disagreement) does not translate easily into being simply for or against autonomy.

Similarly, an ethic of all-inclusiveness is too simplistic. Differential judgments will be made all the time; ethics says we should justify those judgments. A call to avoid all such judgments can only be made in a discourse that is safely separated from the real world. The writers producing such calls are almost always involved in deciding whose work gets published and who will be admitted to their graduate programs. It is hard to avoid the sense that many academics pride themselves on keeping their hands clean—and they do so only by ignoring their own daily acts of judging (grades, for starters) and by leaving the dirty work to be done by others. Yes, many of our excluding judgments are outrageous. But I am convinced that the proper ethical response is not some general condemnation of all judgments. Rather, ethics involves the explicit examination and articulation of our values as they are lived out in our judgments. Every judgment is accountable to those values, and every value should be open to contestation by others. The scene of judgment and its evaluation by others needs to be as public as possible. Obscurity here, as elsewhere, serves the privileged (those who have the power to exclude) better than the vast majority.

THE WORLD-WIDE WEB

My department hired two assistant professors in instructional technologies and I felt intimations of old fogeyism. Here, I thought, is the first new thing coming down the pike on which I will pass. It's all well and good for them, but I can see my way safely to retirement without having mastered or used the Web, being ignorant (and proud of it) of chat-rooms, and never having to teach a distance-learning course.

Two years later, I am not so sure. My essential activities—read, think, discuss, talk, write, grade papers—are starting to look a little different. I don't think computers will change everything. But they will change some things, are doing so already, and academics (even in the humanities) are not going to be able to hold out much longer.

The predicted impacts on written work have been slow to materialize. But I like the formal possibilities, especially for tiered texts. An overture would hit all the main themes, and then readers could click on various items to get fuller expositions, supporting arguments, references, and even full source materials. As a writer, the flexibility of different organizational strategies appeals to me. Since I am one of the few people I know who is addicted to reading books from cover to cover, I'm more wary as a reader. My reading habits may be less flexible. I find contemporary magazine (and grade-school textbook) layout, with its side-bars and boxes (anything to disrupt continuous reading over several pages), deeply annoying. I crave the consecutive when reading, even while finding it less than satisfactory for much of what I want to say when writing. Hence tiered texts of discrete, consecutive parts make sense to me.

New publishing formats—digital, on-line, or otherwise—strike me as neither here nor there unless they shift possible audiences. To put something on the Web strikes me as equivalent to putting it in a drawer, not because I care about the refereeing process, but because there is no targeted, no designated, audience. The academic who publishes a book that sells 800 copies can still feel read if that book is taken up by his or her field. There are, in other words, all kinds of institutional venues for the book. By contrast, the novelist who sells 5000 copies will much more likely feel his book has sunk without a trace, perched on several thousand public library shelves. (Of course, many academic books also generate that feeling, but not if they sell 5000 copies.) The Web is so amorphous, so unorganized, so (in a word) a-institutional, that, despite its touted dialogic capacities, publishing on it seems a wanton disregard of the desire to reach an audience for an academic like myself who has gained a place in the institutional conversation. The time and energy required to write are hard to summon—and the effort is driven (once the institutional ladder has been climbed) by the urge to connect with the reader. I cannot imagine the reader provided by the World Wide Web. This imaginative incapacity on my part defines the gap between me and the younger scholar who is Web oriented. I ask "why bother?" where my younger colleagues see the very place in which they want their work to appear. Of course, one usually assumes the visibility of pieces that appear in the places one reads. When I start using the Web more, perhaps I'll start believing that others like me will see and read what's on the Web. I can't predict if that will happen. My old fogeyism hangs in the balance.

XENOPHOBIA

The next person who says, knowingly, that "Derrida and his ilk haven't been taken seriously in France for years" should be condemned to a year of reading only Lacan—in French. The same anti-theory zealots who derided American academics for slavishly granting authority to all things French now appeal to the authority of reported French disdain for all things poststructuralist. The national identity of ideas is irrelevant; the idea of national identity needs to be exploded.

A YAULD YIRR

I've ended up with something between a rant and an essay. I began with the hope of conveying why my reaction to theorists and anti-theorists alike is so often "a plague on both your houses." I don't want to be a curmudgeon, or one of those smug and nasty types who congratulate themselves on speaking home truths no one wants to hear. (These supposedly lonely truth-tellers, from Allan to Harold Bloom, have consistently found larger audiences than the conformist cowards they sneer at.) I take it that academics (especially) have a duty to be optimistic, since pessimism is the easy road to doing nothing, to taking the world's ills in stride. So if I yirr (snarl or growl as a dog does), I must be yauld (active, vigorous) about it—and in the service of an active moving forward. What really irks me are tunnel vision, narrowness of scope and purpose, and disdain for work that explores different questions, follows different protocols, and has different aspirations from one's own. Relieved of the most serious threats to life and granted the space and time for reflection and inquiry, academics should respond by opening up the vistas of themselves, their colleagues, their students, and whatever audience they can reach beyond the academy. Theory, broadly conceived, has encouraged such opening more than it has shut it down. Evidence of active, challenging, expansive academic work is all around us—and that's cheering news.

ZARATHUSTRA

The temptation is to close with prophecies. Theory has brought to academics the anxieties of fashion. What is the next new thing? Will I look outdated? How do I stay ahead of the curve?

In fact, the pace of change seems to have slowed down. We seem to be in a phase of assimilating, sifting through, and putting into practice the various new concepts and approaches theory suggests. There has been no "big" theoretical book that "everyone" must read since Judith Butler's *Gender Trouble* and Eve Sedgwick's *Epistemology of the Closet*, both of which are now more than ten years old. Another—more troubling—sign is that there are no forty-something European figures who are as known or read now as Habermas, Foucault, and Derrida were at that age. This fact is troublesome, and reflects a broken tie with Europe, severed by the retirement of the émigré generation that staffed American universities after fleeing Nazi Europe. Returning to the mono-lingualism of seventy years ago (made only marginally less isolating by the ascendance of English as a global language), American universities may now simply be less capable of attending to foreign-born ideas than they were thirty years ago. It is not as if the loss of the European connection has been accompanied by any great strides toward connection with the rest of the globe. Intellectual globalization is barely an idea, and nowhere near a reality, irrespective of economic developments.

But the absence of new Derridas and Foucaults on the scene also suggests a pluralism that seems both positive and abiding. For a very short space in the 1960s (during the student movements that did sprout up all around the world) and an equally short time in the 1980s (when the term "postmodernism" did seem to capture some essential features of the time), our era fleetingly possessed a unity, an identity. But these moments dissolved into times whose varied characteristics are belied by any overarching designation. No one figure represents in himself or in his work our era; no intellectual movement speaks to every aspect of our "condition." There is too much going on in too many different places. Such pluralism makes it foolhardy to predict what the future will look like, what will win out, what fade away. I think that the best we can hope (and should work) for is that pluralism itself is our future, that no one of the various viewpoints competing for attention manages to win general acclaim and crowd out the others. Which just might be my own way of proclaiming that god is dead.

CHAPTER 4

Humanists, Cultural Authority, and the University

Two quasi-public debates stirred the thoughts that comprise this chapter. The first concerned faculty salaries at the University of North Carolina, Chapel Hill, where I teach. In a state where the median household income in 1998 was $36,985 and 13.8 percent of the population was under the poverty level of $17,029 for a family of four, UNC tried to make the case that faculty salaries—which averaged $51,000 for assistant professors and $86,000 for full professors—were not "competitive." (These figures exclude the medical school and, thus, are not artificially high. There is no available breakdown for salaries in the humanities, but my sense is that they deviate at most $10,000 from the cited numbers. Starting salaries for assistant professors in the English department are currently in the mid to high 40s.) These salaries place UNC 34th out of 84 Research I and AAU Institutions in faculty compensation.[1] The university asked the state legislature for an appropriations increase that would match an increase of 25 percent in tuition over three years, with the money specifically earmarked for increased faculty salaries and increased aid for students of demonstrated need. In-state tuition in 1998–99 was $2262, already a 56 percent increase from 1993–94's $1454. Out of state tuition was $11,428. 82 percent of our students are from North Carolina.

1. Figures are for 1998–99. Sources: "In US, Poverty at Lowest Since '79," *Raleigh News & Observer*, Sept. 27, 2000: 1A, 15A. UNC figures are from the Office of Institutional Research and are available on its web site: www.aid.unc.edu/ir. Subsequent figures are from the same source unless otherwise noted.

The internal faculty debate over this issue divided into three camps, each of which published a position paper in the state's newspapers. The first group made the market argument that UNC's preeminence as a research university required that it pay competitive salaries—and then added that UNC's research, reputation, graduates, and entrepreneurial spin-offs contributed mightily to the state's booming economy. The second group supported the students' opposition to a tuition increase, advocating adherence to the state constitution's provision that "the General Assembly shall provide the benefits of The University of North Carolina and other public institutions of higher education, as far as practicable, be extended to the people of the State free of expense." Legislative appropriations had shrunk from 42.5 percent in 1986 to 31.3 percent in 1996 of the university's total annual revenues. The state was withdrawing its support of a public university and shifting the burden to students, a strategy necessitated during a time of economic prosperity by large tax cuts during the 1990s. This group advocated a more holistic appraisal of the university's problems—including scandalously low wages for support staff and a crumbling infrastructure—in relation to the "depublicization" of the university.

The third group lamented the obsession with "peer institutions" and *US News and World Report* rankings, arguing that the particular ethos of UNC had eroded with the arrival of increasingly bureaucratic and impersonal modes of "accountability" and increasing pressure on faculty to achieve "national prominence" in one's field as opposed to contributing to the local intellectual community of colleagues and students. Play that game in evaluating faculty and, of course, they will develop no loyalty to the institution and will bolt for the first job that pays more. Repair of local working conditions in defiance of the university's "rationalization" (in Max Weber's sense) would do far more for faculty retention than salary increases. We needed to resist the one-size-fits-all model of what a university should be and how it should be ranked.

Although far more sympathetic with the second and third groups, I found myself in sharp disagreement with them all. For a start, no one liked it when I insisted that UNC is welfare for the upper middle classes. The tuition is outrageously low, especially when 56 percent of incoming students in 1999 reported a family income of over $75,000, just about twice the state's overall median.[2] Tuition will never cover the whole cost of a

2. Figures are from the 1999 Freshman Survey taken at UNC, Chapel Hill, administered by CIRP (Cooperative Institutional Research Program). This survey offers the following

college education; subsidies from various other sources will always be necessary. A progressive financial aid system can insure access for all students—and is more likely to be tolerated than a genuinely progressive state-wide income tax. Cuts in tuition aid over the past twenty years contribute to the fact that "in 1979 kids from the top socioeconomic quarter of American families were four times more likely to get a college degree than those from the bottom quarter; now they are ten times more likely."[3] Higher education, in other words, has played a major role in American society's steady movement toward plutocracy. The upper middle class should at least have to pay a substantial tuition toward the maintenance of the institution that secures its social and economic standing.

Even more telling is the disproportionate share of North Carolina's education budget that goes to its flagship campus. Chapel Hill has 15,400 undergraduates, about 12 percent of the total enrolled in the 16 campus UNC system. Add graduate students and Chapel Hill enrolls 16 percent of all students studying at a UNC system campus. But UNC, Chapel Hill, receives 25 percent of the system's annual budget.[4] The contrast with public K-12 education in North Carolina is even more stark. The state ranks 38th in annual per student expenditure, at $5,315 in 1995–96 when the national average was $6,392. Only Georgia and South Carolina had lower average SAT scores for its high school graduates in 1997–98.[5] The governor's big initiative over the past five years was to raise starting teacher salaries in K-12 to $25,000 by the year 2000, a goal that was accomplished.

UNC, Chapel Hill, in other words, is a rich school in a poor state. Or, more accurately, it is a privileged school in a moderately prosperous state that has a long history of neglecting the education of the many while supporting the education of the few. (That history, of course, is connected first and foremost to segregation and, then, to desegregation. After 1960, public schools were underfunded because many whites fled to "private academies.") To call for increased state allocations to Chapel Hill in view of

---

figures nationally for highly selective public universities: 48 percent with family incomes of $75,000 or more, and for all public universities: 38 percent with family incomes $75,000 or higher. My thanks to Lynn Williford for tracking down this information for me.

3. Rorty (1998, 86). Rorty cites Karen Arenson, "Cuts in Tuition Assistance Put College beyond Reach of Poorest Students," New York Times, Jan. 27, 1997, B1. Of course, other factors contribute to the class profile of our students, including access to better (public or private) schools before college with the resultant more competitive SAT scores when applying to college.

4. These numbers come from the website of the UNC system's General Administration, www.ga.unc.edu and from UNC, Chapel Hill's web page, www.unc.edu

5. Figures are from the *Digest of Educational Statistics 1999.*

more pressing needs elsewhere in public education looked to me like a formula for perpetuating and even widening the gap between haves and have-nots. To whine publicly about faculty salaries when public school teachers and our own support staff were abominably paid was worse than insensitive. Thus I found myself the sole advocate for a raise in tuition that would free state revenues to be allocated elsewhere.

It would be easy to say that I was taking a position contrary to my colleagues' and my own economic interest, so they inevitably rejected it. I think the situation was far more complex. The money was an important factor. I hope to write in the future about the constant and nerve-wracking anxieties about money that plague most American families earning less than $125,000 a year.[6] I will only relate here that UNC issued its faculty Diners Club cards last year for use during university-related travel. Four months later, we received a directive that their personal use was forbidden. It seems a significant portion of the faculty had maxed out the card's credit line within weeks of receiving it.

Beneath the money worries, however, lurked a more general and truly bitter sense of being ill-used. A conviction that one is overworked and under-appreciated is perhaps endemic to any hierarchical organization, but is exacerbated by the peculiarly individualistic structure of academic achievements. The academic career is almost entirely self-fashioned. You're on your own, baby. The projects are self-generated and, by and large, the work is all done by one person, who is also responsible for securing the time and funding that permit the work to get done. That work, often called "my own work," is also separate from the teaching which takes much of the professor's time—and which is barely noticed unless done extremely well or extremely poorly. (The model is different in the sciences, where there is less teaching and more research collaboration.) Yet this academic free agent is peculiarly dependent on the recognition of others, their appreciation and reward of the individual's efforts. Most academics were praised throughout their school years—and suffer greatly from a dearth of praise, a being-taken-for-granted, as adults.

But I want to insist that this personal grievance connected to local neglect is not the whole story either. The more general grievance is that academic work is undervalued by society. When salary matters are discussed, aca-

6. Schor (1998, 7) cites a survey in which 27 percent of respondents earning over $100,000 a year, 39 percent earning from $75,000 to $100,000, and 50 percent earning from $25,000 to $35,000 report, "I cannot afford to buy everything I need." A more objective measure is that 63 percent of households earning between $50,000 and $100,000 are in credit card debt (19).

demics don't talk about how much more than school teachers they make, but about how much less than other professionals—doctors, lawyers, MBAs. "I am as smart, I have invested as much time and money in my education, as these others, but I am making a sacrifice to do the work of education." The market discounts the academic's abilities, the academic's work. Students and their families won't pay the full cost of education and, increasingly, the state won't either. The difference has to be made up by private benefactors, by corporations contracting for specific services, and by the willingness of talented people to take lower salaries in return for various amenities such as significant autonomy. This bargain rankles.

For whatever reasons—maybe I am just a sweet-tempered guy—I don't feel these grievances. I am impatient with, annoyed and even outraged by, the pissing and moaning of many academics. (Admittedly, this salary issue brought out the worst in everyone.) Perhaps it's because I spent twelve years teaching in less wealthy schools before arriving at UNC instead of coming straight to Chapel Hill from grad school at Yale or Harvard. I often want to send my colleagues for a three year stint at Fayetteville State University or East Durham High School when I hear them complaining. More globally, I have always been amazed at how privileged academics are. (When I said just that to colleagues, while I was earning $37,000 at my job prior to UNC, a furious argument ensued.) What strikes me is not that the market undervalues our work, but that it values it at all—and consistently at a price above the median paid to all workers. Why should our work be more valuable, better compensated, than the work of most Americans? I just don't have the sense of entitlement, of self-assured conviction that what I do is important and necessary, that would sustain the complaint of being under-appreciated. That some people like what I do, and that I am paid enough to keep doing it within an institution that enables me to do the work, seems miraculous. Maybe this is a class thing. The university afforded me an escape from the quotidian world of drudgery that was my family's fate prior to my generation. What I do feels so little like work as I understood that burden when growing up that I am amazed I get paid to do it.

But this is still not the whole story. I want to ratchet the analysis up another step—and introduce the second debate that motivated this chapter. The complaint that the market undervalues academic work can take a very different tack. Humanities professors, by and large, are paid less than non-humanities professors because of "market forces." These same market forces stand to blame for the decline of the humanities both within the university and within the general society. This decline has been slow, but steady, over the past 150 years at least. Objective measures would be fewer humanities majors, a shrinking portion of required and offered courses coming from humanities disciplines, and a loosening link between a "liberal arts education" and social status.[7]

Right now I am neither interested in analyzing this decline nor in predicting the humanities' future. My focus here is on the way that the values associated with the humanities, or most likely to be central to those working in the humanities, have been on the defensive for a long time. Adherents of the humanities have felt constrained to be public advocates, to convince a mostly indifferent and sometimes hostile society of the humanities' value in every sense of the term "value." In the bluntest terms, the humanities condemn "commercial culture" for neglecting and/or scorning the knowledge, insights, and ways of being-in-the-world that the humanities offer. Either humanists must show that a liberal education has market value or they must argue for the value of other goods which do not provide an obvious financial return on money invested. In most cases, humanists have taken both tacks.[8]

I have been part of an on-going colloquium at the National Humanities Center on "Liberalism and its Contexts."[9] We have mostly focused on

7. In fact, the statistics tell a complicated story. If we start from 1950, the percentage of English majors among all undergraduate degrees granted looks remarkably stable, moving from 3.99 percent in 1950 to 4.21 percent in 1996–97. But that hides a large spike from 1960 (5.13 percent) to the high of 1967–68 (7.59 percent), followed by precipitous decline through the 1970s to the low of 3.50 percent in 1979–80. The 1980s brought a small run-up to 4.83 percent in 1990–91, and then a steady decline to the current 4.21 percent. The figures for history majors are fairly similar, but show a more decided long-term decline, moving from 3.13 percent in 1950 to a peak of 5.58 percent in 1967–68, a low of 1.66 percent in 1985–86, and a current 2.15 percent (1996–97). Interestingly, bachelor's degrees in business have declined through the 1990s, although they still represent 19 percent of all undergraduate degrees in 1996–97, down from 23.66 percent in 1989–90. The big growth areas in the 1990s have been agriculture, biological and life sciences, and health professions. (Source: Franklin, 2000).

8. See Hutcheon, 2000, for a succinct rendition of almost all the arguments humanists in the university employ to defend their work. Her final sentence covers nearly all the bases, claiming both economic and non-economic benefits: "Skills are part of the picture, but only part; those broader educational goals are desirable and important both for the general economic and social well-being of the nation and for the personal and professional life of the informed and thoughtful citizen—and voter" (4).

9. This Sawyer seminar is funded by the Mellon Foundation. My thoughts here were formulated particularly in response to Gary Wihl's paper presented to the seminar, "Individualism and Liberalism in the Poetry of Walt Whitman." Wihl critiques the "abstract" individualism of procedural or simply rights-focused liberalism in order to advocate the more "robust" individualism that can be found in other liberal writers, noticeably Emerson, Thoreau, and Whitman.

nineteenth-century arguments for and with liberalism, although we have ranged more widely than that. Once again, I find myself at odds with most of my colleagues. (I may be sweet-tempered, but I also seem to be perversely contrarian.) At issue is what might be characterized as a diffident, pluralist liberalism (which I advocate) and a culturalist liberalism. Most of the colloquium's members accept that commercial culture offers a reprehensible way of life, and openly advocate a more "robust" liberalism that will offer an alternative to the market. Commercial culture only offers selves who are rational maximizers of interest, passive consumers, or mechanical drudges; the "cash nexus," however understood, only generates lives of quiet or not-so-quiet desperation. If liberalism is diffident, if it is understood as merely a neutral by-stander that provides the political infrastructure for commercial culture's existence, then liberalism must be rejected. The total triumph of the market cannot be accepted.

Luckily, according to their story, there is another liberalism, a more activist liberalism. This liberalism comes in two forms, both of which rest on the foundation of rights that negatively define the state's limits, rights that are the centerpiece of diffident liberalism. State action liberalism interferes in the market to counter extreme economic inequalities, to protect the public health and the environment, to forbid the growth of monopolies, and to alleviate the misery of the sick, aged, and otherwise unemployed. In this liberalism, citizenship entails not only negative liberties, but also positive welfare claims to which the state must respond. State action liberalism addresses the economic failings of the market. It accepts that individual flourishing is the *raison d'être*, the legitimation, of liberal polities, and thus provides state remediation when and where the market fails to provide the resources necessary to flourish. Since I will only return to this branch of liberalism in passing, let me say right now that I am all for it.

Culturalist liberalism is hardly antagonistic to state action liberalism. In fact, the two are usually understood as complementary; it is my desire to disentangle the two, endorsing the one but not the other, that leads me to disagree with my National Humanities Center colleagues. Fundamentally, the culturalist liberals believe that individual flourishing requires not just financial resources and physical security, but also certain skills, knowledge, competencies, and values. In a word—our contemporary word—flourishing requires an "identity," a way-of-being-in-the-world and of being-with-others that gives individuality substance and individual existence meaning. The participants in the seminar have amply demonstrated this culturalist tradition within liberalism. (Rosenblum [1987] is a central text for this argument.) That is, various thinkers who are committed to individual liberty are also concerned with the process of *Bildung*, of identity formation within culture, in order to create individuals fully capable of enjoying the freedoms liberal polities will afford them. (As I will discuss in the next two chapters, what I am calling culturalism can also take anti-liberal and a-liberal forms. Here I am confining myself to its liberal manifestations.) Mill, Arnold, and Emerson represent this liberal tradition, which merges Romantic paradigms of self-actualization with Enlightenment commitments to universal rights. Here is a vision of individual and society that counters, even subsumes, a vision that sees the world as all market. A richer culture, one that attends to the "full humanity" of persons, is offered in place of the attenuated, partial, and thin culture of the market. Individuals are called to participate in, form their identities in relation to, this richer culture.

I have my doubts. As a pluralist, I am not in favor of letting the market determine all human relations or all human desires. But I want to encourage suspicion about the culturalist alternative, which looks equally anti-pluralist to me. The culturalist alternative to the market is so attractive to humanists because they are continually aggrieved at the market's undervaluation of what they do. Here, in one fell swoop, the humanist lays claim to the cultural authority s/he thinks rightfully his or hers. The arena of identity formation is shifted from commercial culture to the school, where the humanist presides. And the cultural authority that the humanist might not acquire in a full and fair competition of diverse models of selfhood is now underwritten by the state. The humanists' importance is assured, and they are even given their own institution (or, at least, part of that institution) through which to enforce it. I am extremely wary of the humanists' turn to state power to shore up their visions of the qualities that the more general culture ignores or derides. In addition, it raises my hackles when professors assume that education is a self-evident good, obviously benign. Complacent confidence in their own virtue follows. To be most suspicious of that which serves our own interests, and even more our own cherished self-images, seems a good rule of thumb to me.

I do not advocate the abolishment of compulsory education or the state's abandonment of education to the private market (whether through a voucher system or other means). Since education is currently the primary means toward economic well-being, it is crucial that the state do everything in its power to provide equal educational opportunity to all its ens. (The failure of government—federal, state, and local—in the ed States to provide anything like an equal education to all children nply documented in Kozol [1992].) My concern here is how intellec-ᴛᴜᴀᴌs, particularly humanist intellectuals, use schools and the university to acquire cultural authority even as they continually complain that they do not have as much authority as they deserve. Those complaints almost always involve the denigration of other sources of cultural values, attitudes, and identification.

Three historical points about the institution of compulsory education must be stressed. The first is that required schooling is a creation of the liberal state, as if the extraordinary freedom granted to adults in liberal polities must be purchased at the price of an unprecedented subjection of children to the state. The terror of what freedom would produce necessitated the long indoctrination of citizens during childhood. This desire to make citizens worthy or capable of freedom is tied directly to the transformation of liberal polities into democratic ones during the 19th century. Liberal and conservative elites all shared a fear of the *demos*. The necessity of subordination and deference was the conservative response to that fear; the necessity of education was the liberal response. For Mill and Arnold, the masses' ignorance is alarming, but their weak-willed susceptibility to outside influences is even more alarming. Citizens must be given the wherewithal to resist the blandishments of demagogues and crass commercialism. A strong, non-anarchistic democracy will go hand-in-hand with the ability to keep the market in its place, only one facet of a more complex society. While education schemes evidence a laudable faith in the potential capacities of the people, their dark underside is the conviction that the people are only ready for democracy if they become more like us, the educated and enlightened ones who will serve as their teachers. Fear of democracy and fear of commercial culture merge in writers like Tocqueville and Flaubert, then get carried into the twentieth century as condemnations of "mass culture" and worries about the ways that "mass media" influence political opinions. In sum, the state got involved in education because it wanted to control its citizens, not because it wanted to undercut or supplement the selves shaped by commercial culture.[10]

Secondly, education, almost from the start, gets tied to nationalism, to the effort to bind citizens to the state through patriotism. I need not rehearse the details of nationalism's origins in the period from 1750 to 1850;

10. Tony La Vopa of the Sawyer Seminar will recognize his influence on this paragraph.

that work has been done elsewhere.[11] States needed large citizen armies during the Napoleonic period, but were also susceptible to the intellectual fear that the dissolution of traditional communities and the growth of cities dissolved the "social glue" that mitigated the individualistic competition of each against each. Liberal individualism and the growth of capitalist economic relations were underwritten by a nationalism that seemed to guarantee that the center would hold and that a common cause would unite the individuals freed to pursue their own life projects and their own economic good. School becomes a key place for inculcating this common tie to the nation.

Third, far from being hostile to commerce, school is, from the beginning, tied to training for employment, not just to responsible citizenship and patriotic sentiments. That literacy and technical competence contributed to national prosperity was a truism by 1870, and the last third of the nineteenth-century links educational credentials (especially high school and college degrees) to a readiness for employment that still provides the economic rationale for students' efforts today. The tug-of-war between schools as sites of vocational training and non-instrumental cultural education begins almost at the same time as the establishment of required schooling for all.

So school was never solely the humanists' preserve. Liberal polities had multiple, though not particularly compatible, aims in establishing public education, and I would argue that the development of education over the past 130 years has only proliferated those aims. Once securely in place, it is no wonder that various different social groups would strive to get a foothold in the schools, to use them to further their own designs on children and the polity. If the state ever had much control over schools, it lost that control long ago. Schools are inefficient shapers of identity partly because students are subjected to so many messages in school. (I discussed other causes of schools' inefficiencies in chapter 2.) I am always skeptical of arguments, inspired by Foucault, that stress the state's powers of subject-formation.[12] For a start, the liberal state is not, in theory or aspiration,

11. Among a multitude of recent studies, Anderson (1991) has been especially influential. He points to "the large cluster of new political entities that sprang up in the Western hemisphere between 1776 and 1838, all of which self-consciously defined themselves as nations" (46)

12. Miller (1993) provides one example of such arguments. The "cultural-capitalist state," he writes, "needs to produce a sense of oneness among increasingly heterogeneous populations at a time when political systems are under question by new social movements and the internationalization of cultures and economies. It works to forge a loyalty to market

the Hegelian state. It does not explicitly aim for a unified whole of which it is the consummate expression and within which individuals are fully articulated. Even its reliance on nationalism is usually refracted through the "land" more than through the "state." That's why fiercely patriotic Americans can also be fiercely anti-government. Furthermore, the contemporary state is a multi-headed beast, with a limited ability to insure how its directives are enacted in practice. The state's left hand often does not know how its right hand is counteracting it, while its functionaries are often using state institutions and power to pursue their own agendas. The ability of the state to act consistently across time and in different places is extremely limited.

Humanist teachers are in the belly of this confused and stumbling beast, and my argument is that they should not dream of more effective state power or more effective pedagogies as techniques for the furthering of their particular vision of the good life. Let's try, instead, to affirm the inefficiencies and contradictions of schooling while also being somewhat more skeptical about the humanist vision. What evidence do we have that the masses are not prepared for citizenship; that the masses lead thin, attenuated lives; that alienation, narcissism, or schizophrenia characterize the modern individual;[13] or that the humanist holds the key for escaping these desperate conditions?

Intellectuals—in flight from family, religion, business, and local communities—not surprisingly scorn the sites that anchor identity formation for most people. The republic of letters, the realm of ideas, and professional cohorts have afforded intellectuals the means to escape from local bonds they found narrow and constricting. But does that escape necessitate or justify denigrating those left behind? Is it possible to lead a good life in total ignorance of Nietzsche or Shakespeare or Virginia Woolf? Intellectuals hardly have exclusive claims to moral probity. And it is not obvious that "culture" in an Arnoldian sense is a firmer bulwark against

---

economics and parliamentary democracy, as well as a sustainable society through the formation of cultural citizens, docile but efficient participants in that economy-society mix" (xii). This account suggests a unity of purpose for "the state" that I find hard to credit.

13. "Alienation" comes from Marx (1978), especially the section entitled "Alienated Labor." The term subsequently figures prominently in Western Marxist and existentialist diagnoses of the ills of humans under modern economic and social conditions. "Narcissism" comes from Lasch (1979) and "schizophrenia" from Jameson (1991, esp. pp. 25–31). These three terms, and these three writers, are only cited here as representative of a long-standing tradition of critique that insists that individuals lived maimed, unsatisfactory lives in modern societies, with capitalism and/or liberalism often cited as cause.

commercialism than family, religion, or local commitments. What intellectuals consume is different, but they consume as avidly as every one else does, and with more means (usually) to do so.

I am not arguing for ignorance or against education. I am saying that humanists have not made a convincing case, either in their apologetics or in their behavior, for the benefits of the liberal education they espouse (whether that espousal takes the traditional form of extolling exposure to the great books or the less content-specific form of extolling the development of "critical thinking skills.") Education is one among many sites of identity formation, and I think we teachers would be better off thinking of education as adding to the mix rather than as correcting the deficiencies of the other sites. We are not our students' saviors in an otherwise utterly deplorable world. To think that we are saviors guarantees our condemnation of them when they reject our wares, and of society at large for not valuing us for our indispensable work. Our students' benefiting from what we can offer them does not depend on their repudiation of their non-school based identifications. The crux here is a caricatured picture of commercial culture dear to many humanists, one that overstates that culture's triumph in our time and its utter lack of praiseworthy qualities. This is a picture formed, by the way, on the flimsiest grounds; if scholars presumed to characterize the Renaissance in utter ignorance of texts from the era or academic studies of it, we would deny their work publication. But humanists don't read the massive written record of the business world, nor pay much attention to academics who have studied business culture. Cultural studies needs an ethnography of business to match its sophisticated ethnographies of consumers. Then we would stand a chance of getting past the fatuous opinions of commerce that now pass unchallenged.

The same tendency toward wholesale contempt can be found in many intellectuals' attitudes toward family, religion, and patriotism. The fetishization of "critical thinking" and "distance" in much intellectual work exhibits this suspicion of satisfied belonging. I share all these prejudices of the intellectual, but I think we should avoid transforming such prejudices into justifications for our authoritative rewriting of students' identities. I do aspire to change my students' lives by prompting them to reevaluate their primary commitments, but the goal of being explicit about the components of identity does not inevitably necessitate their repudiation.

In a pluralistic culture, school needs to take its chances among multiple sites of identification. In my diffident view, liberals should be extremely wary of all appeals to state power, especially in matters involving the formation of beliefs and of decisions about how to live one's life. Does that mean the state should get out of education altogether? No. For three reasons, at least.

First, education is an absolute necessity for participation in the contemporary economy. State action is necessary to rectify inequities of inherited wealth and status. Plus (arguably) the state has an interest in general economic prosperity. A well educated workforce is a benefit to the nation—and benefits citizens individually as well. It is worth adding that even if education is geared toward its economic benefits, targeted training for specific jobs would not provide the greatest return. Intellectual skills of a more general order are, in any time frame but the extreme short term, more valuable. Humanist forms of education can be justified economically, which is not to slight or recommend abandoning non-economic justifications.

Second, society benefits from the codification of received knowledge and the effort to reexamine and extend that knowledge. It is simply not true that a free market will, on its own, produce anything and everything deemed valuable. Citizens in a democracy have every reason to look to the state to supply goods the market will not, just as they look to the state to rectify market created inequities in certain crucial domains (health, opportunity, care for the elderly). The arts and humanities, especially in the United States, often depend on state subsidies, yet find it hard to legitimate such expenditures in terms of utility. The educative value of the arts and humanities is generally conceded and, thus, their position in schools is fairly secure (the humanities more so than the arts). But their value as repositories of knowledge and producers of new knowledge is less universally accepted, mostly because prevailing paradigms of knowledge do not easily accommodate what the arts and humanities offer. Such disputes aside, my general point is that markets can fail to provide what at least some people value, and the state may be used by citizens to overcome that deficiency. Education is so generally valuable that the state should be enjoined to provide it for all.

Finally, the state has some interest in knitting its various citizens together into "a society." This is tricky, but the events of the past twelve years in Eastern Europe, Canada, and elsewhere have made me reevaluate my prior conviction that fears of anarchy or anomie are usually unjustified, that centripetal forces in modern societies outweigh centrifugal ones. As a pluralist, I still want to be a minimalist here. The key is the co-existence of different individuals and groups, not their merger into a whole. But my understanding of democracy includes the belief that selves are socially constituted through their relations with others and that democracy, beyond its procedural elements, points toward transformative public, dialogic interactions among citizens. These connections are only possible if lines of communication across various differences remain open. The state can and should be used to overcome segregation of every sort: racial, economic, status, ethnic, etc. Democracy needs public spaces where everyone intermingles. The market has proved itself a great separator in many, albeit not all, ways. It divides (into "niches") to conquer and creates spaces that, by a kind of economic filtering, encourage people to associate only with their own kind. Much advertising, of course, relies on the ploy of linking ownership of this thing to becoming one of this desired kind. It is typical of American liberalism that the state has only tried to establish truly inclusive public spheres (in schools and workplaces primarily) fitfully and often ineffectually. The rights of private property have been allowed to supplant fully open public spaces throughout American history. The current permission for wealthy partisans to crowd out full public debate during elections is only the latest instance. Since the geographical segregation of money and race in our country leads to radically unequal schools, a voucher system—tied to need and serving to shatter the local funding of schools in favor of more centralized, equal funding— looks potentially attractive. But the fact that vouchers would enable a market-like fragmentation of schooling, with every self-defined identity group setting up a school, is for me the decisive argument against them. Schools exist not just as repositories of received knowledge, but also as sites of inclusive pubic interaction where the need and means to communicate across lines of difference are acknowledged and provided. Let me only add that schools—and the state—cannot do this work alone. If such pubic interactions only take place under state compulsion, then society is in parlous condition. I agree with those who argue that a vibrant, voluntary "civil society" is crucial to the survival of pluralistic democratic polities.[14] The state cannot create the cultural conditions for sustaining democracy by fiat, just as it cannot unilaterally shape the identities of the students it educates.

14. The relation of "civil society" to the state in democratic polities has been a major topic in political theory for the past fifteen years, inspired by the actions of dissidents in Eastern Europe, especially in Poland, before 1989. See Cohen and Arato (1992) for a comprehensive overview of the subject. Also useful are Keane (1988), and Calhoun (1992).

Given these arguments in favor of state-run, compulsory education, my final position does not look very consistent. Humanist intellectuals should resist the temptation to use state authority to bolster their particular vision of the good life, their particular belief that commercial culture bears all before it and produces miserable, pathetic, deficient, and passive selves. The intellectuals' visions must take their chances in the general rhetorical cacophony that is a democratic society. Yet I would also acknowledge the market's extraordinary power, not so much in relation to the content it purveys as in relation to its ability to shape the form taken by civil society, the non-state public sphere. The market's tendency to give wealthy voices an advantage over non-wealthy ones and to segregate groups of citizens from one another can and should be remedied by state action. Since education has become a necessity, and since we have decided that the state should supply this necessity, then intellectuals may use their institutional platform for promulgating views not likely to get a full airing in commercial fora. But they should not enlist state power to gain their views additional leverage on their audience's endorsement.

We often distinguish authority from power by saying that power compels obedience irrespective of assent whereas authority garners agreement and respect that are freely given. In a pluralistic society, cultural authority should be diffuse, with many possible allegiances available for citizens. These various allegiances and the multiple cultural identities that derive from them will not all be compatible and they will not, in their aggregation, yield a unified culture. The state should promote interaction across lines of difference, should create public spaces where such dialogue occurs, and should monitor access to such spaces to insure equality. The state may even subsidize certain groups and voices when they lack the resources the market provides to other groups for appearances in public spaces. But the state should not endorse any particular cultural vision, just as the state should not align itself with any particular religion.

Accepting this position creates a fairly sharp distinction between cultural politics and economic politics, though this will never be totally unambiguous, since there will always be troublesome borderline cases. In matters of resource allocation and economic justice, the parties involved appeal for state action, either from the legislature or the courts. They want the state to divide the pie in certain ways, or they want the state to remedy market effects. But those who wish to transform the primary allegiances, the values and beliefs, of their fellow citizens cannot (or, I am arguing, should not) appeal for state action. Instead, they must direct their efforts directly to the citizenry. Of course, that amorphous audience is much harder to contact and much harder to get a response from. So the temptation to address the state instead is ever present. My argument is that those engaged in cultural politics can only ask the state to act to provide access, non-segregation, and equality in the public spheres in which their rhetorical appeals will be made. Given the current situation in the United States, even this limited role for the state gives it plenty to do. But we shouldn't confuse the need for massive intervention in the form of the public sphere for the state's endorsement of any particular cultural vision's content.

My argument with my Humanities Center colleagues also has a theoretical dimension. I want to resist totalized characterizations of culture that posit a centralized source of identity. So I argue that liberalism does not name a culture, that it is not an adequate or useful covering term for the complex and plural conditions in Western societies since 1750. Thus liberalism should neither be seen as the origin of contemporary forms of selfhood nor blamed for not offering an alternative form of selfhood when capitalism is considered the dominant shaper of selves. Liberalism is better understood as a response to pluralism, to the multiple and non-shared identifications of citizens. Historically crucial was the recognition (only after much bloodshed) that unity of religious belief had been lost forever in the wake of the Protestant Reformation; thus modern polities had to discover how to exist in spite of fundamental religious differences. Liberalism, then, is a set of strategies for organizing political life in the face of diversity. It obscures the specifically political questions that liberalism addresses to make liberalism solely responsible for identity formations that occur at multiple sites within a society. Some of these sites are certainly more sympathetic to liberal political arrangements than others, and we might even claim that some of these sites are consonant with certain liberal priorities (such as peace and individual well-being). But the many sites stand in complex and varied relationship to liberalism. Liberalism, then, is neither the cause of contemporary forms of selfhood nor the remedy (if a remedy is needed).

I, of course, cannot enforce my diffident liberalism, or my attempt to reign in more grandiose accounts of what liberalism encompasses. I can only try to persuade you (as I will continue to do in the next two chapters) that totalized explanations of social and identity formations are less productive for a democratic politics than decentralized, pluralistic ones. And I believe that it is both analytically and practically useful to separate questions of institutional political responses (such as tolerance, individual rights, freedoms of speech, movement, and association) to pluralism and to capitalism (remedial state action) from efforts to foster pluralism in face of the forces that oppose it (one possible task of cultural politics). One crucial pay-off of this analytic separation is its reminder that politics does not entirely take place within the purview of the state. State-to-citizen relationships are political, but I am with Hannah Arendt in believing that we lose much of what can be valuable in politics if we ignore citizen-to-citizen relationships in public spaces—relationships that are, ideally, unmediated by the state. Diffident liberalism aims for that ideal. For that reason, my plea is that practitioners of cultural politics form allegiances with the state only under extreme duress. I do not want a "national cultural policy" emanating from the NEH or any other governmental agency, as some of my National Humanities Center colleagues advocate.

THE UNIVERSITY

My argument so far mostly pertains to compulsory education prior to university. How does a pluralist account of culture alter our understanding of the university? Basically, I agree with John Guillory and Bill Readings that the university can no longer legitimate itself as the place where young people acquire the culture common to all educated people.[15] The notion that access to status requires a veneer of culture is not entirely dead, but it is certainly dying, especially in America. Bourdieu's account of "cultural capital" does not translate very well from France to the United States. Education, especially a college degree, is more than ever the divider in terms of economic prosperity in America. But status differences, which are less strong in America once you get outside certain very rarefied circles, do not map to initiation into "high" or any other kind of culture of the Arnoldian sort. Pace E. D. Hirsch (1988), there are no specific things the educated person is expected to know. Rather, the educated person is supposed to be "smart"—a portmanteau term that covers any num-

15. Guillory (1993) connects the rise of literary theory to "a certain defunctioning of the literary curriculum, a crisis in the market value of its cultural capital occasioned by the emergence of a professional-managerial class which no longer requires the (primarily literary) cultural capital of the old bourgeoisie" (xii). Readings (1996) argues that the university "has outlived itself, is now a survivor of the era in which it defined itself in terms of the *historical* development, affirmation, and inculcation of national culture" (6).

ber of competencies, the most important of which (perhaps) are the capacities to carve out a prosperous life for self (and family) and to negotiate a successful, non-traumatic career in a constantly changing economic realm.[16]

It doesn't matter what your university degree is *in*—and matters less each year you are removed from campus. (It does matter where your degree is from.) The proliferation of programs and departments at the university over the past thirty years has spawned the multi-versity. There is nothing we give to *all* of our students. (Even Freshman English has gone by the boards as schools adopt Writing-Across-the Curriculum programs.) Each student gets only a part, and each gets different parts, of what the university has to offer.

This situation poses grave problems for the humanities, because their legitimation has almost always been phrased in universalist terms. The argument has been that everyone, even the non-major, needs to read Shakespeare and Dickens and study the French and Russian Revolutions because they are an essential part of our culture, our tradition. We have used the cultural authority accrued by the humanities as the repository of tradition to justify the insistence that all educated persons should read and study literature and history. But now that the goal of being an educated person in that "cultured" sense has lost its hold, the humanities find themselves unprepared to make different kinds of arguments about their value.

Humanists find themselves, as always, threatened by discourses of economic utility. That's an old story, albeit a still important one. But I think a newer story is our current need to make arguments that convince both ourselves and others that while it is true that society does not need all university graduates to have studied Shakespeare, it is valuable for some university graduates to have done so. This, essentially, is the case that physics, sociology, and religious studies have made for years. They don't claim their courses should be required of all students, only that the university should provide the opportunity for some students to study these subjects. I don't think English, history, and philosophy—even if they rely on more general arguments about critical thinking and/or communicative skills in lieu of claims about their specific subject matter—will long be able to convince anyone that they offer access to some essential knowledge, viewpoint, or aptitude that not only cannot be acquired elsewhere in the mul-

16. *Ex post facto* thanks to Jeff Williams, from whom I have stolen this idea.

tiversity, but also should be a required part of every student's education. We humanists have not begun to understand ourselves and to articulate that understanding to those who fund our activities in partial terms yet. That vocabulary, those arguments, need to be developed.

More generally, the university always needs to legitimate itself in the eyes of those within it and those outside of it. Attention to shifting legitimations would indicate shifts in where and how the university feels challenged, as well as shifts in its self-image. While the university's economic utility is always an issue, I think we can identify changes in emphasis lately. The economic benefit of degrees is not currently a big issue. Universities are not particularly anxious about selling themselves to students these days as they were from 1974 to 1994, a time when the number of college-age youths was low and the percentage of those youths attending college was also low. Current realities are clear: getting a degree pays—and thus the percentage of college-age students attending college is at an all-time high.[17]

This influx prompts a different concern: efficiency in credentialing students. Colleges and universities, especially public institutions from the middle-tier on down to the community colleges, are facing tremendous pressure to be cost-effective. Fantasies of distance-learning, which would supposedly lessen capital and maintenance costs for physical plant and possibly labor costs for faculty (although such savings have not manifested themselves anywhere yet), are part of this drive to produce more degrees at lower cost. So is the increasing use of adjunct and part-time faculty. With respect to efficiency, the humanities, with their penchant for small classes and their army of extra PhDs, are especially vulnerable. Moreover, humanities degrees remain economically dubious.

The humanities' response to erosion of tenure lines, the threat of distance learning, and the effort to increase class size has been to preach "quality" over "quantity" or to talk about more intangible public goods, like democratic citizenship, supposedly better served by the way we've educated our students for the past fifty years. I do not disagree with such claims for our deserving a place at the university, or even a modicum of cultural authority. I am even willing to defend our cherished teaching

17. College enrollment rates of high school graduates move from 45.1 percent in 1960 to 55.4 percent in 1969, but then decline through the 1970s (although not back to 1960 levels), bottoming out at 49.3 percent in 1981. Over the past fifteen years there has been a steady rise to the current (1997) all-time high of 62 percent. That number is expected to keep creeping upward. Source: *Digest of Education Statistics 1999*.

methods, although less enthusiastically, since they often hide a lot of laziness combined with a lot of ignorance about the different learning capacities and needs of our students. But we humanists should not expect to convince everyone. A healthy skepticism about our received notions about ourselves is the beginning of understanding how they might sound pretty hollow to the outsiders we are trying to persuade. Camp meetings of beleaguered humanists singing the old tunes to one another do nothing to further our position in public debates. Deep and lasting disagreements characterize a pluralistic culture like ours, and while we need legitimations of our activities that convince ourselves, we also need to consider the possible legitimacy of others' criticisms. We cannot rely on institutional inertia, a few old saws, and some sentimental well-heeled alumni to insure our continued presence on campus. As public money withdraws, private and/or corporate wealth increasingly finances American universities, both public and private. The humanities are unlikely to garner much direct support from bottom-line-driven corporations, but they need to bolster universities' resolve to retain some independence from the supplier of funds, and the tendency of universities to shift their activities toward where the money is. This will be no easy task. Everything in American attitudes toward money since 1970 has run in the direction of those who pay the piper calling the tune. Stock-holders have demanded ever greater profits, thus altering paternalistic firms like Kodak that once offered superb benefit packages and job security for employees while also being a major civic benefactor. I don't have proof (and don't know how I would get it), but my sense is that private donations to the university increasingly are targeted toward specific uses as opposed to "unrestricted gifts." Those who pay tuition—parents and students alike—now often see themselves as customers paying for a service and expect "satisfaction" defined in business-client terms. Tax-payers and their representatives have demanded greater accountability on the part of public agencies, especially schools. (I can't resist noting that such accountability doesn't seem to extend to those who build highways at outrageous costs and with even more outrageous cost over-runs.) We educators are in the tough position of having to legitimate our professional *bona fides,* of having to say that we know better than you do how to educate your children, so you need to pay the bill, but leave us free to create and implement the program of study.

The intensity of these demands from its sources of revenue has everyone at the university on the defensive these days, not just the humanists.

But the humanities have no way to directly generate income. They do not, generally speaking, have a product they can take to market that will secure substantial funds. Their product is education and the cash cow of tuition has just about reached its upper limit. The massive tuition increases of the past twenty years have simply bled that stone dry (except at a few very prestigious schools). There is no more money to be had from students and their parents and the banks from which they loan money. The money chase now is all about the funds needed to augment tuition revenue, which never pays the full ride. The sciences, and to some extent the social sciences, can sell the knowledge they produce in the marketplace. Since the humanities cannot, their fate is more intimately linked to the university's ability to legitimate a certain independence from those who give it money while convincing them to keep the money rolling in. The spenders who want a specific return for their bucks will not be doing business with the humanities' departments.

In this context, I want to list sixteen arguments that universities deploy to legitimate themselves as serving either a generalized public good or as serving the particular needs of its paying clientele. I hope that I have been inclusive here—and would be interested in additions to this list. Most of these will be familiar to my readers, so I do not offer extensive commentary. The various reasons for the university's existence are not all compatible, and they appeal to a wide variety of ways to understand "the good." Part of my point is to illustrate how pluralistic the multiversity is, how many arguments are made about its value. I also hope the list will help my readers think about which arguments are currently ascendant, which less frequently invoked. I have refrained from evaluating the merit of the arguments; the list says nothing more and nothing less than someone in the university legitimates his or her activities this way. Finally, although couched as arguments, I do think that each item listed is tied to things actually being done at the university. In other words, someone at the university is working to realize the vision of the good to which the legitimating argument appeals.

1. *Culture.* The university is a repository of culture, and it transmits that culture to students. Culture is at times understood as a whole, as "common" to the whole society. At other times, culture is understood as multiple and various, with only parts imparted to students.
2. *Civic.* The university produces citizens capable of democracy.

3. *Cultivation.* The university provides the means toward self-formation or personal growth, especially (but not exclusively) in respect to values and meaning. There is a link here between the college experience and maturation. Hence the cultivation of work habits and self-management can also figure here.

4. *Economic worth of the degree.* Beyond the benefit to the individual, the university also provides a means of upward mobility for the able, hence enabling meritocratic access.

5. *Economic impact on the local, state, and/or national economy.* There are various different ways of claiming beneficial economic consequences of the university's existence.

6. *Economic benefits of creating a trained and educated work-force.*

7. *Prestige.* This one is tricky since it is rarely nakedly stated, perhaps because it is less a justification of the university as a social institution and more a justification of this particular institution through comparison with less worthy rivals. There is a lot of talk of "excellence" or of "competitive advantages," but less of the sheer pride in being "No. 1." The brilliance of the US News rankings is their exact replication of the AP rankings of college football and basketball teams, thus transferring the sports fan's obsession with relative status to the more staid ground of the colleges as colleges. Universities attract students and donors and hire faculty on the basis of prestige, just as some faculty activities are geared toward enhancing prestige.

8. *The production of useful knowledge through research.*

9. *The production of useless knowledge through research.* Not as paradoxical as might first appear. "Pure" research may prove useful—socially or economically—in the long term. Universities argue that they can take the long view—and the risk that something might prove utterly useless—because insulated from direct bottom-line concerns. But they will also argue that they can indulge human curiosity, the urge to know, apart from any benefit beyond learning something new.

10. *Autonomy.* The argument here is that freedom, not just from economic pressures but also from ideological, political, or institutional demands, fosters creativity. The new emerges from the unshackled work the university enables. Of course, this argument assumes a positive attitude toward change and novelty. But it is also connected with certain notions of objective knowledge and how it can be obtained. Issues of academic freedom find their place here as well.

11. *Critique.* Another variant of the argument from autonomy. Here the benefit is not new and objective knowledge production, but the untrammeled examination of prevailing norms and beliefs. Critical thinking, the ability and freedom to question everything, is linked to self-stretching, but also to the renovation of society.

12. *Moral.* Similar to critique, but with a much more positive spin. Not so much the critical examination of norms and beliefs as their articulation in a form that solicits others' agreement even as it makes one's own values clear.

13. *Creative.* The university encourages and fosters creativity, intellectually and artistically.

14. *Professional.* The university is a major player in the creation and maintenance of professional competencies, and thus protects (and often provides) the goods and services professionals offer to society.

15. *Utopian.* The university models certain forms of social interaction, as argued in my first chapter. I guess a less utopian version is the idea that our students' "social life" during college is also a valuable learning experience. Certainly, we expect students to "experiment" in various ways (sexually, with drugs, with different living arrangements, with different schedules of work/play/sleep) during their college years.

16. *Community Preserving/Community Creating.* A variant of numbers 1 (Culture) and 15 (Utopian) perhaps, but worth a separate entry. The point here is more the preservation and/or creation of a subculture, a particular communal identity that recognizes its difference from the mainstream or the common. Examples range from Brigham Young University and Bob Jones University to Bryn Mawr and other all-woman colleges.[18] Less extreme would be the social networks that originate in college, where people do expect to meet others who will be life-long friends and (sometimes) business associates. And, of course, lots of students form romantic attachments with people they meet at the university.

What should be obvious from this list is that different constituencies want and expect very different things from the university. I take it that all sixteen arguments appeal to someone—and that none of them appeals to everyone. Some of them more obviously fit with humanists' values than others. The thorny issue is whether any of them directly threatens the continued existence of the humanities or, more drastically, the university. Two

18. I owe this point to my colleague David Whisnant.

dangers lurk. The first is that some of these legitimations could actually lead the university down a path that would destroy its integrity or its ability to work in ways that fulfill its other legitimations. I don't believe this is the case, but not everyone would agree. Many in the humanities would argue that the university should never do work in direct return for a fee. I don't see that radical a distinction between sponsored research and paid-for education. In both cases the professor provides something to someone who pays for it. I won't rehearse the full argument here, but will rest content with highlighting the point of contention. My position is that the university can march forward on all the fronts identified by my list; none of the items necessarily excludes the accomplishment of any of the others. I may not like what that guy over there is doing, but his doing that does not prevent me from doing what I deem valuable.

The second danger seems much more real to me: some of the activities of the multiversity will garner financial, institutional, or popular support at the expense of others. Absolute repudiation of some of the activities may occur at certain universities, but such explicit abandonment of current activities is unlikely to occur across the range of all colleges and universities. But drastic shifts in relative resource allocation and status are possible across the board. The humanities are in decline, not, I think, in absolute as much as in relative terms. That is, there has not been an absolute repudiation of the humanities, but instead more attention paid to and money directed toward activities that respond to legitimations that the humanities do not particularly address.

Not surprisingly, with the decline of legitimation in terms of a common culture, the humanities have turned to other legitimations (self-cultivation, creativity, critical thinking, democratic citizenship). I don't think we humanists need—or are likely to find—many new arguments. I think we need to work from arguments, loyalties, and commitments already in place. Our constituencies will be limited; they will not constitute everyone with a stake in the university, perhaps not even a majority. So we may be in the difficult position of all those who strive for minority rights, access, and resources in a democracy. Our position as a minority might help us learn the new non-universal vocabulary I believe we now need to explain what we do to those who stand outside those activities.

I refuse to mourn the loss of the universal. And I absolutely refuse to hanker after a cultural authority we never really had (its existence is always displaced to an ever-receding past). I also refuse to denigrate those for whom the humanities or the life of the mind are not their chosen path through life. The university is as contradictory, contentious, multi-faceted, and multi-purposed as society at large. It is not our anointed kingdom. The state has a responsibility to maintain the university and a responsibility to insure and increase access to higher education as it becomes increasingly necessary for economic well-being. But that responsibility does not extend to supplementing any authority the functionaries of the university might gain through their thoughtful articulation and promulgation of their view from within it—views then offered (sometimes) to those outside the university as well. Quite the contrary. Our stated views and our displayed activities must do all the work of persuasion on their own.

II

ROADS FROM THE PAST,
PATHS TO A FUTURE

These final three chapters widen the frame in an attempt to locate contemporary intellectual practice in historical and theoretical perspective. Chapters 5 and 6 are, in some ways, two efforts to address the same topic: the implication of intellectuals in a vocabulary dominated by the terms "modernity" and "culture." It is not simply the fact that these terms structure a master narrative of dubious validity that troubles me. I am also struck by the persistent pattern of interpreting particulars (whether events or texts) by elucidating their relation to some hidden substrate, be it a historical period, ideology, the social imaginary, or the dominant culture. We may have escaped the economic reductionism of vulgar Marxism, but varieties of base/superstructure thinking are still the norm. The individual is still understood as an instance of the general, with its variations from the base serving to mark its particularity. And we still favor totalizing general forms that structure the entire social field. Everything is related to everything else, because all things are symptoms or manifestations of the underlying culture. The intellectual's role is to elucidate these relationships in order to make the submerged substrate visible.

Although not usually receptive to deconstructionist doublethink, my attempts in this part of my book to undo these ingrained interpretive habits acknowledge that to think is to generalize *and* struggle to disrupt the reliance on totalizing, systematic maps. I favor two tactics, dearticulation and performative articulation. Neither is explained or exemplified here to my full satisfaction. These chapters are part promissory notes and part stumblings around in the dark. I try, for starters, to think about how we could manage to be pluralists, to think of things as, in some cases, unrelated to one another; to resist, in other words, the patterns of relationship that are already in place in intellectual work. Pluralism begins, we might say, as a work of disaggregation and dearticulation. From there, it moves to the insistence that all relationships are contingent and hence to be understood as the product of human sense-making. To place things in relation to one another is a human action and is best understood as performative. The goal is to take responsibility for these actions and to make them, as much as possible, purposive. Articulations do not reveal some deep structure; the relationships are as much surface phenomenon, with exactly the same ontological weight, as the things related. And the audience's acceptance of any particular articulation is utterly contingent as well. The potentially transformative interactions that characterize democracy as a way of life rest on this double contingency of the patterns of relationship I forge as my way of understanding and shaping the world, and of what happens when I attempt to share that vision with others even as they articulate their own visions. The democratic part rests on the existence of a public space for these multiple articulations, the refusal to privilege any particular vision, and openness to (even eagerness for) these energizing connections with others.

CHAPTER 5

Modernity and Culture, the Victorians and Cultural Studies

John Stuart Mill (1965, 28) begins his 1831 essay "The Spirit of the Age" with the conviction that his very subject matter is new.

> The "Spirit of the Age" is in some measure a novel expression. I do not believe that it is to be met with in any work exceeding fifty years in antiquity. The idea of comparing one's own age with former ages, or with our notion of those which are yet to come, had occurred to philosophers; but it never before was itself the dominant idea of any age.

My thesis in this chapter is, in some ways, a simple one. I will argue that the very enterprise of cultural studies marks our Victorianism. We inherit the proclivity to characterize eras, to read the events and fashions of a particular historical moment as indices of an era's "spirit," its profound way of being, from a group of German-influenced English writers who were the first literary (or artistic) intellectuals cum social critics: S. T. Coleridge, J. S. Mill, Thomas Carlyle, John Ruskin, Matthew Arnold, Harriet Martineau, George Eliot, and William Morris, to name just a few.[1] Overlaid on top of this *Zeitgeist* assumption is its "materialist" twin, which locates a systematic or structural unity in terms such as "capitalism" or "modernity." But my thesis is complicated by the fact that I want to trace the consequences of proceeding from the assumption that an era has a

1. For venerable, but still valuable, studies of Victorian intellectuals, see Holloway (1965), Brantlinger (1977), Goodheart (1978), and Morgan (1990).

spirit and/or a structure, while also trying to be skeptical about that assumption. My exploration of this terrain will unfold in three sections. The first connects the notion of a *Zeitgeist* to the corollary concepts of the "modern" and of "culture." The second considers how the basic categories describing political orientation—left, right, center—since the French Revolution derive from the concept of the modern. Finally, I want to turn back upon my whole essay and speculate on what the critical enterprise would look like if we somehow managed to dispense with the "modern" and "culture" as signposts. This last move is crucial because I am guilty, throughout these pages, of the very patterns I wish to question. I am operating close to the limits of my own intellectual paradigms—which, of course, following *Zeitgeist* logic, I deem others' paradigms as well.

Mill's "The Spirit of the Age" is a great place to start, because it offers just about every notion entailed in the belief that time is divided into "ages" in its first five pages and because its identification of searching out the *Zeitgeist* as itself "the dominant idea of [the] age" already pushes almost to the point of parody the whole enterprise. Mill provides a new way of doing intellectual work, and the concept of "the dominant" is essential to this new paradigm. The spirit of any era cannot be described unless the plurality of actions, motives, and beliefs of human beings is organized according to a rubric which identifies the dominant, the truly determinative. What explains, what gives meaning to, the individual event or utterance? The answer, since 1800, has very often been "modernity," understood as a relational matrix within which particulars are held.

Isobel Armstrong (1993) follows Mill's characterization of his age almost exactly when she stresses the "modernism" of the Victorians, a modernism best indicated by their attention to change.

> Victorian modernism . . . describes itself as belonging to a condition
> of crisis which has emerged directly from economic and cultural
> change. In fact, Victorian poetics begins to conceptualise the idea of
> culture as a category and includes itself within the definition. . . .
> [T]o be 'new' or 'modern' . . . was to confront and self-consciously
> to conceptualise *as* new elements that are still perceived as the
> constitutive forms of our own condition (3).

To understand ourselves—or those from the past whom we study—is to examine the "dominant" or "constitutive" lineaments of thought, belief, values, and practices. And part of being "modern" is to have self-consciously taken up this critical task.

Mary Poovey's work (1988 and 1995) offers a sophisticated and highly influential contemporary version of reading particulars in relation to an overarching modernity. Her theoretical goal is to avoid a simplistic mapping of part to whole; adopting Althussser's definition of ideology, she wants, like him, to short-circuit an "expressive" model in which the part expresses unproblematically the qualities of the modern matrix.[2] Rather, the part stands in tension with that matrix, which it both contests through the inadvertent mobilization of contradictions and "reproduces" (1988, 123) through the symbolic resolution of those contradictions. The novel *David Copperfield* thus "construct[s] the reader as a particular kind of subject—a psychologized, classed, developmental individual" that "*is* the modern subject," *and* also indicates "the contradictions inherent in this subject" (90). The both/and relationship of *David Copperfield* to the ideological constitution of the social field is generalized to all literary texts: "'Literature' cannot exist outside a system of social and institutional relations, and in a society characterized by systematic class and gender inequality, literature reproduces the system that makes it what it is" (123). But literary texts can also "expose the operations of ideology within class society" because "they provide the site at which shared anxieties and tensions can surface as well as be symbolically addressed" (124). Poovey does not consider whether "exposure" might be a subset of "reproduction." In other words, must exposure always threaten an ideology? Is an ideology consciously held always more vulnerable than one that is unexposed? If so, why?

I want to highlight three features of Poovey's work. First, the significance of *David Copperfield* rests on its connection to "shared anxieties" and the construction/exposure of the modern subject. In other words, both meaning and knowledge rely on identifying an overarching constitutive

2. See Poovey (1988, 3), for her definition of ideology. See Althusser (1969, esp. 200–218) for the critique of "expressive totality" and the notions of "uneven development" that Poovey adopts. See also Althusser (1971) for the understanding of ideology on which Poovey draws. Poovey's more recent *Making A Social Body: British Cultural Formation, 1832–1864* (1995) makes much more extensive use of the terms "modernity" and "culture" (especially in chapter 1) than *Uneven Developments* (1988) and, thus, might seem even more suited to my concerns in this chapter. My choice of the earlier book has been governed by the neatness of the example of how she reads *David Copperfield.* I do think the more recent work evidences the same intellectual paradigm, although admittedly stretched to the breaking point since Poovey strives mightily to accept "that modern culture's imaginary totality" is not "effective" (1995, 14) *and* to argue that in "early nineteenth-century Britain . . . the groundwork was laid" for "this representation of a single culture [mass culture]" that "competed with and then gradually replaced another representation, which emphasized the differences among various groups within England" (1995, 2 and 4).

framework (historically limited though it be to one era and one place) to which the literary text is related. Secondly, the critic's work is absolutely vital because that framework is "the very condition of its [the novel's] intelligibility . . . even if the reader is not conscious of this pattern" (90). The epistemically privileged critic describes these conditions of intelligibility.[3] Third, despite Poovey's insistence that "causation is never unidirectional" (18), it is hard to see how texts are more than reactionary in her view. *David Copperfield* "reproduces" (not *produces*) modern subjecthood, which seems inevitable because there is no sense in Poovey that a text could rewrite the very terms of intelligibility. Textual reproductions do introduce differences, but the processes by which fundamental changes (from a premodern to a modern subject, say) would occur are less clear, although we are told "that the conditions that produce both texts and (partly through them) individual subjects are material in the ever elusive last instance"(17). These (material) "conditions of intelligibility," then, are the container within which the parts are held or, to switch metaphors, the subbasement on which all particulars rest.

Only this working assumption justifies the general statements about the Victorian context which undergird all the individual readings in Poovey's book. For example, within the general contention that the movement from the eighteenth to the nineteenth-century can be characterized by "the consolidation of bourgeois power," she can claim that during the Victorian era, "as the liberal discourse of rights and contracts began to dominate representations of social, economic, and political relations . . . virtue was depoliticized, moralized, and associated with the domestic sphere, which was being abstracted at the same time . . . from the so-called public sphere of competition, self-interest, and economic aggression" (10). This dominance of liberal discourses could be and was contested in all kinds of ways in Poovey's readings; what is not possible is to write a text that is not related to the framework of intelligibility created by that dominant discourse. The priority of framework to text justifies the vocabulary of Poovey's literary criticism: texts "expose"(124) contradictions that are "inherent" (90) in the modern subject and in modern ideology.

My uneasiness with this type of criticism stems somewhat from a skepticism about generalizations. To characterize Victorian ideology is always

3. The contradictions in the conditions of intelligibility provide the possibility that readers, as well as critics, "can achieve" some "distance" from the matrix, Poovey tells us (90). But she also says that her "reading" of *David Copperfield* "is not an interpretation that a nineteenth-century audience would have been likely to devise" (89).

ham-handed—and generates both endless revisionist histories that contest previous generalizations by way of citing specific counter-instances and re-peated efforts to stake out ever wider conceptualizations of the fundamental conditions so that everything will be caught in their net. Such generaliza-tions become more vacuous, less perspicacious, the wider they become. The irony of Poovey's work is that she recognizes the need for and brilliantly exemplifies focused engagements with the specific, yet still can only theo-rize the significance of such engagements through anchoring them in the wide generalizations. What I really want to question is not historical accu-racy, but the models of meaning, knowledge, and the social that "Zeitgeist" thinking implies. Must we assume that the meaning of individual acts and texts unfolds against or in relation to the backdrop of a containing social context? What kind of knowledge does work like Poovey's claim to provide and what does it imagine the consequences of producing such knowledge? Must we know the conditions of intelligibility to alter them? Does knowing the conditions of intelligibility in 1850 impact on our rela-tion to the conditions of intelligibility in our own day? Is there any way to keep identified contexts from spiraling out into concatenated relations with other contexts to eventually form a totalized image of the social field?

I want to ask: Is pluralism possible? And I also want to know why plu-ralism is so hard. The logic of criticism seems to push us to ever-widen-ing fields of relation. What would it take to argue that some one thing is not related in any way to some other thing? Any criticism that talks of "shared anxieties" or, even more globally, of "conditions of intelligibility" which are beyond conscious awareness is not likely to recognize unre-lated spheres of human endeavor, except across the gulf that separates one era or one culture from another. Spice up your totality with tensions and contradictions to the max, there will still be a container postulated as guarantor that the bits are in relation to one another.

Before tackling the pluralist question, however, I want to examine the assumptions of *Zeitgeist* thinking a bit further. Such work is oriented to-ward questions of power and identity. It seeks to answer the question "who we are" and to identify what or who made us that way. We express our identities through what we produce and consume, but such expres-sion is constrained (at least) and determined (at worst) by the matrix within which we live. The continual return of cultural studies to the prob-lematic of identity locates it squarely on this terrain.

The names offered for the constitutive framework vary—culture, ide-ology, habitus, lifeworld, national character. The social critic's task is to describe us to ourselves; we live the life underwritten by the present age, but only half-consciously. We are the very stuff of culture, but not fully aware of how culture is the very stuff of each one of our individual selves. We suffer from delusions of individuality.

Of these various names, I am particularly interested in modernity and culture, because of the current prominence of cultural studies, multiculturalism and the like, and because the terms "modernity" and "culture" have a complicated history, sometimes related, sometimes not. *Zeitgeist* discourse is ostensibly temporal. The division of time into "then" and "now," into "premodern" and "modern" is a primary organizing device of intellectual analysis since the end of the eighteenth-century. The whole rhetoric of "development" as applied to nations and to children relies on a unified, holistic model of time in which all humans can be tracked and the location of various behaviors as "modern" or "advanced" is not taken as problematic. This diachronic scale assumes continual change, so that what was modern yesterday will not be particularly modern tomorrow. Change does not necessarily sweep the old away entirely, and so we get Althusser's "uneven developments" or Raymond Williams's (1977, chap. 8) "residual, emergent, and dominant." Such concepts try to explain why the "modern" is not everywhere present in modern times.

Culture enters because once temporal analyses admit different paces of change, it is tempting to isolate the differential spatially in order to still be able to identify the modern. In other words, if the modern is inextricably mixed in with the premodern everywhere, then how does it effectively act out its modernity? The holistic assumptions in the term modernity discourage analyses that cannot separate out the modern from the nonmodern. Grafted on top of the temporal differentiation of modern/nonmodern, then, is a spatial differentiation. These two things both exist in the same moment in time, but one is modern and one is not. How can that be? Culture provides the answer. Some places and the people who inhabit them are less modern, more resistant to change, than others. It is their culture—a set of habits, beliefs, and practices which characterizes them as a group—that explains this resistance.

We can see immediately that the concept of "culture" makes the same unified and holistic assumptions that inform the concept of *Zeitgeist*.[4] But culture stands in an ambiguous relation to temporal discourses. In J. G. Herder's work, "culture" serves to resist the yardstick of modernity; his

4. Much of what I have to say about culture has been influenced by Herbert (1991), which traces English notions of "culture" from 1770 to 1870.

arguments for the incommensurability of cultures claims that modernity does not give us a way to judge all cultures together.[5] Certainly in our own time raising the banner of culture has been a persistent and perhaps the most successful (if never fully so) strategy in battles against modernization. But the holism of culture has also made it easier to characterize peoples as "backward," "primitive," "underdeveloped" and the like; in such cases, the discourses of modernity and of culture work hand in glove.

I am even more interested, however, in how a discourse of culture supplements the temporal discourse of modernity imagistically. If all humans now live in a modern moment, their different relations to the modern can only be figured in spatial terms. The temporal, it seems to me, is inevitably abstract in a way the spatial is not. The modern is an abstract notion to which we are all held accountable. We are judged in terms of our relation to the cutting edge, the up-to-date. But the image of that most current thing is always out ahead of us; it must be continually produced (at various sites from the Hollywood studios to corporate R & D units to "original" academic research) because it is so seldom (if ever) lived. The modern is rarely concretely possessed—and only fleetingly before it becomes obsolete. The spatial is what we live, that messy compromise between the traditional/habitual and the new. If the modern has its own abstract unity by virtue of an imagined development that is not "uneven," then the spatial has the unity of its messy mixture of old and new secured by the concept "culture." Here, we say, is a lived life that coheres, that functions. The unity and holism that informs the notion of *Zeitgeist* attains local habitation and a name in culture, understood in the anthropological sense as "a whole way of life."

Modernity in its full purity is never lived anywhere; thus the (presumed) unity of the lived must be designated otherwise. In some discourses, culture then becomes a way to explain the modern's inability to fully install itself. Proponents of modernization will talk (as does E. B. Tylor in his 1871 classic *Primitive Cultures*) of "survivals," pieces of the past that a culture cannot or will not give up.[6] Dystopic views of modernization will insist that its predilection for endless change dissolves various stabilities (designated as "traditional" and "cultural") necessary to life.

5. See Herder (1969), as well as Berlin (1976).

6. Tylor's (1994; first published in 1871) foundational definition of "culture or civilization, taken in its wide ethnographic sense" as "that complex whole which includes knowledge, belief, arts, morals, law, custom, and any other capabilities and habits acquired by man as a member of society"(1) is followed very quickly by the assertion that various cultural

Mill takes a more middle-of-the-road position: "The first of the leading peculiarities of the present age is, that it is an age of transition. Mankind have outgrown old institutions and old doctrines, and have not yet acquired new ones" (1965, 30). It is commonplace to quote Arnold's "Stanzas from the Grand Chartreuse" at this point—"Wandering between two worlds, one dead, / The other powerless to be born, / With nowhere yet to rest my head"—and to attribute Victorian melancholy and doubt to the fact that Mill was right. The Victorians exist in an uneasy transition from Romanticism to Modernism (if you are doing literary history) and from the premodern to the modern (if you are doing history proper). But my claim is that the very notion of the modern inevitably places us in a moment of transition. The modern is always out in front of us. The abstract ideal of the modern leads us to ask anxiously in every moment, "Are we being modern yet?" And the answer, inevitably, is "not quite yet."

This anxiety can be assuaged somewhat (never fully) by shifting the focus from the temporal (modernity) to the spatial (culture). One strategy is to celebrate what we have now: our culture. Here an attempt is made to escape the tyranny of temporal judgments by affirming what is and has been over what is to come. Culturalism of this sort is a hallmark of Lyotardian postmodernism, which sometimes pursues a policy of trying to value the local and particular apart from the master narrative of progress and development.[7] It's worthwhile to note that culturalism is hardly a new strategy; arguably, the majority of the world's population since 1500 on (meaning, in large part, the non-European populations who had to confront the imposed presence of Europeans) has never been modern, if being modern entails a fundamental valuation of change as continual and as an improvement. What is new in postmodernism is only the first adoption by leftist intellectuals of spatial over temporal priorities.

---

stages "may be consistently arranged as having followed one another in a particular order of development"(14) and by the introduction of the concept of "survivals," which are defined as the "customs, opinions, and so forth, which have been carried by force of habit into a new state of society . . . [and] remain as proofs and examples of an older condition of culture out of which a newer has been evolved" (15).

7. Skepticism about modernity necessarily entails skepticism about postmodernity. For the most part, I think postmodernism is a word that has outlived its usefulness; for a while during the 1980s it did serve to focus attention on a set of intellectual debates and choices. Lyotard's influential *The Postmodern Condition* (1984), specifically, poised the local as incommensurate against larger frameworks that would subsume it. His strategy is culturalist, although his argument is couched in rather different terms. The local in his book abides in "language games" rather than in cultures or sub-cultures.

Culturalism, however, seems only fitfully successful. The lure of the modern is not easy to cast aside. Syncretism—various deals with the devil—seems the order of our day. Even the most fervent attempts to maintain cultural integrity tolerate various kinds of accommodation with the modern, while a self-conscious theatricality inflects many efforts to live traditional cultures. The prefix "re" becomes crucial: cultural practices are re-enacted, re-vitalized, re-produced, re-presented. The staged, ritual character of these events marks their quaintness. They exist only within the charmed space of re-enactment.

I don't want to trivialize all attempts to maintain traditional cultures. Many such efforts are (all too) deadly earnest. But earnest efforts will inevitably court fanaticism because only constant vigilance, an obsession with purity, can keep out all traces of the new. At one end of the spectrum, culturalism is weekend play-acting, dressing in clothes you would never wear during the week, and performing/watching "traditional" activities that have no part in daily modern life. At the other end of the spectrum, culturalism is an attempt to say a thunderous no to modernity in all its forms. Not surprisingly, most expressions of culturalism fall somewhere between these two extremes, leaving us in a hybrid space that feels both unsettled and peculiarly (postmodernly?) ours. When I name my children Kiernan and Siobhan, I really don't know what I am doing, since I long ago opted out of the last piece of my Irish heritage (Roman Catholicism) that marked me in any way Irish. So why this ethnic gesture in naming my children? What bit of Irishness beyond pretty names am I wishing upon them?

A certain kind of contemporary humor plays this doubleness to the hilt. We love the image of the Navaho rug maker who tells us she can only weave while watching TV since the weaving is so monotonous. Tourism and Hollywood play this doubleness somewhat differently. The staged past both calls us to a quaint life less hectic, less comfortable, less complex than our own *and* reassures us of our modernity. We get to be proud of being modern (at least, more modern than them) while also indulging in the fantasy of sloughing off the burden of modernity. The fate of the Victorian as marker of the past in the late twentieth-century reveals that our current time-sense not only involves a modernity always fading out in front of us into the far future, but also the receding of the past. If my students are any indication, the past in 2000 comes in two flavors: Victorian and then some obscure, undifferentiated far past beyond the Victorian, a time when people lived in castles (or was it caves?) and knights in armor tilted at dinosaurs. Where their period was the modern for Mill, Carlyle, and Ruskin, the Victorian is now quintessentially the past, the period against which we gauge our own modern-ness. The Bloomsbury group played a large role in this transformation of the Victorian into the non-modern by organizing the (subsequently) endlessly repeated narrative of our (ambivalent) progress around sexuality. No re-staging of Victorian life is complete without reassuring us that we are more enlightened sexually than those repressed Victorians. (For my students, interestingly, the salient belief is not that the Victorians were sexually repressed, but that all their marriages were arranged by tyrannical parents.) Yet many of these re-stagings also ruefully contrast the complexities of our sexual world against the simplicities of the Victorian (when men were men, and women were women—and they liked it that way). The film version of *A Room with a View* offers a perfect example. It pushes Forster's tale from Edwardian times firmly back into the Victorian. Then it ridicules Victorian prudishness throughout. But we also get the joyous innocence of the men's naked bathing, untroubled by the threat of homosexuality (either Forster's or our own).

The recent *Wings of the Dove* is more interesting. The narrative is located in a transitional period, *between* the Victorian and the modern. From my point of view, of course, the issue isn't whether such a transitional time ever really existed, but that viewing any time as transitional is one of the hallmarks of the problematic of the modern. The film, however, locates that transitional moment in the past, not in the here and now (as Mill and Arnold do). Still, the film is trying to break down the easy assumption that we know who the Victorians are (repressed pre-moderns) and who we are (enlightened moderns). And it tries to make us see that James's characters, although dressed in ways we associate with simpler times, occupy a social landscape every bit as complex, as unscripted and under-normed, as our own. That is, the rules of the game, which designate social standing and suitable sexual partners, are all changing in the world the film presents, so that the possibilities for and significance of actions are radically unclear. The film suggests that things are in flux, that our assumption of simpler, more innocent, times is backward projection, not historical accuracy.

To the question "Are we being modern yet?" the only possible answer is "Yes and No." No, we will never be fully modern, because the modern is out in front of us. Yes, we are modern because immersed in constant change, the surest sign of modernity. If we live in a world where change is the norm, then we live in the modern world. The modern is its own continual negation. Anything substantial, no matter how advanced, will yield in its turn to the even further advanced. We cannot, substantively, be modern. But we can (must?) have the *form* of modernity, a form which requires an odd ascesis, a withholding of full investment in any substantial thing. Computers offer an extreme version of this relationship to things and time. A computer is outdated a month after its purchase. This obsolescence is not simply a result of our cultivated craving for the new, but stems also from the need to be in touch with our contemporaries.[8] We cannot communicate with others if we lag behind them. We all need to be on the same page in the book of (modern) time. But how can we be on the same page in a speed-reading world of constant change? "Culture" is a term that taps the brakes. We can say something about the here and now, identify regularities and stabilities within the horizon of change, through the concept of culture. It is our pole star within the swirling heavens.

Let me summarize the argument thus far before taking up the way we chart political positions in relation to this narrative of modernity. What interests me is the organization of much intellectual work around two concepts which I see as related to each other supplementally. The temporal concept judges events, practices, and social structures according to their modernity, their development. But this model also posits a holistic matrix within which change occurs. Modernity is a dynamic whole, nowhere fully present, but a process that figures prominently (often determinately) in the constitution of particulars. The spatial concept "culture" gives the here and now a coherence that modernity (always in transition) cannot provide. Various elements of culture can be judged as more or less modern. Culture can be a rallying point against the blackmail of the modern, but it also assuages the anxiety of not being modern enough. Maybe we are not fully modern yet, but that culture over there is even less modern than us.

"Modernity" and "culture" between them organize a huge amount of our intellectual landscape (most prevalently in the humanities and the social sciences). Mapping the particular to the modern and/or to the cultural began with the Victorians and has become particularly prominent

8. See Douglas and Isherwood (1979) for an argument that consumption is always about social involvement and thus primarily oriented toward gaining information and establishing social relations. We must buy computers in order not to be poor, if we accept their assertion that "the rightful measure of poverty . . . is not possessions, but social involvement" (11).

among American academics during the past twenty years.[9] Current efforts to map the Victorian (either to characterize a shared Victorian culture or to identify the clashing forces within a contradiction-ridden social matrix) hoist certain Victorian writers (Mill, Carlyle, and Ruskin especially) on their own petard.

I now want to turn to the use of modernity as a political measuring rod. The terms "left" and "right" in their political sense are contemporaneous with the "discovery of time" and the birth of the term "culture."[10] Dating from the French Revolution, left and right are coordinated with responses to change. Actually there are three possibilities: left, right, and liberal. The liberal is the champion of modernity, at home in its cities, and a proponent of its economic and social arrangements, which are legitimated as the best possible (in an imperfect world) way to approach justice (on the basis of meritocracy) and freedom (civil rights and free enterprise). Mill is, of course, the great spokesman for liberalism in the Victorian age. And he, along with Arnold, points toward one version (the Ted Kennedy variety) of twentieth-century liberalism when he abandons *laissez-faire* positions in favor of state interference in training, protecting, and rewarding citizen-workers. In the late twentieth-century, we think of *laissez-faire* liberals as conservatives or rightists, sometimes called neo-conservatives, less often called neo-liberals. The last label is the most accurate historically. The important point here is that the definition of left and right in the United States today represents the complete triumph of liberalism which has split in two since 1789, thus giving us our current internecine struggles between interventionist and *laissez-faire* liberals. Both groups are proponents of modernity, which means they favor economic and technological growth, change, and innovation. They support rights-based democracy, and they are adherents of market economics.

Liberalism's middle-aged paunch has pushed nonliberal versions of left and right to the margins. Nonliberal positions are characterized by at-

9. Michaels (1996) writes: "[I]f we return to the revised version of the question with which we began—which myths do Americans believe—we can see that culture, not visitors, races or even history, is the correct answer. Americans, especially American academics, believe in the myth of culture; indeed, with respect to American academics, the point could be put more strongly—we do not simply believe in the myth of culture, many of us have accepted as our primary professional responsibility the elaboration and promulgation of the myth" (13–14).

10. For an argument that historical paradigms of thought are a late-eighteenth-century and nineteenth-century phenomenon, see Toulmin and Goodfield (1965). For accounts of "culture" as a concept dating from the same period, see Jenks (1993), Williams (1976), and Kroeber and Kluckhorn (1960).

tempts to reject modernity *tout court*. (As with culturalism, such attempts in politics are often compromised in one way or another, which yields the usual obsessions with purity and the inevitable schismatic breakdowns into splinter groups asserting their integrity against the complicities of their erstwhile allies.) The rightists can be characterized as premoderns, nostalgic for premodern social and economic arrangements. During the Victorian era, rightists were often medievalists, pointing to that age of faith and social hierarchies as a model for a just and well-ordered society. The defining concern of true-blue rightism is order. The right's prime objection to modernity is its chaos, its anomie, its individualistic anarchy. Thus, when a liberal like Arnold plays the anarchy card in a text like *Culture and Anarchy*, he is halfway to becoming a reactionary. In this view, modern political and social arrangements undermine all authority and leave the unchecked individual to do as he pleases, while modern economic arrangements promote the war of all against all in unbridled competition. Modern society lacks any "social glue," principles of authority or bonds of affection, respect, or obligation that establish relations beyond interest-driven give-and-take in political and economic bargaining. Patriotism, and its cousins ethnic and racial loyalties/hatreds, have, in practice, proved the most potent elixirs concocted to prevent modern societies dissolving into the individualistic war of each against all. Perhaps if we could reassess the threat and lose this fixation on the bogeyman of anomie, we would be spared cures that have been disastrous while addressing a disease that has never manifested itself.

In our own day, premodernism flourishes fitfully among "cultural conservatives," a group the Republican Party in the United States managed to incorporate and exploit during the 1980s, but which has damaged that party in presidential elections in the 1990s. The increased visibility of culturalism and various fundamentalisms in religion during the last quarter of the twentieth century demonstrates that abhorrence of modernity and all its works still exists. For much of the world's population, modernity has brought no palpable benefits, and the program of jettisoning the modern entirely in favor of the premodern "survivals" which have persisted alongside the modern has gained new and vocal adherents. Such movements have highlighted the extent to which modernity is the province of (primarily professional) élites. Workers in the West were brought into modernity's fold before World War II through nationalistic patriotism, racism, or brute force, and after World War II through economic participation in prosperity. But the move toward a global economy has widened the economic gap between professional (upper) middle classes and less skilled (lower) middle classes, a widening that has made the cultural gaps (which had never disappeared) between these two groups prominent once again.

There are various litmus tests for attitudes toward the modern, for marking the gulf between the sophisticated élites who feel at home in modernity and the much larger numbers who have never experienced modernity as anything more than a threat. Three such tests are attitudes toward religion, cities, and ethnic identities. The liberal proponent of modernity (whether Democrat or Republican) is likely to be a-religious, at ease in large cities (even if living in the suburbs), and unlikely to take ethnic identity very seriously (professional identity is probably primary; family life, while crucial, is not organized ethnically for élites, who marry along class lines, not ethnic ones). The élites—and the two political parties—are not going to roll back modernity significantly. But each party needs to court constituencies that are hostile to modernity in ways the élites are not. And when, as has happened in the Republican Party, the non-élites manage to move from being the foot-soldiers to being elected representatives, disarray can follow as the modernism of the business class clashes with the premodernism of the cultural right.

But what of the radical left? If the radical right are premodernists, does that make the radical left postmodernists? If only it were that simple. The nineteenth-century radical left divides between the Marxists and the anarchists.[11] Bypassing theoretical and/or factual accuracy somewhat, let me say that Marxism's great strength and its great flaw as a political pro-

11. What, you might ask, about left Hegelians and their descendants, later in the century, the social democrats? In my *Postmodernism and Its Critics* (1991), I have tried in chapter 4 to delineate a left Hegelian position that is neither Marxist nor liberal. Such a position dovetails with some (but hardly all) elements of contemporary communitarianism (of the Charles Taylor rather than the Alasdair MacIntyre variety) while also picking up some hints from attempts to resuscitate a republican civic virtue tradition. But I think now that left Hegelianism is more liberal than not—and certainly liberal in its attitudes toward modernity, change, and individual rights. Liberalism is a capacious house, and I think we need to come to terms with its variants, instead of believing we can reject it wholesale. We can no more banish liberalism by fiat than we can make the modern disappear. Liberalism and the modern (along with capitalism, patriarchy, racism, imperialism, etc.) are the nontotalized horizons within which we operate, and the clean choice of affirmation/rejection should be swapped for the messy task of working through the details of what opportunities (for good and for evil) our intellectual, political, and emotional predilections, our past, and our present afford us (fully recognizing that different groups and individuals located within this horizon have different purposes which inflect their assessment of possibilities). In other words, liberalism is no more of a piece than modernity is. I remain a left Hegelian (or a "radical democrat" in today's parlance), but I think this position stands in a more complex relationship to liberalism than "it is" or "it isn't" can encompass.

gram are one and the same: it ignores all cultural objections to modernity and hence all protests against how modernity destroys "ways of life." Therefore Marxism is only interested in modernity's economic sins, how it creates "poverty amidst plenty." The typical Marxist is the engaged intellectual (not the proletariat he tries to woo to the party) and he, like other élites, is at home in modernity and its godless frenetic cities. He doesn't so much reject modernity as he expects to come out on its other side. Modernity is a stage on the way to socialism—and much of modernity will survive into the socialist future. Marxism, in other words, can only appeal to those who are temperamentally modern, not to premodernists. A leftist political party can only attract premodernists if it succeeds in getting them to check all their cultural allegiances at the door and focus political activity on the sole issue of a bigger slice of the economic pie. The cultural recidivism of our times followed from the discovery by Reagan's Republicans and Thatcher's Conservatives that if played right, certain hot-button cultural issues like flag-burning could supplant economic interest. (Of course, it didn't hurt that Reagan was playing off the oil-crisis inflation of the 70s and Thatcher off the same energy crisis, symbolically centered around the coal miners in Britain.)

Anarchism is less easy to track, but the energies of the *enragé* must be noted because they are also with us today. By tapping into culturalist energies through the thematics of hostility to the state, reverence for religious and social authority, abhorrence of modern cities (figured as a-religious, homosexual, and the home of nonworking non-whites), and traditional family values, political fanatics have unleashed a rage that has spawned para-military groups, violent confrontations with federal agencies (especially out West), and "domestic terrorism" (the Oklahoma City and Atlanta bombings, as well as the blowing up of various abortion clinics around the country). The left's engagement with these energies has been troubled. Starting with the civil rights and student movements of the 1960s, but accelerating with the "identity politics" of the 1970s and 1980s, the left has tried to face up to the fact that economic issues are not primary for some constituencies still willing to associate their politics with the left. It turns out that the indignities most crucial to many people willing to take vigorous political action involve issues of equality, recognition, appreciation, respect, and tolerance more than economic concerns. For people who want to be taken seriously on their own terms—and want to resist changes that seem to threaten those terms—traditional leftist economic issues and tactics (the ballot, strikes, revolutions) are less compelling than cultural issues (or representation and recognition) and symbolic tactics (demonstrations, civil disobedience, media access and coverage).[12]

If this analysis is correct, then postmodernism (as an intellectual movement) can be read as the left's attempt to process the fact that its political agenda cannot simply be the transformation of modernity's economic arrangements within the context of a general acceptance of the modern. Rather, the left has to re-invent itself, first by grasping just what are the complaints/grievances of the groups crudely lumped under the inadequate label of "identity politics," and secondly by thinking through a social vision which gets at the root causes of the abuses that underlie those grievances. I think this work has hardly begun. Old (economist) ways of thinking are hard to put aside, although I'd say the most progress has been made on this front. Less successful has been the attempt to understand fully the stakes in cultural politics for groups on both sides. For example, despite all the current focus (both theoretical and historical) on racism, analyses of intolerance are never going to get us very far until the powerful appeal of racism can be presented in nonpathologized terms. So long as leftist intellectuals provide descriptions of *their* benightedness, the gap between those intellectuals and their purported allies cannot be closed.[13]

Along with its repudiation of Marxist economism, postmodern theory has (more fitfully) considered the left's entire relation to modernity. Various bits and pieces of the modern (its addiction to universalist arguments and solutions, for example) have been questioned, and there have also been repeated flirtations with anarchistic jettisoning of the modern altogether. But neither total rejection nor Habermas's attempted embrace of modernity's unfinished emancipatory project has proved attractive to many. The dramatic choices the postmodernist debate of the 80s appeared to offer have faded into a more meticulous project of picking through, piece by piece, the modernist heritage, figuring where and how each piece

12. My characterization of these leftist, but non-economically motivated, political agents connects up to long-standing controversies about the "new Left," "the new social movements," and "identity politics." Readers will find the essays collected in Nicholson and Seidman (1995); Rajchman (1995); and Charles Taylor et al. (1994) a good place to start.

13. I am attracted to, without having worked out all the implications of, the "principle of symmetry" promoted by Barbara Herrnstein Smith (1997, chap. 3). The principle recommends that we take as a starting assumption that others with whom we disagree have as reasonable a basis for their beliefs as I have for mine. The difficulty of enacting the principle becomes apparent when that other is someone who strongly believes in racial differences. But it is equally hard to imagine progress in an argument in which the only move is my repetition that you are wrong—really, truly, and fundamentally wrong.

might be useful or harmful. Such salvage work is hardly heady; it yields few moments of stunning, all-illuminating epiphany. As a result, we passed through the millennium in a peculiarly undramatic way. The ending of the twentieth-century brought neither a whimper nor a bang. Perhaps we peaked too soon, but that's fine by me. (I'm prone to semi-serious baby-boom determinism; that we hit the millennium in middle-age may account for its not living up to its hype.) 1989 put the apocalyptic East-West face-off to bed in an inconclusive non-ending which was at least semi-triumphant given the possible scenarios. The big one was never dropped. If our current situation is innumerable intractable local conflicts, each of which requires sustained, fine-grained attention with a minimum of general commitments/beliefs if any solution is to be found, should we bemoan the lost clarity of global schemes, globally envisioned progress, and enemies identified as evil empires? I don't think so.

The political stakes, then, in my desire to question the Victorian heritage that has us gauge political positions and possibilities in relation to modernity lie in my conviction that the terms "left" and "right" have lost their usefulness, and that holistic covering terms such as "modernity," "capitalism," "disciplinary society," "patriarchy," "socialism," and the like are similarly more of a hindrance than a help.[14] We need more nuanced, more particularist analyses that consider situational utility, situational harm. Progress here would be greatly enhanced by abandoning the belief that modernity is of a piece, that each element of contemporary life stands in relation to other elements more or less modern, and by acknowledging that modernist themes like "universal rights" cannot be judged apart from the situations in which they are deployed. Current appeals to the "global economy" are the blackmail of the modern in a new guise. "Survivals" (in Tylor's sense) like France's social safety nets cannot survive long, the pundits assure us, for only streamlined modern economies will be able to compete. Retaining any local differences that hamper productivity or subtract the cost of social goods from the shareholders' bottom line will prove short-sighted and self-destructive. The price paid for local difference, of uneven development, is too high.

The left would do better to resist such holistic analyses and the prescriptions they warrant. Its political analyses and programs should be uncou-

14. J. K. Gibson-Graham's wonderful *The End of Capitalism (as We Knew It)* (1996) provides a sustained attempt to consider the political and epistemological consequences of abandoning the term and concept "capitalism."

pled from both a sensibility that says yes or no to modernity *tout court* and from theories that identify any new practice as the thin edge of the wedge. Production for export markets is not necessarily bad, does not necessarily destroy local communities, while some local communities are hardly to be celebrated and protected. All the grounds for judgment and decision are in the details of the particular situation. Instead of trying to hold out against modernity, or of bemoaning the fact of being already implicated in some way with the modern, the left might try to stop taking the modern as a yardstick. Certain actions (for example, rural industrialization or the growth of web-based communication) need not carry certain inevitable consequences. Modernization does not everywhere take the same form and have the same results. If we can disconnect individual actions from the overarching matrix of the modern, we can be more attentive to the very different consequences that can follow from similar actions taken at different times in different places and handled differently. We should cherish what works, but recognize how much doesn't—while recognizing that modernity does not prescript results. Yes, there are various pressures of various sorts, including the pressures of a world economic situation, but various creative responses to those pressures are always a possibility.

Such pragmatic particularism comes with its own attendant risks. But that is to be expected; much of the point is that theory and its models cannot offer magical nostrums that protect us from failure. What worked elsewhere may not work here and now. The temptation can be to cultivate one's garden, to build enclaves (restricted, "intentional" communities) against the general uncertainty. The watchwords could become "family" and "community," two local forms of relatedness that eschew connection or intervention in wider social structures named "state," "corporation," or "United Nations."

In such a climate, images of the Victorian can function to reinforce a certain sheltered ideal of community. All the recent films set in that generalized English past that covers Jane Austen to E. M. Forster are essentially drawing-room comedies or melodramas. These films ignore the hungry forties specifically and the working classes generally, while presenting an astoundingly insular view of England when we consider that the time period in question saw England at its most expansive, that is, as ruler of the empire on which the sun never set. We get England only. Even the recent spate of (vaguely anti-English) films set in Scotland and Ireland all avoid the 1850 to 1910 time period. (A counter-example, *Mrs. Brown*, gives us the ultra-devoted Scottish servant to the British monarch, not the Scottish rebel.) The golden age of Victoria provides a very popular contemporary image of domestic felicity—domestic in both its senses of confined to the family home and confined to the home country. Contented relatedness is a function of sealed-off relations, in unremarked tension with the outward directed imperial grasp of the actual historical period. Depicted this way, the Victorian dovetails with a prominent isolationist mood in a prosperous America and England disinclined to take much responsibility for, or remediating action toward, the less well-off, either abroad or at home.

My point in this section has been that our way of understanding the political categories left and right has shrunk since the early part of the Victorian period, because political and intellectual élites (for the most part) have lost the sense that these categories chart fundamental orientations to modernity itself. Modernity is not at stake in our politics; left and right are defined within a framework that takes modernity as the unalterable given, and thus focuses only on possible maneuvers within modernity. The narrow focus of contemporary filmic representations of the Victorian replays this narrowing of possible political positions and political options in contemporary two-party democracy in both England and the United States. To re-ask the question of modernity gives us a useful alternative take on what is at issue in contemporary politics and on the vicissitudes of the two major parties in both countries over the past thirty-five years. Postmodernism can be seen as the intellectual discourse that attempts (especially from the left's point of view) to reconfigure the primarily economic view of politics that prevailed before the 1960s. However, we can also view postmodernism as calling us to eschew the fixation on modernity altogether, to organize our thinking along entirely different lines, to stop being modernists in exactly the way the Victorians were modernist: that is, in taking modernity as the key reference point when examining allegiances, beliefs, practices, and outcomes. In other words, I believe that my raising the question of modernity in the way I do in this essay is part and parcel of an effort to rethink the whole political landscape, to get beyond inherited (and currently very confused) configurations of left and right.

The reader will have noted that this chapter, thus far, commits the very sin it strives to describe. I have characterized a certain type of cultural criticism as modern and have claimed that we and the Victorians are both modern since we practice that type of criticism. To say that critical generalization since 1800 is usually temporally and/or culturally organized is to enact the very critical move to which I am trying to draw attention. As recent (1975–1995) criticism geared toward uncovering ideological taken-for-granteds amply demonstrates, even tonally neutral accounts of unacknowledged assumptions convey a skeptical, if not downright denunciatory, relation to the material described. Some positions, it seems, are hard to occupy self-consciously. If, as an ideology or a *Zeitgeist* critic, you are doomed to be no different from those whom you critique, does the critique lose all its value? Or is there some pay-off for self-consciousness, for the examined life? Is there any way to use self-consciousness about the intellectual paradigm this essay discusses?

From the outset, let's acknowledge a fascinating, if perhaps, infinite regress here. *Zeitgeist* thinking would suggest we pose this question: "What about the current moment allows the paradigm of *Zeitgeist* thought to become a consciously raised issue?" What in the temper of our times or in our current intellectual situation allows us to identify, as Walter Benn Michaels (1996) does, a belief in culture as our prevailing myth and to examine the structures and consequences of that belief? I have, as you can imagine, various thoughts on this topic that I would love to try out on you, the gentle reader, for plausibility. But that path leads back into the labyrinth just when I want to consider if we can by-pass the labyrinth. Can we do our intellectual work in other ways?

One solution, of course, is to opt for pure particularity, for singularity. Certain strains in poststructuralism (especially in Derrida, Deleuze, and Foucault) point us in this direction.[15] These writers indicate a tension between the particular and the categories by which we envelop it, and consider (at least tentatively) the possibility of encountering the specific thing without subsuming it under a more general term. The problem of such an approach is dramatically conveyed by the Borges story, *Funes the Memorius*. The title character has perceptions so fine that today's tree is completely different to him than yesterday's, so much so that they cannot be identified by the same name or grouped in a single category. Funes is an idiot; the narrator tells us he "suspect[s] . . . that [Funes] was not very capable of thought. To think is to forget a difference, to generalize, to abstract (1962, 115)." Funes finds the world overwhelming and ends up in bed in a darkened room, the only way he can survive in a world of countless singularities impressing themselves upon him.

15. See Foucault (1979, 251–55), and (1980, 42–45) for passages that indicate his attempt to disconnect appearances from a "depth hermeneutic" and that locate their meaning in essences or identities hidden from view.

Still, it is tempting to pursue the Foucauldian dream of taking appearances as all there is, thus eschewing our habitual mapping of appearances to identity, essence, causal matrices, or deep foundational regularities like culture. Yes, singularities are inflected by, gain significance through, their relations and interactions with other singularities. And many of these relations may exist over fairly long stretches of time, institutionalized and maintained by various social arrangements, some of which are enforced against opposition. But there is no reason to think that these various relations and these various arrangements map onto some deeper and unifying reality that is acquired differently, is possessed unconsciously and thus more tenaciously, and is more fundamental than any of our other beliefs about the world and our place in it. The systematic relationships and fiercely held commitments that do exist are human products, no more and no less than my casual preference for blue over yellow shirts. Depending on context, what is casual now could become all-important and vice versa; there are a variety of ways in which we acquire beliefs and commitments, none of which is more fundamental or exists on a deeper level than any other. Similarly, there are many different kinds of social pressure (power) brought to bear on individual belief formation and such pressure is brought to bear in many different ways, but none operates on a different level than any of the others, and they form cohesive or contradiction-ridden wholes only as a result of specific human actions aimed at establishing such encompassing relations among things. We live in a world where lots of energy is expended trying to change each other's minds and actions; such efforts often involve attempts to rescript the meaning of things through recontextualization and forging new connections. The results of such efforts are mixed.

Because the results are mixed, my argument throughout this essay has been skeptical of any easy generalizations about what constitutes either Victorianism or our own moment. My argument suggests that it makes sense to identify various specific conditions of specific historical moments; we might even claim that some of these conditions are "modern," meaning that they did not exist prior to some designated date (say 1600). But we should avoid thinking that there is some substrate called "modernity" or "Western (or American or English) culture" which actively structures the relations of all of these conditions to one another. The elements of the modern exist in contingent, problematic, and ever-changing relation to one another. In other words, the elements are not necessarily related to one another at all. We live in a modern world, but it is not systematic in the way that terms like "modernity" would have us believe. My approach suggests that we ask: who (in any particular historical or cultural analysis) is trying to make what kind of connection between what elements of the past and what elements of the present; and how; and why? Relationships and meanings are forged through various (contingent) human actions, one of which is the telling of stories in fiction and film, another of which is making interpretive arguments in criticism.

I will close by indicating, all too briefly, that Hannah Arendt's thoughts on story-telling and judgment might help us re-orient our notion of what criticism can accomplish. Arendt, especially in the posthumous *Life of the Mind* (1981), was committed to an ontology of appearances.[16] The real for Arendt is that which exists between humans in publicly apprehensible forms. But the real is not purely singular in Arendt because of the requirements of story-telling and judgment. Story-telling is necessary for two reasons: to maintain the reality of that which is not itself apprehensible now and to consider the meaning of the real. Things appear. Many of these "things" are human deeds (action) or the products of human efforts (work). Action and work would seem futile if they left no on-going impress on the world. Work's legacy is very often the things it creates which now furnish our world. But action that does not create a material object depends on stories for preservation—and for an impact on future deeds.

Stories, however, do more than just memorialize. Appearances are not self-evident; their possible meanings unfold over time through a process of re-telling. Story-telling records, but it is also productive. The story elaborates and speculates; it ponders possible ways of being in the world as exemplified by the actions it relates. Here is where story connects to judgment. Each of us has to decide how to live a life. Or, if that is too grand, each of us has various decisions to make in various situations. We are guided, certainly, by the particulars of the situation, which include our particular purposes as well as the possibilities afforded by the situation and our estimate of possible success. In other words, judgment involves gauging what is possible in these circumstances in relation to what I desire to achieve. Any situation offers a number (more than one but less than

16. I discuss Arendt's notions of story-telling and judgment in detail in McGowan (1998, chap. 3). Arendt's own texts on these topics are widely scattered, from the essays on Lessing, Isak Dinesen, and Walter Benjamin in *Men in Dark Times* (1968), and the essay "Truth in Politics" in *Between Past and Future* (New York: Penguin, 1977), to the posthumous *Lectures on Kant's Political Philosophy* (1982). See Arendt (1981, 42–46) for the most succinct statement of her ontology of appearances.

infinity) of options for action. Judgment entails both identifying the options and choosing among them. Stories often offer examples of creative or otherwise extraordinary actions that invite us to expand our notions of the possible.

What has this model of the interaction among situations, stories, and judgments have to do with academic work which explains *Bleak House* by mapping it onto typical Victorian attitudes or (in the more sophisticated version of this kind of work) to a constitutive Victorian social field? Primarily I think it shifts the focus of our mapping efforts. Judgment aided by stories still must decide which stories (among many) are relevant to the situation at hand—and in what ways those stories are instructive. No fit is perfect; we are always proceeding by analogy and approximation. The fluidity of the process is crucial, since the absence of exactitude keeps judgment supple and creative in the attempt to respond to novel circumstances. My suggestion, then, is to re-orient our relationship to various elements of the past. Instead of understanding the element's meaning as a function of its dynamic relation to the defining discourses, ideology, or beliefs of its age or culture, we should be considering what elements of the past can mean in relation to our purposes in the present. Instead of viewing things that appear as indices of who they (the Victorians) were and/or who we (postmoderns?) are, those things would be elaborated through stories that ponder what we might become. Instead of asking (anxiously) "are we being modern yet?" and looking over our shoulders for the preceptor who bears the report card registering how well we've passed the test, we would see in stories of the past images of being in the world that tell us there are multiple ways to be human and that we are engaged in the project of living out some of those ways.

Whether such an approach would lessen the pressure on the "we" which I invoke in the previous sentences is an open question. I hope that a focus on the future we are trying to enable rather than describing the characteristics of the past might make images of the "we" more fluid, less a group solidarity we necessarily share or can be blamed for not accepting than forms of human relatedness that must be continually re-created.[17] The "we" is precisely what the storyteller, the user of discourse, is trying to create through the appeal to an audience, with success in that endeavor blessedly hard to achieve and only temporarily stable even when

17. I highly recommend Young (1995) for a way of thinking about the existence of groups that gets us beyond the stalemate of essentialized identities versus mobilized differences.

achieved. Just as the elements of the modern do not cohere into an all-encompassing "modernity" which organizes them once and for all in one way, so individual human existences touch each other in some ways and in some times, but not in others. Just exactly what connections are made and when is the product of human action, not the result of systemizing unities that lurk beneath or behind or beyond that contact of humans, one with another.

CHAPTER 6

The Narrative of Culture:
A Burkean Perspective

I. SKEPTICAL MUSINGS,
OR AGAINST CULTURALISM

My starting point is a deep skepticism about the term "culture." My skepticism takes two forms: one political, the other epistemological. To make the political point will require a (greatly truncated) genealogy of the term. Our contemporary infatuation/enthrallment with culture has complicated roots which I am going to dramatize with a partial (in all senses of the word) narrative about how a conservative, Romantic concept was appropriated by twentieth-century Western Marxism. This narrative lies aslant models of culture and agency offered by cultural studies and by poststructuralist versions of the performative—both influenced by them and taking up different issues than them.

If we go back to Romanticism—German Romantics such as Herder and the Brothers Grimm, English Romantics such as Coleridge and Carlyle—culture enters the scene as a player in the struggle with science for explanatory power. My take on Romanticism—hardly novel, but hardly uncontroversial—is that these writers attempt to recuperate under another name what religion represented in the Enlightenment battles between religion (figured as superstition by *les philosophes*) and science/philosophy/reason. The Romantics accept that religion is a dead letter, but work to revivify spiritual factors that, according to them, scientific materialism ignored. (Abrams [1971] offers one standard version of this argument.) One branch of Romanticism takes the tactic of championing an animistic, living Nature to pose against the dead mechanical nature of science; but another version of Romanticism turns to culture, not nature, as the locus of what transcends reason. There are intangibles—like *esprit de corps,* patriotism, English phlegm—that science can not recognize, but which have consequences in the world we inhabit. Culture acts as a substance term, the "stuff" to which such intangibles adhere as we struggle (in a post-Enlightenment age) to give them a local habitation and a name—and to consider their production, their coherence, and their reproduction. Culture, then, is a repository for all kinds of things that Enlightenment reason threatens to exclude.[1] Let the word "culturalism" designate those who appeal to culture in order to insist "that ideas and practices have their foundation in neither logic nor empirical science, that ideas and practices fall beyond the scope of deductive and inductive reason, that ideas and practices are neither rational nor irrational but rather *non*rational" (Shweder, 1984, 28).

Culture as a repository of the extra-rational and supra-sensible is a curious amalgam of left and right, especially from an early to mid-twentieth-century perspective. Traditionally, leftist thought—dominated by Marx—embraces Enlightenment reason, the aspiration to rational control, and a hostility to religion and nationalism (insofar as the Workers' International represents the height of leftist aspirations). But just as, in our post-Marxist era, these clear lines of leftist allegiance have been blurred by postmodernist attacks on Western reason and by the identity politics of new social movements, the first Romantic adherents of culture—dare we say of a "cultural politics"—are not easily characterized as left or right. This is as true of Edmund Burke (purported godfather of conservatism) as it is of the Tory Radicals who combine Burke's paeans to tradition, cultural values, and hierarchical authority with denunciations of capitalism that are as ferocious as anything Marx ever penned. Burke—like Coleridge, Carlyle, Disraeli, and Ruskin after him—already saw that capitalism is the great destroyer of traditional social life, that capitalism itself is the

1. Critiques of Enlightenment reason are, of course, standard fare in post-structuralist theory. Two crucial sources for this critique are Horkheimer and Adorno (1972) and Foucault (1965). Many of the most repeated post-structuralist criticisms can be found in Romantic writers, especially German Romantics. See, for one example, Herder (1993), along with Berlin's (1976) discussion of Herder's critique of the Enlightenment.

direct manifestation of instrumental reason put to work. Culture is trotted out as the champion which will do battle for all that is about to be lost.

Despite the teaser of my title, the Burke in whom I am primarily interested is Kenneth, not Edmund. But we need to think a bit more about Edmund now in order to gauge just how conservative the notion of culture is. Burke's *Reflections on the Revolution in France* (1993; first published 1791) establishes (at an incredibly early date) the battle lines between tradition and modernity, a move paralleled by the contemporary establishment of *droit* and *gauche* by the French revolutionaries themselves.[2] I think it fair to say that the narrative of a transition from the traditional to the modern is the founding gesture of history (as it comes down to us from Hegel), sociology, and anthropology. Each of these discourses is built upon the supposition that the West has undergone a "great transformation," to use the title of Polanyi's (1944) classic work on the birth of capitalism. This transformation is figured as progress or as loss in different versions. Societies are characterized in relation to their position on a time line of development, in a continuum from advanced to primitive. And, again quite quickly, the self gets mapped on an analogous time line, from primitive childhood to an appropriate maturity. In one of its manifestations (which are multiple, complex, and contradictory), "culture" stands as the spatial marker between "traditional" (primitive) and "modern"—a necessary supplement to the temporal line of development, a way of accounting for the fact that some societies that exist now (in "modern times") are categorized as "pre-modern" (as discussed in the preceding chapter.)

Burke's thought is conservative (reactionary and nostalgic) insofar as he argues against modernity in favor of tradition, against change in favor of continuity. But Burke also introduces two themes that are less consistently conservative: a downplaying of human agency in the making of history and an emphasis on the situated, communal component of human individuality. Michael Oakeshott, perhaps this century's greatest conservative thinker, takes this mistrust of human agency as his starting

2. Eagleton (1995, chap. 2) provides a superb reading of how Burke relies on culture to enable authority to win allegiance and obedience from those over whom it holds sway. "At the centre of Burke's political thought lies the belief that colonial power must cling tenaciously to the contours of a native culture . . . . It was the violation of this principle which led to the loss of America, and which has wreaked havoc in Ireland. To achieve hegemony, colonial rule must be refracted through the traditions of those it governs, miming their cultural gestures and conforming to their customs . . . . It is thus that power will found itself securely" (40–41).

point.[3] The great evils of our century, he insists, stem from a misplaced faith in rationalism, a belief that humans can plan and then implement a better world. Just as we muck up breathing once we start thinking about it, deliberate interventions into ongoing social processes invariably cause more harm than good. Here is Burke's insistence that culture is like a living organism, which changes "naturally" according to its own rhythms and needs, and which is beyond rational comprehension. The would-be physician is just a meddler, someone who has no real idea of how the various parts of the organism interact, and who is just blindly experimenting with a hubris unjustified by the results he actually can procure. Things are better left alone to work themselves out in their own way, according to their own wisdom—a wisdom that far exceeds anything human ingenuity or reason could devise.

Such an attitude might very well seem the quintessence of conservatism until we remember that laissez-faire is the very cornerstone of nineteenth-century liberalism and of the neo-liberalism of our own day. A mistrust of planned collective action can co-exist with a recommendation for rational individual action (admittedly, where "rational" is pared down to mean self-interest) in ways that come to praise capitalism and modernity, not to bury them. Similarly, even Marx's attack on liberal political economy maintains an element of not trusting human action to bring about the desired socialist future. The dialectic will do that work for us. Of course, Marx usually claims that the revolutionary action of the proletariat is also necessary, but the point is that an uneasiness with human action makes its appearance in the writers ranging from Burke to Smith to Marx, which suggests that such uneasiness is not exclusively conservative, liberal, or radical. More likely, the concern is with the legitimacy of human action. What claim does such action have on others? Why should others join in the efforts of one group or (even more problematically) obey the strictures of that group?

Modernity is often associated with a crisis in authority, as the traditional non-human sources of authority are replaced by human ones. In a writer like Kant, reason serves as the principle of authority, the self-legislating

3. Oakeshott (1962) writes: "How deeply the rationalist disposition of mind has invaded our political thought and practice is illustrated by the extent to which traditions of behavior have given place to ideologies, the extent to which the politics of destruction and creation have been substituted for the politics of repair, the consciously planned and deliberately executed being considered (for that reason) better than what has grown up and established itself *unconsciously* over a period of time" (21, my emphasis).

inner voice that every man (this view is gendered; it's hardly clear if women and children have reason) possesses. In non-Kantian, more Romantic figures, culture functions as the supra-individual principle of authority to which individual humans feel bound, and over which no individual human has control. The fact that a culture is both "ours" and beyond the control of any particular person or group can make culture seem a safeguard against tyranny in a modern age in which transcendent forms of authority have been lost. Certainly Burke conceives of culture as precisely a semi-transcendent guarantee against abusive power.

Culture is, also, of course a collective term, and as such it stands against the individualism of capitalism as conceived by Smith and the other proponents of enlightened self-interest. It doesn't take too much extrapolation from Burke to argue that he presents identity as intersubjectively constituted and that he understands achievement of the good life as contingent upon full participation in a human community. Such a critique of liberal individualism is not confined to conservatives. Various leftist utopian visions, along with some aspects of Marx, look toward a fuller public life, while even a liberal like John Dewey (1980) critiques capitalism for its destruction of the public sphere. The activist liberalism (of the Ted Kennedy sort) which defines the most commonly understood meaning of the term "liberal" in our own day stands as firmly against the laissez-faire, individualistic liberalism of Smith and Bentham as Burke would. In this configuration, culture is often used to designate binding loyalties and shared values that exist apart from—or even that serve to mitigate—the sheer individualism of competitive market exchanges.

I recognize the usefulness of culture to counter laissez-faire capitalism or even tyranny through the naming of motivations and concerns that escape an individualistic social calculus. But my skepticism about culture's political usefulness stems from the indirection of the means it proposes for political intervention and the hopelessness about possible success that it encourages. I don't think these two are unrelated; resorting to indirect means is a strategy inspired by despair. To explain this connection requires the second part of my genealogy: how a mostly conservative culturalism (used to authorize the traditional way things are done against conscious, rational critique and/or action) comes to the practitioners of "cultural studies" in the late twentieth century refracted through the radical Marxist tradition. The linchpin is the fact that "culture" names a social collectivity that both explains the failure of the Marxist collective agent, the proletariat, to act in the predicted ways *and* serves as a displaced site for the collective action that the leftist looks to inspire. It is through culture that the proletariat has been rendered quiescent, and it is within culture that the leftist intellectual (and/or empowered and hence nonquiescent couch potatoes) can do the radical work that the working class hasn't done economically or politically.

Marx's allegiance to Enlightenment rationality explains his lack of interest in culture, his dismissal of it as mere superstructural froth. (Yes, I do recognize that this dismissal is not consistent and, like all searchers for the subtle Marx, the Marx who avoids the "vulgar Marxism" of the base/superstructure model, I have dutifully read *The Eighteenth Brumaire*. But allow me, for the sake of considering Marx's legacy, to stress that Marx's emphasis on the economic base is the most obvious facet of his views on culture, views that will only be rendered more subtle by much later commentators.) The other result of Marx's Enlightenment rationalism, the result that seems most fatal to us in our own particular post-communist moment, is his confident faith in human rational action. Marx reduces public questions to matters of economic welfare—and he believes that rational action (what he calls "administration") can insure welfare for all. Politics understood as the agonistic give-and-take of public debate among citizens—debate spurred not just by different interests, but also by the fact that what is the best course for collective action is never obvious—disappears in Marx's communist utopia. It seems terribly clear now (it was suspected by many in the past) that Marx's hostility to politics was anti-democratic, since democracy is the most intensely political of governmental forms. Marx utterly misses the fact that in politics (as I have just defined it, with a huge debt to Hannah Arendt [1958, chaps. 2 and 5]), the process is as important (probably more important) than the result. It is in the give-and-take of the debate that one has a political existence at all, that one acts in front of and with others.

In his impatience with political wrangles, with the literally unending process of political contestation, and with his belief that each problem has one and only one correct solution, Marx authorizes administration by experts, which proves to be one very characteristic form of modern tyranny.[4] Maybe we would find such tyranny acceptable if it worked. But there also seems to be an imp in the machine. So it is not just that Marx's hostility to politics has bad consequences, but that he severely underestimated the

---

4. Weber [1964, 324–41] and Foucault [1979] are just two of the many writers who have delineated this form of tyranny for us.

problems to be faced. No administration, no matter how capable, seems up to the task of creating a just society. To anticipate my argument a bit: culture has come to be one name we conjure up to explain these intractable difficulties. Consider the failure of the civil rights movement and the legal reforms that it won to appreciably better the economic lot of a majority of African-Americans in this country. Cultural factors—from an ineradicable racism among whites to a culture of poverty among blacks— are trotted out to explain that stateways cannot change folkways, and that the optimism of the 1960s about the effects of legislated integration were obviously unwarranted.

My argument is that the first versions of this use of culture to explain the disappointment of optimistic hopes can be found in Western Marxism, most obviously in Horkheimer and Adorno (1972, 120–67), but also in Gramsci (1971, 24–43 and 419–72) and Marcuse (1964, ix–83). I have said (with, I hope, pardonable exaggeration) elsewhere that Western Marxism can be best understood as the attempt to correct, sometimes it seems to reverse altogether, the base/superstructure model and the economic determinism to which it is linked.[5] There are various reasons why so many twentieth-century Marxists are obsessed with cultural causes, but—to simplify a complex tale—one crucial factor is the need to explain why the proletariat has not been revolutionary despite the fact that it is in their "rational" self-interest to be so. (Let me confess that the logic of Marx's position still enchants me; the worker is so obviously getting screwed that his or her lack of perpetual rage *is* baffling.) With the renewed emphasis on "ideology" (spurred by the publication of the hitherto unknown *The German Ideology* in 1933) and the subsequent formulation of theories of ideology and hegemony that stress the proletariat's manufactured consent to the economic and political relationships of capitalist society, we get the confluence of two intellectual currents, one of which (the Romantic discourse of culture) was largely forged as a hostile reaction to the other

5. "These contemporary Marxists do not appeal to the economic in the last instance or in any instance, granting a complete autonomy to the cultural processes by which subjects are constituted and meaning produced. The forefathers of Western Marxism . . . already attack 'vulgar' Marxism's reduction of consciousness, interest, and motivation to economic concerns; they begin to examine cultural processes for explanations of why groups believe certain things and act in certain ways. Such an emphasis brings the issue of 'ideology' to the fore, with the concomitant notion of 'false consciousness' (fostered by 'reification' [Lukacs], or 'the culture industry' [Horkheimer and Adorno], 'repressive desublimation' [Marcuse], or 'hegemony' [Gramsci], or other non-economic means of obscuring class conflict)"(McGowan, 1989, 242–43).

(Enlightenment rationalism). The significant, if rather paradoxical, result is that the Western Marxists—heirs to a writer who considers culture, when at all, in the narrow sense of works by the ancient Greeks and Goethe—have produced one of the richest and most influential discourses about culture in this century, spurred on by the deficiencies of the great Karl himself. This fact becomes especially significant at a time when our received twentieth-century notions of left and right need to be revised. If we attend to Western Marxism's notions of culture—and consider those notions' relation to Romanticism—Tory Radical positions will not seem so incomprehensible, so incoherent, to us. We are in a period during which we have to reassess our political commitments, and a first step might be to consider such commitments without reference to whether they are left or right. I don't know quite how to accomplish such a jettisoning of what are by now second-nature categories, just as I don't quite know how we could jettison the organizing narrative of a transition into modernity, but I suspect the results of getting rid of one, the other, or both of these inheritances would be beneficial. The current sorry state of the Democratic (in the US) and Labour (in the UK) parties is not just (although it is partly) the left's loss of political courage. It is also that the terms "left" and "right" are increasingly irrelevant to our current situation—a fact that is simultaneously a crucial opportunity and a significant danger for academic practitioners of cultural studies.

In any case, the current academic prestige enjoyed by the word "culture" stems, in large part, from the many Marxist meditations on the word in this century. This is not to deny the importance of the anthropological and sociological discourses about culture. But much of the work in those disciplines, just like the work of many social historians, has been motivated by leftist aspirations and influenced by Marxist theorists. Thus, culture, along with its Romantic associations as those things which reason cannot recognize, has been consistently associated with the popular and hence with resistance to rule by experts from the "top down."

This link of culture to the popular is, needless to say, tricky. Here's an abbreviated argument that accounts for the connection of culture in someone like Matthew Arnold with what we now call "high" culture, and with the authoritative power of a state that inculcates that high culture through compulsory education (a subject I worried at length in chapters 2 and 4). Culture in Herder and the Brothers Grimm is part of the pathos-laden attempt by a variety of Romantic artists—Wordsworth and Coleridge's *Literary Ballads* offer an example—to gain a contact with the "folk" they deem has been lost. Culture's power, then, is not just its embodiment of motivations and loyalties deeper than reason, but also its connection to the "people." If only the energies of the "people," the demos, could be tapped and brought to bear on modern society. Once such a power is identified, it is no surprise that competition over its appropriation should commence. Arnold makes it very plain that it is the hearts and minds of the "populace," the people, that is at stake in his plan for hegemony of high culture.[6] Hence, I take it that high culture is produced as a response to the invention of "popular culture" as a category by the Romantics.[7]

In the populist culturalism promulgated by the Romantics, culture is the unofficial, the unorganized, and the residual (those practices which evade, one way or another, the onslaught of modernity).[8] Culture is precisely that which is killed by administration, institutionalization, rationalization. Thus, as has often been noted, there is a poignant paradox to the efforts of Romantic folklorists, as there is to the efforts of anthropologists a little later on. The very writing down of oral traditions, the very studying of folkways, participates in the processes that overwhelm the

6. The most relevant text is, of course, *Culture and Anarchy* (1965a). But see also Arnold's fascinating essay, "Democracy" (1993).

7. Although no one ever remembers it, since they are so busy accusing Horkheimer and Adorno of mandarinism, the claim that "serious art" is a secondary creation which marks the bourgeoisie's retreat from the populace, is made in the "culture industry" essay. Unlike Arnold, Horkheimer and Adorno do not think that "high" culture can serve to elevate the populace; instead, they see the split in art between "serious" and "light" as indicative of the split between the classes in bourgeois society. They write: "'Light' art as such, distraction, is not a decadent form. Anyone who complains that it is a betrayal of pure expression is under an illusion about society. The purity of bourgeois art, which hypostasized itself as a world of freedom in contrast to what was happening in the material world, was from the beginning bought by the exclusion of the lower classes—with whose cause, the real universality, art keeps faith precisely by its freedom from the ends of false universality . . . . Light art has been the shadow of autonomous art. It is the social bad conscience of serious art. The truth which the latter necessarily lacked because of its social premises gives the other the semblance of legitimacy. The division itself is the truth: it does at least express the negativity of the culture which the different spheres constitute. Least of all can the antithesis be reconciled by absorbing light into serious art, or vice versa" (1972, 135). This analysis should throw a damper on more naïve, unproblematized celebrations of a collapse of the distinction between popular and high art as actually accomplished or as obviously politically valuable.

8. For the term "residual," see Williams (1977, 121–27). Williams talks of cultural forms as "dominant," "emergent," or "residual" and exploits this time lag (or lack of exact alignment) between cultural forms/practices and the forms/practices of other social realms (particularly the economic) to locate potential sites of popular resistance to capitalism—a work carried on by various practitioners of cultural studies, perhaps most notably John Fiske (1989).

culture being recorded. Folklore and anthropology are species of elegy that contribute to the killing of the object they eulogize.

Yet the new ideology of culture also installs culture as the foundation of identity and of motivation. Emotional investment in what one does and is stems from the ground of culture. Thus, preservation of a vital culture is seen as crucially in the state's interest. So much is at stake that the state can hardly forego efforts to control, direct, and foster cultural activities, even as all such efforts are also seen as the surest means for killing culture off. It's like telling someone to be happy. States create a number of mausoleums (museums, universities, staged festivals and holidays) in which the corpses of culture are displayed—under conditions in which a simulated life is enacted. Radical intellectuals (along with other intellectuals) have often played the court jesters, the desperate MCs, at such displays. No wonder they have dreamed of biting the hand that feeds them and of escaping these haunts of the living dead to find the "real" and "authentic" culture of the folk in those corners hidden out of modernity's sight. Yet the ever-present bad faith of this gesture has never been shaken off. Radical intellectuals are always pilgrims from modernity and, thus, the harbinger of its appropriation of the authentic culture they discover. (This fate is only hastened by the occupational inability of intellectuals to keep their mouths shut; their discoveries are always a prelude to publication.) Even more telling, radical intellectuals rarely return to their own roots. Instead, resistance to the powers that be is always presented as occurring at an other cultural site; they see the cultural heritage from which they come as already completely co-opted. They try to take up a place in another's culture, even while knowing that just such occupation by outsiders who desire to go native is the harbinger of the very co-optation they are fleeing.

All this said, I can now articulate my skepticism about the usefulness of culture as a tool in political contestations. Culture seems to me linked to despair for three reasons. First, culture is used to designate tangled, intractable complexes of messy irrational stuff unamenable to direct human action. While it is crucial in any democratic polity to stress that there is not any unmediated or automatic connection between individual actions and their results, such an insistence is not the same thing as saying that the gremlins of factors that lie beyond our control (either our own unconsciouses, the complexity—even the perversity—of the universe, or the intricacies of culture) make efforts at direct, purposive action at best futile and at worst harmful. Culture all too often serves as a way to throw up our hands and say that no potentially successful means of human intervention can be identified. Admittedly, this is the extreme, the conservative, view.

But, to turn to my second point, this view has a more radical variant. Here is the first of my complaints about the indirection of a cultural politics. Under the cover of theories of ideology and/or of representation, cultural politics often despairs of the capabilities of reasoned political argument. The other side, this line goes, have done a much better job of winning the people's consent through a series of manipulative cultural representations that play on their fears and desires. Direct contestation of this sneaky other side will be unavailing; what we need to do is beat them at their own game, create our own representations that will connect up to emotionally charged material. The problem with this view is not just its glaring condescension, but also its equally glaring inconsistency. It posits that people are generally swayed by emotional, non-discursive, and highly complex cultural images, yet would deny that one's own position was formulated out of the same materials. The would-be cultural politician will offer you good reasons for why he or she takes a certain position but at the same time has no faith that those reasons would prove persuasive to others. The hidden logic here, of course, is that anyone who believes something different from me couldn't possibly have good reasons to do so; they must have been tricked into it.[9] And the kicker is an unexpected addendum: that such trickery cannot be undone by proffered reasons, but only by a counter-magic, by trickery in the opposite direction.

I admit that I have entered here into the highly contested and highly complex issue of belief formation. I am not trying to say that belief formation is utterly rational—no matter how rational might be defined. But I am saying that most people, when challenged, can offer reasons for their beliefs—and that, crucially, a democratic politics is dependent on the public rendering of such beliefs in confrontations between people of differing beliefs. To utterly despair of the rational character of beliefs (in this minimal sense of articulable reasons) and to discount from the start the reasons

9. Smith (1997) describes " 'epistemic self-privileging' or 'epistemic asymmetry': that is, our inclination to believe that we believe the true and sensible things we do because they are true and sensible, while other people believe the foolish and outrageous things they do because there is something the matter with those people" (xvi). Smith challenges herself and us to replace this asymmetry with a symmetry that begins from the assumptions that others have reasons for their beliefs as I do for mine. Theories of ideology and hegemony trouble me because they seem especially prone to asymmetry and because it seems to me that an assumption of symmetry is crucial to successful democratic interchange.

offered by those with whom one disagrees (as rationalizations or delusions) is to undermine democratic processes before they can even begin.[10] My argument is that the term "culture"—and the strategies of the cultural politics that follow from an emphasis on culture—often indicate a despair about reasoned forms of belief formation and of direct interchanges about commitments by those who disagree. I am suggesting that this despair comes from the Western Marxist attempt to explain why the proletariat, if they are rational, did not believe what Marxism says they should believe.

Finally, my third reason for thinking "culture" problematically useful for a democratic politics is that cultural politics, it seems to me, inevitably takes its stand on very shaky representational ground. There are various ways to say this, but perhaps the most convenient way will be to stress culture's essentialism. Culture has become the favored term by which to designate all the factors that combine to make some person who he or she is or some group what it is. As Kenneth Burke constantly reminds us, representation in both its linguistic and its political usage relies on synecdoche, the taking of the part as standing in for the whole. But the legitimacy of such truncated presentation, the question of what gets left out by presenting this part, will always trouble synecdochic representation. Hence indirection appears built into the very concept of culture, since the all-encompassing wholeness of what the term is to designate means that culture can never be directly presented in itself, in all its fullness. We are always only put in touch with the effects of culture, not with the thing itself. And this generates endless disputes about who or what can "speak for" culture.

Now, I have already indicated that I am no enemy to endless disputes. But disputes about accurate representation appear to me to point in the

10. Let me try to make my position clear at this crucial point in my argument. I do not think that we can establish some hard and fast distinction between rational and irrational arguments and persuasion. Thus I do not think that we can invoke such a distinction to police what speech is allowed in public and what is not. But the lack of firm distinctions, of a continuum, does not mean a dearth of possible rhetorical strategies. Theories of hegemony and ideology often greatly reduce the number of possible rhetorical strategies deemed possibly effective. Yet these very theories are usually presented in a language the very theory claims to be ineffective. Intellectuals, I am suggesting, should have the courage of their own way of forming convictions—which means thinking of their own forms of contestation, argumentation, and persuasion as continuous (and often overlapping) with forms they would use in non-academic public arenas. Among the things contested in a democratic public sphere are the rhetorical modes that will be deemed appropriate and found convincing. It is conceding far too much if we delimit from the outset certain modes, just as it is assuming way too much if we think any given mode can be deemed legitimate and effective by definition or fiat (as sometimes seems to be the case in Habermas's work).

wrong direction—backward toward origins instead of forward toward the world our actions are trying to create. A view of culture that gets obsessed with questions of accurate representation is not sufficiently open to transformation. Yet the risk and potential of democratic interaction is that the participants will be transformed. (It is in order to pursue the dynamics of transformation that I will turn to Kenneth Burke in the second half of this chapter.) The focus on the indirection of synecdochic representation, with its constant reference back to the absent whole that cannot be brought on stage, seems to me a way of insisting that identity is something to be honored even as it is withheld, as opposed to bringing identity fully into play, where it might be worked upon, even transformed, not just recognized. What I am suggesting is that culture, even as figured and appealed to by the most "radical" of the new social movements, is a safe refuge, a thing held apart from the processes of democratic contestation—and that the indirect representation of culture and identity are the means for maintaining its separation. I hardly intend a simple condemnation of the new social movements here.[11] As has often been noted, they are better at preserving rights that are threatened than at expanding the capabilities afforded citizens in contemporary societies. But we should hardly belittle the need for—and any success in—combating encroaching state power. Appeals to identity and to cultural preservation have proved efficacious in various ways—and it is more an indictment of our diminished democracies than of the new social movements to say that contemporary politics has found it hard to move beyond such defenses of what is already possessed. But what I dislike about the indirection of cultural politics is that it does not envision identity itself as something to be worked upon in the processes of politics, as something that will be forged and transformed in the very activity of politics. The self—and culture, such at it is—is created in and through politics, not exclusively (there are other types of human interaction that are not political), but crucially.[12] Only if the self and culture are directly brought into the political can such creative work be done.

11. I am guilty here (as elsewhere) of oversimplification. The women's health clinics or community shelters created by feminists, like the various health education efforts of gay organizations, are examples of creative, pro-active public action undertaken by the "new social movements." See Bickford (1996, 175–87) for a good overview of the various types of citizen action now occurring in the United States.

12. There are, I am afraid, a number of Arendtian assumptions in this sentence that I cannot fully unpack here. My basic intuition is that "culture" as a marker of differences and of values and identities to which individuals are loyal needs to be understood as a *public*

So much for my political skepticism. Now, more briefly, my epistemological doubts. At issue here is the explanatory power of the term "culture"—and, then, of the very existence of the thing the term names. To be
schematic about it, culture seems to me a prime example of the kind of
"effect" that is then designated as a "cause" in Nietzsche's analysis of the
persistent reversal of cause-and-effect relationships.[13] Culture is used to
name a causal power that is not reason (either in its diminished form as
economic rationality or in any more expansive form, say Kant's triumvi-
rate of pure reason, practical reason, and judgment). Culture serves as the
site of difference since reason, if we grant its universal presence in all humans (not something always granted), dictates the same answer to each
problem. Culture offers an explanation for, marks, the distinctive preferences and choices which appear neither universal nor eccentrically individual. Culture designates an aggregate of humans who share values,
tastes, habits, patterns of work, kinship and family organization, and various other features of a "thick" life-world, features that post-Enlightenment
thought no longer views as having any claim to being universally binding.
I want to emphasize this last point: that culture as a concept only becomes
thinkable in the aftermath of the Enlightenment de-universalization of large
parts of human life. Contemporary (i.e., postmodern) reappraisals of the
Enlightenment have focused so persistently on critiquing and disman-
tling what is left of Enlightenment universalism that we have forgotten
that this whole genre of critique was begun by the Enlightenment itself.
The ur-case is religion. The Enlightenment strove to make Europeans indifferent to religious differences, to see the choice of religious belief as
particular to specific social groups or to particular individuals and as requiring no response from the state which imposes uniformity in other
matters (say, in forbidding murder or requiring the payment of taxes)

---

marker. That is, culture is connected to forms of identity production that take place in public and are valued both for the ways that they render a public sphere vital and the ways that
each citizen can be "recognized" within that public sphere. What happens between family
members or between friends need not (although at times it can) be public this way. The political, then, refers to the processes that produce a public sphere and the activities that are
enabled by the existence of that public space. I want to think of "culture" as politically, and
as publicly, created, which motivates (in part) my move toward the performative in the second half of this chapter.

13. See Nietzsche (1968, sec. 479) which reads (in part): "The fragment of outer world of
which we are conscious is born after an effect from outside has impressed itself upon us,
and is subsequently projected as its 'cause'—In the phenomenalism of the 'inner world' we
invert the chronological order of cause and effect. The fundamental fact of 'inner experience' is that the cause is imagined after the effect has taken place."

where universality is appropriate. Religious preference, of course, becomes just one of the many choices given over the "private" sphere, while an attempt is made to foster a corresponding ethos of tolerance. We are used to linking the private with individualism, but for writers like Burke and Coleridge "culture" carries many of the features of the private, most crucially as designating an area in which state interference is both wrong (since it violates certain inalienable freedoms) and disastrous (since it always makes people's lives worse).

Of course, culturalism is not the same as individualism even if it occupies some of the same territory vis-à-vis the state and vis-à-vis universalist reason. Culturalism drastically mitigates the claims to autonomy inherent in individualism, claims which are certainly implausible as soon as one begins to think about how individuals make choices or reach self-understanding or acquire an individual identity. What gives culture its surface plausibility is that few things are universally uniform among humans, yet the absolutely unique is also rare. Differences tend to congregate, to be found in clumps. So the observed reality is less than universal gatherings of similar behavior and beliefs, and culture is the posited power that causes the clumping. In other words, following Nietzsche, the cause (the observation that some people act similarly) comes first. That observation causes the effect, which is our invention of the term culture to explain that observation. We then take our invented (ex post facto) explanation and retrospectively claim that it existed prior to our observation; it (culture), we now say, actually caused the observed behavior. Cause and effect are inverted.

Anthropology, sociology, political science, psychology, and linguistics are the most prominent of the social or human sciences which have arisen in the attempt to specify more concretely just how culture works its magic. How are individuals initiated into a culture (socialization or acculturation or interpellation)? How do cultures enforce conformity? How is deviance produced, regulated, possible at all? How do cultures respond to encounters with other cultures (what kinds of boundary maintenance are required; what kinds of borrowings occur)? How do cultures manage to persist over time (social reproduction)? How do cultures change without collapsing entirely? How is a culture differentiated within itself? What is the relation of culture to non-cultural elements in a human community; or are all elements cultural? These are some of the recurring questions the social sciences address.

Some of the answers to these questions are more persuasive than others, but it seems to me that one rather overwhelming difficulty faces every attempt to use "culture" to explain groupings of similar behavior and beliefs. It may make sense to speak of the culture of a small, isolated group if two rather stringent conditions apply: uniformity of beliefs and behaviors among its members, and the almost complete absence of the kinds of specialization and differentiation that follows from the division of labor, the division of classes or sexes, or any other kinds of separations that would give some individuals markedly different experiences, knowledges, purposes, or beliefs than other individuals. In other words, in highly differentiated societies, the use of the term culture to designate the society as a whole seems untenable. There is just too much variation in attitudes and behavior for cultural generalizations about Americans or the French to work very well. Culture appears to rest on an essentialism that cannot stand up to scrutiny very long. And if we try to soften that essentialism by way of something like Wittgensteinian family resemblances, the problems still seem close to insuperable. Furthermore, I am inclined to believe someone like Eric Wolf (1982), who suggests that the "tribes" anthropologists study are not much, if any, more culturally uniform than any modern society. The attribution of such uniformity to "primitive" societies says more about our own longings for harmonious uniformity— the myth of the Golden Age—than it does about the groups studied. Margaret Mead's vision of New Guinea is akin to Ruskin's vision of the Gothic age of faith and Arnold's vision of Greek sweetness and light. It just warn't so.

Faced with the difficulty of mapping culture onto society (where society is understood as the geographically bounded aggregation of a people under one government, though this usage hardly exhausts the term, since we say European society as well as English society), the fall-back position for those who wish to retain a large-scale notion of culture is to map culture onto a shared language and/or shared ethnicity. The difficulties of both strategies are notorious. Are English, Australian, Scottish and Irish cultures all the same because their members all speak English? And how strong a claim do we want to make about the extent to which language determines thought, perception, and belief? Recent reports indicate that the old stand-by of the Sapir-Whorf hypothesis, the Inuit's twenty-five words for snow, is a myth, as is the report of those South American Indians (or is it Australian aborigines?) who don't see the figures on the screen when shown a Western movie. Appeals to ethnic determinants are even more dubious, largely because nothing any one can do manages to keep ethnic divisions intact. How much Celtic blood must one have to be a

Celt? And what test could ever ascertain whether one had the requisite percentage or not? To prove the identity by way of the behavior one displayed would be the ultimate in circular reasoning.

From those who decide to abandon the possibility of locating culture at the level of society, we get a proliferation of cultures or sub-cultures. The culture of drag racing, the culture of drag queens, the sub-culture of teenage gangs, the sub-culture of the Kiwanis clubs. (It would be interesting to see if a detailed look at the actual usage of the term "sub-culture" instead of "culture" revealed a consistent pattern; my sense is that the terms are used willy-nilly, one for the other once the scale is small enough. Thus, drag racers can form a culture or a sub-culture, but we wouldn't say English sub-culture. But there may be discernible connotative differences in the way the two terms are used.) This proliferation appears to follow one law: where ever any two are joined together in a practice, there a culture shall be. The result is that culture appears at every level of analysis, from the trans-historical and trans-social (Judeo-Christian culture) to the socially specific (American culture) to the socially and historically specific (nineteenth-century American culture) to the local (youth culture, grunge culture, Southern culture, country club culture). Am I the only one who begins at this point to suspect that culture has little explanatory power, that it is a ghost in the machine, pulled out of the hat after a pattern of shared behaviors is observed in order—supposedly—to explain how that pattern was formed?

Of course not. Christopher Herbert's superb *Culture and Anomie* (1991) expresses the skeptical point of view succinctly: "[T]he entity that Tylor names 'culture' takes on a distinctly hypothetical or conjectural character and reveals itself to be a thing the existence of which in space and time can never be demonstrated, only posited ahead of time as a device for organizing one's data. It is, this line of reflection suggests, a fiction that exists to gratify a passion or an institutional demand for certain kinds of interpretive work" (10–11). Clifford Geertz (1973) admits that this problem has dogged anthropology even as he offers his own notion of "ordered clusters of significant symbols" as the solution: "If the scientific study of culture has lagged, bogged down often in mere descriptivism, it has been in large part because its very subject matter is elusive. The initial problem of any science—defining its object of study in such a manner as to render it susceptible to analysis—has here turned out to be unusually hard to solve" (362–62). Might we be better off without the concept of culture? At the very least, we need to be wary of its uses, attuned to the work it is given to do, and the claims it is consigned to bear whenever it appears. I am going to shift gears now and begin to rehabilitate "culture," but I do so extremely tentatively. Skepticism of the term still has seventy percent of my allegiance.

II. TARRYING WITH THE PERFORMATIVE

Even while culture itself is invisible, its palpable effects appear more real than ever. Who would deny in the 1990s that culture is tremendously powerful? Loyalty to and identification with a culture, of which nationalism is one variant, ethnic pride and prejudice another, appears to be the dominant passion of our time, the supreme motive of the most vigorous actors on the public stage. Here's where the abbreviated history of the term "culture" that I have offered might help. Culture, from the start, was a performative term, one that called into existence a force to be posed against Enlightenment rationality, a motive to be posed against economic self-interest, a loyalty to certain received ways of life to be posed against both rationalist reformers (like the Jacobins or Bentham) and capitalist innovation. It has often been noted—and just as often held against it—that loyalty to culture is almost always reactionary in every sense of that term. Such loyalty tends to be negative, to exist as a defensive resistance to change, without any positive plan of action itself beyond a desire to return to the status quo ante—which is vastly complicated as a political platform, insofar as that remembered past often never existed. If the dream of revolution, with its corollary attempt to imagine radically transformative action, was the left's mainstay for two hundred years (from 1789 to 1989), the performative projection of a grounded past has been the right's mainstay. And it is an indication of the crisis of the left today that it has lost the dream of revolution and now relies on its own versions of culturalism—either the politics of identity or an oxymoronic "multiculturalism"—to counter a right that is stronger than ever. With dreams of revolution lost, local resistance to capitalism (which respects neither persons nor noneconomic social groupings) often seems the best hope available, and there is no denying that defenders of a culture have proved just about the most resolute and most successful resisters. What cannot fail to impress any observer—left or right—is the sheer persistence of certain symbols and issues. Think of the school prayer issue or the fight against Darwinian evolution. Machiavelli (1975, 97) said men will eventually forget—or at least stop fighting against—anything so long as you don't confiscate their property or their women, but the late twentieth century proves him wrong. What people seem to never forget is what they see as outside attempts to shape their way of life.

If "culture" refers to nothing at all, then why such passion? An answer may rest in focusing on the performative words that speak culture. I use performative here in the very broad sense of a verbal utterance that creates the thing it enunciates instead of referring to the thing it enunciates. (The term, of course, comes from Austin [1975 and 1979].) The contrast is between the utterance: "The book is on my desk" and the utterance "I promise to bring the book to you." The first sentence describes a state of affairs in the world that pre-exists the statement. Before I said a word, the book was on the desk. The second sentence creates a state of affairs. The promise did not exist until I said "I promise." A performative, then, is a use of speech that alters the world, that changes or adds to reality.

How does the performative effect this change? It is true that human beings change the world by physical work upon it. The action of cutting down a forest alters reality. Speech acts, however, do not perform physical changes, although they may be vital initiatory moments in a sequence that does lead to physical changes. My promise can certainly lead to my taking the book off my desk and bringing it to you. But human speech acts do not work like the creative fiat, "Let there be light." The physical world usually does not jump to do our bidding—with the crucial possible exception of other human beings (and certain animals). I say "Close the window" and my son walks over and closes the window (one out of ten times anyway). Pretty neat. How come that works? Primarily because the pre-existing relationship of father to son (which involves authority, affection, ambivalence . . .) gives my command/request a "perlocutionary force."[14] Austin recognizes that his introduction of the category of performatives also requires "a new doctrine about all the possible forces of utterances" (1979, 251), and is explicit about the ways that performatives are often dependent on authority-establishing institutions for their force. Only the judge can say "I sentence you to life imprisonment," and it be a sentence, while the perlocutionary force of that utterance will rest on various contingent facts about that court, its jurisdiction, the government, the sentenced, etc.

14. Austin (1975, 101) introduces the notion of the "perlocutionary" to designate the "consequential effects upon the feelings, thoughts, or actions of the audience, or of the speaker, or of other persons" of an utterance.

Other performatives, like promises or insults, while relying on conventions, do not necessarily rely on formal institutional conditions nor on pre-existing relations (authoritative or otherwise) between speaker and auditor. There is the possibility that performatives *establish* a new relationship between the parties. My insulting you does not presuppose any determinative prior relationship between us, and may in fact be radically discontinuous with any prior relationship we might have had. And my insult may lead to all kinds of future actions that alter my life and yours. Expanding somewhat on Austin's definition of the performative, we reach Burke's notion of "symbolic action" as the "dancing of an attitude," the enunciation of an orientation toward the person or thing spoken of or to. With Burke, I want to think of how speech acts establish, reinforce, or transform the *relations* between human beings or between human beings and things. To alter those relations is often to alter the world, sometimes immediately, sometimes less immediately.

How might we characterize uses of the word "culture" as performative? I want to offer two models here (hardly meant to be exhaustive of the possibilities). The first pertains to the discourses by which we order our world. Culture is a projected, imagined, or fictional category, which gathers together and organizes empirical entities. Since our categories, however, serve as heuristics that guide perception, adherence to the semantic term "culture" actually guarantees the perception of what the researcher sets out to find. The semantic category thus creates, rather than reflects or refers to, the entity it names. Such a process is hardly unconsequential, but a meta-theoretical description of a process (like this one) has no impact on the process's consequences. Fictional categorizations have real effects precisely because they alter the relations between people and the world, as well as between people and other people. It makes a difference whether I understand the difference between me and you as cultural, genetic, temperamental, or racial.

It seems to me that this first model is basically what Stuart Hall assumes when he uses "hegemony" and "articulation" as key terms for cultural studies. For Hall, there is a social struggle over the terms that will serve as the primary organizing categories of reality.[15] Such terms articulate the

15. "This approach replaces the notion of fixed ideological meanings and class-inscribed ideologies with the concepts of ideological terrains of struggle and the task of ideological transformation. It is the general movement in this direction, away from an abstract general theory of ideology, and towards the more concrete analysis of how, in particular historical situations, ideas 'organize human masses, and create the terrain on which men move, acquire consciousness of their position, struggle, etc.,' which makes . . . Gramsci (from whom that quotation is taken) a figure of seminal importance" (Hall, 1996, 41).

world and hence serve to delineate what it is possible to do. The most fundamental site of political action, then, becomes this discursive site of contestation, where social actors struggle both to replace their categories with ours (or mine) and to "resignify" existing categories in ways more amenable to our (my) purposes.

I have three worries about Hall's project. First, as my parentheses in the previous paragraph indicate, I think that the hypothesis of constant struggle puts a huge pressure on collective agency. Hall, quite consistently, believes that collectivities must be created through the discursive categorization that is social struggle. But, it seems to me, that more attention to both the historical aggregates in a particular society and the institutional matrix which (at least to some extent) frames how and where struggle occurs is needed to temper the tendency to declare that discourse bears all before it. I like the way that Hall's work puts everything into motion, and I suspect that what I am trying to do in this essay is close in spirit to his project. But I think that he tends to short-change the institutional structuring of contestation and the varied investments which agents bring to interactions. Secondly, as the first section of this essay indicates, I am not sure that battling hard over the significations of the word "culture" is the most productive course to follow right now. Finally, what meaning can the word "productive" in the previous sentence have? Discourse-centered theories flirt with seeing us as determined by the categories we utilize. If purposes, if judgments of what is productive or useful to do, follow from the discourse within which we operate, then what any agent brings to the struggle is unclear and how the struggle might actually transform the parties to it—and the social order they inhabit—is also unclear. Obviously, terms like "resignification," "hybridity," and "subculture" are utilized to do the work of designating discursive regimes that are not hermetic monads. The theoretical and ethical dilemma, it seems to me, is to avoid swinging wildly between the poles of a monolithic "dominant discourse" and an anarchistic proclamation of total difference, utter and incommensurate singularities. The problem here is describing relative stabilities in a world of change and thinking about what kinds of stabilities are enabling. And this work would have to be connected to considering how purposes are formed and judgments made, both ethical (is this right? and should this be done?) and practical (can this be done? and should it be done now in lieu of other possible actions?).

The second model of the performative I want to suggest is more social, less discursive, and seems to me more promising. Here the focus would be on action taken in public. In terms of culture, such action produces the very identities to which it seemingly refers. It may be the case that no collective identity can be created without appealing to something that ostensibly holds the group together. But the call for the group to gather as a group in public can always fail. It is, in other words, the group's staging of itself that makes it a group. No matter what the appeal to a past, the group no longer exists on the day when it can no longer manage to appear. So, in a very practical way, the group's existence is predicated on its ability to function as a group in the future, on the next occasion that it is called to form. Identities of any sort (of which cultural identities are one variant) are rhetorical constructs; that is, identities exist only in the in-between space traversed by speakers and audiences. In ritual, we might say, speaker and audience are merged in one. Rituals tend to be affirmations to the participants that they still exist, hence the almost inevitable linking of ritual with doubt and insecurity, with a response to endangerment. But the larger point is that identities require to be performed in a space that has both an actor and a witness.

Although the actor and the witness can be the same person, the performance still needs to be visible (think of a diary or rituals of meals for a person who lives alone). The performance occupies a space that is public (because visible), interactional, and intersubjective. To fully pursue its public dimension would require a discussion of Hannah Arendt on politics and the public/private distinction as well as a discussion of Ludwig Wittgenstein's private language argument. To fully explore its interactional component leads to an encounter with William James, John Dewey, and George Herbert Mead. The rest of this essay offers the beginnings of such an encounter, but through the work of Kenneth Burke. I just assume Burke's pragmatism here; certainly, I read and use him in ways fully consonant with pragmatism's interactional account of the relation of individual agents to others and to the world. My focus is on how an interactionist emphasis shifts our understanding of the performative. Ultimately, I argue that this model of the performative gives us another way to think about "culture," one that designates a more modest range for the term's applicability than the one history has given us, but a usage I think helpful for various purposes.

My Burkean model of the performative is contrasted (alas, only implicitly because of space limitations) to the Derridean performative (and its development in Judith Butler's work)[16] and the dramatistic performa-

16. The key texts are Derrida (1988) and Butler (1990).

tive that can be culled from a certain way of reading Burke's own work. Stand warned, then, that mine is a very pointed use of Burke, pursued because Burke offers me a convenient way to present certain pragmatist themes I want to take up against prevailing Derridean models of the performative. What Burke offers an intersubjectivity richer than the face-off between subject and Law in Butler, in whose solipsistic-tending work actual others—except the abjected—rarely appear; temporality that is not just the repetition with a difference of Derrida; and a transformative agonistics which points toward a public space less bounded and orderly than the space of interaction imagined in more dramatistic models of the performative. Only half-jokingly, I would suggest that Burke's own work is such a mess because he finds disorderly chaos not only congenial but generative.

III. AT LONG LAST, BURKE

I need to start by telling you something about Burke's understanding of "symbolic action"—which I take as his version of the performative. Burkean speech acts "are answers to questions posed by the situation in which they arose. They are not merely answers, they are *strategic* answers, *stylized* answers. . . . So I should propose an initial working distinction between 'strategies' and 'situations,' whereby we think of poetry (I here use the term to include any work of critical or imaginative cast) as the adopting of various strategies for the encompassing of situations. These strategies size up situations, name their structure and outstanding ingredients, and name them in a way that contains an attitude toward them" (1973, 1).[17] These acts of naming can be seen as narrative because they are oriented toward action, toward the future state of affairs that will be produced by the relationship established to the situation by the speaker's words. We cannot stand still in Burke's version of pragmatism (nor in Dewey's). The flow of time continually presents new situations to which we must react, within which and toward which we must "orient" ourselves. And such orientation always aims at amelioration at worst, improvement at best. Our specific purposes arise out of situations and the opportunities they afford us, but our general purpose is the best accom-

17. Note here Burke's peculiar use of the word "poetry." I will use "poetry" and the "poetic" in Burke's sense throughout the rest of this essay, although it is the "temporality" or "narrative" dimension of the poetic (in his sense) that I want to stress.

modation possible with the ever-changing circumstances in which we find ourselves. Action aims to alter the world in the direction of improvement. This hardly means progress is inevitable. Action can lead to unintended disasters. But it does mean that Burke thinks we must intend progress, must act to make things better. Even the traditionalist, the one who wants to preserve the way things are, must actively work at such preservation, because time is continually moving us into new situations. The traditionalist is always having to re-create a "lost" present and is thus oriented (as much as the progressive) toward making things better than they currently are.

Two further Burkean distinctions must be introduced before we can return to the issue at hand: "culture" as a performative. Both distinctions point toward Burke's complicated and ambivalent stance toward realism.[18] To be absolutely clear: by realism here I mean "naive realism," the unproblematized acceptance that the things we encounter in experience— through our senses—are real. Burke mixes this use of the term "realism" with another usage, which refers to the holistic vision that manages most successfully to "encompass" all that a situation entails. I hope my discussion will show how this mixed usage is plausible even though I neither justify it nor explore some of the problems it causes. First, Burke differentiates "*practical* acts" from "symbolic acts," adding that this "distinction, clear enough in its extremes, [is not] to be dropped simply because there is a borderline area wherein many practical acts take on a symbolic ingredient" (1973, 9). The "symbolic act," Burke tells us, "is the dancing of an attitude," but taking an attitude toward something is distinct from (albeit often related to) acting physically upon something. There is an "empirical nature . . . grounded in the realm of non-symbolic, or extra-symbolic motion" (1973, xvi), and while symbolic acts may set a chain of events into motion, they also may not. Poetry sometimes makes something happen. It is less clear if Burke believes that practical action can occur without a prior (symbolic) act of naming. Can we act without some orientation, some "sizing up" of the situation?

Burke's second distinction follows his understanding of three terms: magic, poetry, and science. Burke's use of these three terms—and his account of their relation to one another as different species of speech acts— is hardly consistent. He is most steady in his depictions of science as pursuing the misguided hope of a "pure" naming that designates the

18. My understanding of Burke's realism accords, I am happy to report, with Wess's (1996) account of Burke's "rhetorical realism" in his excellent book.

thing-in-itself in a neutral language purged of all human purposes and desires and of all contingent, contextual factors. Since linguistic utterance places the speaker in relation to the thing named, all utterances are situational and purposive for Burke. We only speak of things for a reason, so neutral or disinterested speech simply does not occur. And Burke offers his own version of the standard arguments that logical positivism's own desires for a neutral language violate—and cannot be validated by—its own standards of "objectivity." (See 1973, 138–67.)

Poised against "science" are "magic" and "poetry." "The choice here," according to Burke, "is not a choice between magic and no magic, but a choice between magics that vary in their degree of approximation to the truth" (1973, 6). The issue, we might say, is just how powerful words can be—and Burke doesn't quite know where to come down on this one. At times, Burke says that words are almost all. He is fascinated with Freud's "talking cure" as a kind of magic. The "accuracy" or "truth" of the patient's retelling of the past is irrelevant to the cure's efficacy. Misnaming of that past, Burke implies, may even be more effective—although, strictly speaking, once in the realm of memories, it is hard to see how we could distinguish a true naming from a misnaming, especially since Freud deliberately rules out going outside of the analytic situation to consult other witnesses to that past. In any case, the renaming of a situation can be powerful indeed, irrespective of the accuracy of the naming. For example: Paul tells Jenny that he is upset because Tom was brusque with him. Jenny replies that Tom has been troubled by family problems lately. This renaming of the cause for Tom's brusqueness assuages Paul's fears that he has offended Tom. The magic works even if Jenny has utterly misread Tom's action. Burke offers similar examples of transformation through renaming throughout his work.

But Burke has two reasons for not succumbing entirely to the wholesale belief that "nothing 'tis but talking makes it so." He holds to the common-sense view that word magic reaches its limits (in some cases at least) by running up against the facts. He writes in the 1966 preface to *The Philosophy of Literary Form* that "I have found it necessary to emphasize this point because, over the years, my constant concern with 'symbolicity' has often been *interpreted* in the spirit *exactly* contrary to my notions of 'reality'" (1973, xvi). He does not believe "that our world is 'nothing but' the things we say about it. On the contrary, alas. There's many a time when what we call a 'food' should have been called a 'poison.' And if our ancestors had but hit upon too many of such misnomers, we'd not be here now" (xvi). The utterly "subjective"—or, to be trans-individual, the utterly "human"—has a wider range of play, of possibility, than the utterly "objective" in Burke, but the human, too, meets its limits, is not alone in the world. Situations and the strategies devised in response to them are interactional, are the place where subject and object are co-related, and both are shaped through their determination by and of the other.

More interesting for my purposes in this essay is Burke's second reason for resisting magic in the name of poetry. We can capture the spirit of Burke's aims if we say he critiques magic as too partial. Its partiality stems from its production out of fears, desires, wishes, and the like; but its partiality also reflects its taking only the speaker into account and acting as if the speaker's vision could be imposed upon the world and others. Again, Burke is fully aware that such impositions are, in certain cases, possible. He hardly undersells the word's power. In fact, he wants to secure that power for poetry. But he also wants to explore—and insist upon—the word's limits. And one way to describe those limits is to say that any particular word, any particular utterance, any particular sizing up of a situation, is partial. To take such parts for the whole is to fall prey to what Burke calls "the synecdochic fallacy" (1973, 148). Poetry, in Burke's lexicon, stands in for that (ideal) form of speech that is "complete," that "encompasses " a situation entirely, that "would attempt to *attain a full moral act* by attaining a perspective *atop all the conflicts of attitude*" (1973, 148). The poetic ideal is a "progressive encompassment that does not admit of mutual exclusion" (1973, 145).

To say that Burke consistently rejects the partial in favor of the complete is to acknowledge—as he himself openly does—his fundamental Hegelianism. Current uses of the word "culture," we might say, embody our postmodern ambivalent Hegelianism. Insofar as it names a totality (however small), culture is a Hegelian term. Insofar as culture is used to designate separated entities deemed incommensurate, it is fiercely anti-Hegelian. The wind is mostly blowing in anti-Hegelian directions these days.[19] Nevertheless, I want to explore in the rest of this essay the resources Burke's pragmatic Hegelianism (or Hegelian pragmatism) has to offer for the recuperation (a good Hegelian term) of the term culture from my skeptical account of it—and for offering a useful complication of our current notions (derived from Derrida and Butler or Hall) of the performative. We can begin with Burke's characterization of his "realistic" po-

19. See McGowan (1991, 43–61) for a discussion of recent thought's fascination with and fear of Hegel.

sition against what he calls the "naturalistic" position, which adopts the kind of nominalistic skepticism found in my discussion of culture. Not surprisingly, he finds nominalism too partial, too individualistic. We can, he writes, "sum up the distinction between realism and nominalism . . . by saying that *realism considered individuals as members of a group* and that *nominalism considered groups as aggregates of individuals.* . . . [T]he natural-ist-nominalist perspective finally leads to the assumption that the devices employed in a *group* act are mere 'illusions,' and that the 'scientific truth' about human relations is discovered from an individualistic point of view, from outside the requirements of group action" (1973, 126). Culture re-enters here as the name for the pressure that the presence of others places on any agent's sizing up of a situation. The circumstances in which agents find themselves include and involve others. Any "scientific" accounting of the factors that come into play in the interaction of agent and situation must include the agent's relation to others if it is to be complete.

Culture need not be taken as some occult, mysterious repository of val-ues and inclinations. Rather, it can refer to the ways in which agents mon-itor, are sensitive and responsive to, and are influenced by the expected (ahead of time) and actual (after the act) reactions of others. I am on terri-tory related to Derrida's and Butler's thinking on "repetition" and "cita-tionality" here, but with a much greater emphasis on the context-specific and conscious bringing-to-bear upon that context of "cultural" knowl-edge and capacities. In sizing up situations, in forming attitudes toward them, and in making decisions about appropriate courses of action, agents rely on a fund of knowledge that includes their past experience in situ-ations judged as similar, but also knowledge about actions performed by others in similar situations, and general guidelines and ethical principles learned from others (in either formal or informal ways). Because one of the things agents usually desire in any situation is to achieve and main-tain a satisfactory relation to others, "the requirements of group action," of action in a setting that is social, are among the factors a realistic as-sessment (i.e., one that aims to be encompassing, not partial) takes into account.

Culture, in this view, is not some deep structure, but a readily apparent consequence of the fact that agents live amidst others and care about the quality of their relations to those others, and that work upon those rela-tions constitutes a large proportion of human actions. (Or, alternatively, that there are very few actions that do not have some consequence on our relation to others, even when those actions also have other consequences.)

The extent to which culture exists "inside" selves, its migration from something that exists between selves in their relation to one another to something that exists as knowledge and values that the self brings to bear (seemingly without external prompting) when sizing up situations, only indicates the self's temporal nature, its accretion of experiences and its calling on those experiences to guide it in new situations. Since pragmatism posits that agents seek comfortable and ameliorative solutions to the questions posed by situations, it is no surprise that the pressure of others' presence in the world tends to work in centripetal, not centrifugal, fashion. Behavior clumps together because clumping furthers the ability of numerous selves living in close proximity to one another to get along reasonably well.

This description probably makes culture as a factor within the scene of action look too "presentist." An overly dramatistic reading of Burke might tend toward relying too heavily on what is present in the moment of interaction. My emphasis on narrative is designed precisely to acknowledge that everything relevant to an interaction is not physically on stage. Not only does the agent carry into the scene the "baggage" from his past, but also, as we will see in a moment, "culture" is a term that can indicate an awareness that the situation itself has a past. Furthermore, actions are not always witnessed immediately. Often, others know of my actions only through subsequent consequences which impact upon them. Interactions have a temporal dimension both because they do not occur *ex nihilo* and because they do not occur in a vacuum. One of the reasons to prefer the term "interaction" to "action" is this attempt to indicate the full range of connections, of interrelationships, in which any singular action is enmeshed. The emphasis in this account (which contrasts starkly with the account of action implied by the Derridean performative) is on the relationships established, altered, and maintained by actions understood as interactions.

Note that such a pragmatist account of culture neither makes culture the sole determining factor in any action nor claims that culture will supplant other considerations. Culture is not the cause of last appeal here, but only one of the elements agents consider when confronting a situation. And culture is not something that lies "behind" or "beneath" situations; it is just one of the components at the interactional site that is a situation. Both the continual novelty of and the absolute particularity of situations means that the cultural baggage the experienced self carries into a situation is never determinative. Selves must judge how this new situation is similar or dissimilar to others encountered in the past—a judgment that includes considering which others in my world are likely to be impacted by and thus responsive to my actions in this case. Such judgments mean that "culture" (like "facts" themselves) is situational, that its manifestations in any particular instance of human action is the product of an interaction among the judgments made by an experienced self in relation to the circumstances facing her at this moment. Hence, culture can only designate one set of factors influencing action (the set of factors, roughly speaking, that pertain to the "meaning" of my action for myself and for others) and, moreover, a set of factors continually transformed by the processes of experience. Culture only exists as it is performed, enacted, in its repetitions (habitual and ritual acts), and its transformations.

Culture is a moving target, and we can only give the word a useful specificity if we reference such uses to the pressures an agent took into account when making a decision.[20] Vagaries about cultural predilections apart from how they came into play in specific situations deserve our epistemological skepticism, while even cultural explanations tied to specifics are shaped by an ex post facto plausibility which always deserves suspicion prior to credence. Culture, we might say, is the articulation, after the fact, of the calculations I made about others' possible responses to the courses of action I was considering. But surely we often act without much consideration at all, especially without much consideration of what others might think. If "culture" names the cluster of factors that represent an acknowledgment of the people to whom we feel "answerable" when we act (and that group of people will shift according to the action we are performing), then anxiety about the possibility that agents will not feel answerable to anyone begins to explain the huge social investment in pedagogic institutions geared to inculcate "cultural values."

In other words, since the behavior of others is one of the factors we try to control when facing the world (through situations), it should come as no surprise that various efforts are made to influence others. Such efforts are made in the name of numerous considerations, one of which, after 1800, is "culture." Once the concept "culture" exists, agents try to actively shape culture and also appeal to others to adhere to, preserve, create, and

20. Since I have only just encountered his work, I haven't determined the extent to which the position I am taking here accords with the "modest materialism" proposed by Dan Sperber (1996). But I recommend Sperber's lucid book, if only for its presentation of a position almost completely at odds with everything taken for granted by literary theory.

honor various behaviors, beliefs, and values which are articulated under the umbrella of the concept. Thus, the term is performative in another sense apart from its naming the intersubjective factors any agent considers when facing any situation. "Culture" is one rubric under which the performative strives to create collective identities by articulating a unity of experiences, beliefs, and behavior that various agents are called to "recognize" as their own—and as what they "share" with a designated set of other agents. Thus, "culture" becomes a way to create the very entity to which it claims to refer.

Burke's work is an important resource because it helps us to think about the temporality of this performative work. Burke recognizes that our transformative relation to situations, oriented toward the future of a re-formed relation of self to the elements comprising that situation, is poised against the weight of the past. Situations come to us already named, and at stake is who does that naming, and what kind of power those prior namings possess. My attitudinal naming of this present situation is oriented toward the projected results of my interaction with it. But my naming also responds to the past, which is carried by my experienced self and by the significances already attached to this current situation through previous namings. "Real" entities are named and re-named by numerous speakers and, hence, meaning is not conferred by the individual speaker, but is the product of the sometimes competing (even conflictual), sometimes consonant, speech acts of many. Likewise, situations may be novel in this particular moment, but that hardly means situations are utterly new-born in each successive moment. Their novelty here and now is overladen with the accounts of them which constitute (at least in part) their past and influence their reality for the agent in the present. Confronted with a person, we immediately (automatically, as it were) judge whether the person is an "American" or not, a judgment usually aided by that person's carrying the outward signs (appropriate clothing, certain pronunciations and usages of English, etc.) that accord with previous ascriptions of nationality to it.

The word "culture," then, besides referring to the pressures exerted by the fact that agents live in intersubjective settings and the performative attempt to forge certain collective identifications, can also indicate that significance (produced by acts of naming) is not solely the provenance of selves but the product of a multitude of signifying acts. That these acts do not reinforce one another, that no single, nonproblematic, or uncontested significance emerges in many cases, should neither surprise nor disturb us. In fact, if the pressure of others' responses exerts a centripetal force, the novelty of situations and the multiplicity of acts of naming provide the centrifugal forces that make change common. Culture, in the sense this paragraph is stressing, refers to the process of meaning's formation, not to its product.

Culture is no single product, which is why this understanding of the term stands in tension to its use to designate an unproblematically posited set of shared values or orientations. Or, to put it another way, the denial of culture as a single product suggests that we interpret as performative, as an attempt to create what it designates, any utterance that declares that cultural unity exists. Such a declaration can only be seen as an attempt to forge such a unity out of a prior multiplicity. Emphasizing process over product highlights the nonsubjective creation of meaning, which thus does return "culture" to the time-worn place of designating a certain kind of individual impotence. But pragmatism sees the emphasis on process as a way of freeing us from the dead hand of the past. Because meaning is always in process, our primary concern should not be in delineating *the* meaning of this situation or the causes that bring us to this moment, but instead on the possible ways to go on from here. Process means that acts of naming are always transformative, always supplements to the already named. There is no absolute transformation. We don't begin from nowhere, since just as situations come to us already label-laden, so each agent begins from a set of commitments, loyalties, other agents to whom he or she feels answerable, and habitual strategies of relation to various realities. But selves and situations are transformed through their interaction in the on-going process of meaning-creation.

Burke offers three different paradigms of the narrative of culture. The first is the "magical" Burke (found most "purely" in *Permanence and Change* [1965]), who offers a performative word magic through which the world is utterly transformed. The power of naming overwhelms the forces of nature. "One casts out demons by a vocabulary of *conversion*, by an *incongruous* naming, by calling them *the very thing in all the world they are not*" (1965, 133). Burke here is close to a kind of heroic (meaning purely, wildly optimistic) Nietzscheanism, akin to that found in William James's "The Will to Believe." Human energy and belief can transform the world. This naive, can-do attitude not only hooks up with American pragmatism (precisely the aspect of pragmatism recently lambasted by John Patrick Diggins [1994]), but also to the recurrent complaints that Whitman and Emerson lack a sense of evil. We have seen already that Burke later repudiates readings of his work that link him to a belief in the word's absolute power to remake the world.

Instead, we get two more complicated narratives in Burke's later works. It is not clear how the two fit together; they may in fact be utterly inconsistent with each other. For reasons of space, I will not consider their interconnection here, but simply treat each in turn. The first couples magical re-naming with scapegoating. Burke's notion of the performative becomes fully narrative at the point when he realizes that transformation always involves movement—the change from the situation as it exists prior to the intervention of the word and/or the action to the situation after it has been acted upon (whether symbolically or physically). Any transformation, Burke insists, has two elements: the incorporation or adoption of that element of the situation which is embraced and carried forward into the future, and the rejection of that element of the situation which is to be left behind. Action changes, transforms situations, and that means working with, "taking up," some of the possibilities afforded by the situation, and neglecting others. A "complete" account of any action must acknowledge what has been left behind, and Burke finds such acknowledgment in the various forms of scapegoating that can be detected in any "poetic" narrative.

I do not want to linger on Burke's account of scapegoating here, but do want to mention four features of his account that both fit with and stand in salutary tension with poststructuralist ethics' obsession with the exclusion of the other. First, Burke's interest in figures of speech, in tropes, derives from this sensitivity to the fact that every act of re-naming is selective. When we "judge" a new situation and then name it, we are assessing not only those elements in the situation we wish to emphasize and pursue, but also the situation's relation (relations of similarity/dissimilarity, proximity/distance, cause/effect, container/contained etc.) to other situations. Any naming, then, is tropic because it involves applying a name that was used in past situations to a new situation that is not utterly the same. Thus, the name must inevitably highlight some potentials in the situation and obscure others. Second, scapegoating in Burke is part of a narrative and so must be "thought" in relation to what it enables, to how it allows us (in Wittgenstein's phrase) to "go on." As in other versions of pragmatist thought, the justification of scapegoating lies in what it makes possible to do. We cannot do everything in any given situation; the choice of what to do is predicated on the basis of priorities and purposes articulated to the others to whom one is answerable. There is no blanket condemnation of scapegoating; rather there is the situational need to explain the choices one has made. Third, Burke designates a variety of strategies by which scapegoating can be acknowledged, even while recognizing that its necessity is not always understood, that it can be and is denied at times. In other words, scapegoating comes in a variety of different forms and we need to evaluate, to articulate, an "attitude" toward those various forms. This hardly means that self-conscious scapegoating *tout court* will be preferable to unconscious scapegoating. But it is to reiterate that scapegoating cannot be condemned or praised apart from particular situations and that there are options (the choice amidst which makes significant differences) in the ways that scapegoating is enacted. Finally, Burke seeks to ameliorate the potential harms of scapegoating by way of a resolute holism rather than by a celebration of particularity.[21] His interest in "the socialization of losses" (1973, 50–51) and in the correction of synecdoche's partiality by the "humility" (1969, 514) of an irony that aims for "total form (this 'perspective of perspectives')" (1969, 512) indicates Burke's belief that scapegoating is least harmful when its burden is borne by all.

The final narrative of culture offered by Burke can be called his "realistic" paradigm. This is the Burke I have primarily relied on in commenting on what the concept of "culture" might mean, the Burke who seems to me most fully pragmatist (as opposed to the caricature of pragmatism that the "magical" Burke offers, the caricature seized upon by Diggins). By denying the fact/value distinction, the realist Burke does not so much deny magic as incorporate it. Our "stylized answers" to the questions posed by situations combine the hortatory with a "sizing up" of the facts. Thus our namings and the actions predicated upon them unite a realistic appraisal of circumstances with the desires we bring to the interactions, the ways in which we hope to transform the world to better suit our needs. Because the agent's "magic" is not all-powerful, because one cannot simply impose one's will on the world, Burke's "realism" aims to overcome partiality and its inevitable failures by opening the agent up to a more holistic, more collective, relationship to situations. Locked into partiality, infuriated by the resistances offered by reality and others to the will, the agent will resort to self-righteous scapegoating, the designation of obstructive enemies. For Burke, such conflicts are fixed and

21. Without much exaggeration, we can call Burke's holistic approach the diametrical opposite to Lyotard's approach in *The Differend* (1988).

non-transformative. They do not allow us to "go on." They stop the move-ment of time, the processes of meaning creation and transformative ac-tion. The narrative of culture can be arrested if the other elements of a sit-uation are simply resisted by the self.

In the Appendix on "The Four Master Tropes" in *A Grammar of Motives*, Burke appeals to "irony" as the solvent which will dissolve the fixity of a confrontational relationship of self to world, self with other. "Irony arises when one tries, by the interaction of terms upon one another, to produce a *development* which uses all the terms. Hence, from the stand-point of this total form (this 'perspective of perspectives'), none of the participating 'sub-perspectives' can be treated as either precisely right or precisely wrong. They are all voices, or personalities, or positions, in-tegrally affecting one another. When the dialectic is correctly formed, they are the number of characteristics needed to produce the total de-velopment" (1969, 512). Burke's surprising use of "irony" as the trope of dialectical development indicates the disinvestment from any particular (partial) position required to keep the dialectic moving. If our namings are always accompanied with the understanding that they are (to use Peirce's phrase) "fallibilistic," then we are unlikely to claim any one po-sition as a resting-place. Irony, in other words, acknowledges that the "truth" or "reality" of one's namings is not up to the agent alone, but to the location of those namings amidst the circumstances in which the agent speaks and the others she addresses. And even a temporarily ad-equate naming will, because it generates responses from others and be-cause circumstances change as time moves on and the world is acted upon, push time forward in ways that render that naming inadequate to-morrow.

The narrative of culture, then, is a succession of namings in a perpetual call and response that establishes the on-going relations among self, world, and others, relations that individual performatives strive to shape, to change for the better, but which no action can permanently arrest, de-spite the continual temptation to do just that. If we cannot stop time, how-ever, it is just as crucial to stress that we cannot unilaterally create the sit-uations in which we find ourselves. The poststructuralist stress (in Derrida and Judith Butler) on the repetitive, citational component of per-formatives focuses our attention on culture as it figures as the dead hand of the past, of authority (or Law) that positions us as subjects capable of speech. What those poststructuralist accounts shy away from (a reluc-tance indicated by their ignoring what Arendt finds the most political speech act, the promise[22]) is the way that performatives (the dancing of an enunciated attitude or the doing of something with words) establish a relationship between speaker and circumstance, speaker and other, a relationship that carries into the future as commitment and as a map of possible and impossible actions with, toward, or against those circumstances and those others. If the performative is shaped by the past, it is equally a projection of a future in its commitment to a way of being in the world with these situations and with these others. All of which is another way of saying that the past which inhabits my present performatives is not just the past of the Law, but also the past of my own prior performances, my own promises.

IV. TOWARD A DEMOCRATIC CULTURE

Let me just suggest, all too briefly and partially, the project for which this chapter serves as a starting place, a clearing of the ground.. Basically, I see three things as being at stake here, all three of them absolutely central to what I take to be the pragmatist effort to foster a democratic polity. First, an attempt is being made to articulate a theory of action. (I take another stab at this theory in chapter eight.) That theory is trying to locate the self's capabilities amidst the enabling/constraining (always both at the same time) influence of circumstances and others. Selves are situated—and so are their capabilities to act. And that theory of action also insists that selves are temporal and that the temporality of action—shaped by a past, oriented toward a future—is a vital constituent of an adequate account. Second, the identification of the self's capabilities reinstates the task of considering ethical judgments among different courses of action. Irony, as Burke describes it, is primarily an ethical term. Even if one were to argue (as ethicists often are tempted to do) that the world would "objectively" be a better place if we were all more "fallibilistic" about our namings, more oriented to process and less to fixity, still the call for such attitudes is made to agents who are presumed to have some options open to them in these matters. Once we reach this realm of appeal to agents

22. "The grammar of action: that action is the only human faculty that demands a plurality of men; and the syntax of power: that power is the only attribute which applies solely to the worldly in-between space by which men are mutually related, combine in the act of foundation by virtue of the making and keeping of promises, which, in the realm of politics, may well be the highest human faculty" (Arendt, 1980, 175).

who make choices, I take it that we have reached the realm of ethics. Finally, pragmatism becomes political when it projects images of human collectivity. Issues of culture (what it means and how it can be produced and used) become significant when enlisted in the political program of forming the kind of sociality the writer desires. That form of sociality is democracy for Burke—and it depends crucially on the on-going transformative interaction of self with others. As for Dewey, the problem for Burke is fostering a "culture of democracy." Among the elements of such a culture would be a public space for the performance of transformative interactions between self and others, an openness to change, and a "humility" that recognizes one's own partiality and, hence, one's need for others, even those most different others whom one is tempted to scapegoat. "True irony, . . . irony that really does justify the attribute of 'humility,' is not superior to the enemy. . . . True irony, humble irony, is based upon a sense of fundamental kinship with the enemy, as one *needs* him, is *indebted* to him, is not merely outside him as an observer, but contains him *within*, being consubstantial with him" (1969, 514).

CHAPTER 7

Toward a Pragmatist Pluralism

I have recommended pluralism often enough in the preceding chapters to owe my reader a fuller account of it. The topic is one that mostly still lies out in front of me, waiting to be explored. But I will try here to indicate some of the intuitions that make me want to light out for that territory and some of the topography's looming features. These are "notes" toward a fully articulated position. The writers I take as my guides are hardly the only pluralists out there; they just happen to be the ones I have been influenced by.

Let me begin, for clarity's sake, by identifying five variants of pluralism in the intellectual tradition. I would like to be faithful to all five of these but will admit that they are rarely considered together, and I have not yet worked out if they can really all be held together consistently. As Nicholas Rescher puts it, "Even pluralism itself—the doctrine that any substantial question admits of a variety of plausible but mutually conflicting responses—lies open to a plurality of versions and constructions" (1995, 79).[1] It might be more faithful to the spirit of pluralism to see them as incommensurate; certainly they occupy very different discursive universes. The "pragmatic" qualifier in my title indicates not just that I come

---

1. Rescher (1995) provides a very useful overview of the issues involved in taking a pluralist position, although I ultimately disagree with his insistence on a single world and single truth of which there are multiple versions. McLennan's (1995) introductory volume is also superb; it is directed more toward issues in the social sciences, while Rescher attends to more purely philosophical debates.

to pluralism through pragmatism, but also that my account of selves in complex situations comes from pragmatism. William James is the guiding spirit here and we may take two passages from *Pragmatism* (1975; originally 1907) for beacons: "The pragmatism or pluralism which I defend has to fall back on a certain ultimate hardihood, a certain willingness to live without assurances or guarantees" (290), and more epigrammatically, "Nothing outside of the flux secures the issue of it" (125).

Pluralism 1 is found in Ludwig Wittgenstein and J. L. Austin. This is the pluralism that inspires Wittgenstein's epigraph for *Philosophical Investigations* (1958): "I'll teach you differences" (from Shakespeare's *King Lear*). Wittgenstein and Austin were interested in the variety of different ways we use language and were especially committed to overcoming the positivist tendency to see one kind of statement—assertion—as primary and/or as the ur-form of "sense." Humans do a lot of different things and, thus, they use words in many different ways. The plurality of doing and saying should not be reduced when we attempt to describe, and especially to explain, this multitude. "Everything is what it is and not another thing," says Bishop Butler (in Ignatieff, 1999, 51), but it proves very hard not to convert things into manifestations, effects, parts, stages, or appearances (deceptive or otherwise) of other things, once we begin intellectual work. The metaphor of "family resemblances" is one way Wittgenstein tries to salvage particularity, even when similarities and relationships to other things are acknowledged. As a son, my identity is significantly shaped by my relationship to other family members, and specific similarities can be noted. Pluralism will insist on the existence of many different shades of relation, each of which qualifies the particular in different ways. And it will resist the tendency of systematic thought to build ever larger networks of relation that subtend all the particulars in view. Austin offers a "general warning in philosophy. It seems to be . . . readily assumed that if we can only discover the true meanings of each of a cluster of key terms, . . . then it must without question transpire that each will fit into place in some single, interlocking, consistent, conceptual scheme. Not only is there no reason to assume this, but all historical probability is against it[.] . . . We may cheerfully use, and with weight, terms which are not so much head-on incompatible as simply disparate, which just do not fit in or even on" (1979, 203). The difficulty of thinking "disparateness" should not be underestimated.

Pluralism 2 is Nelson Goodman's notion of multiple possible adequate descriptions of a given situation. Goodman's pluralism is pragmatist in the William James/John Dewey tradition, with an emphasis on appropriate and possible responses rather than on adequate descriptions. "For a categorical system, what needs to be shown is not that it is true but what it can do," writes Goodman (1978, 129). Different vocabularies enable different actions in the world, and since our actions re-form the world, Goodman speaks of multiple "ways of worldmaking." Even if we accept that external circumstances limit the available options of speech and/or action, those circumstances never dictate one, and only one, possible response. And Goodman insists that circumstances must be understood as worlds constituted by prior human actions. He eloquently sums up his position: "The many stuffs—matter, energy, waves, phenomena—that worlds are made of are made along with the worlds. But made from what? Not from nothing, after all, but *from other worlds*. Worldmaking as we know it always starts from worlds already on hand; the making is a remaking . . . . My interest here is . . . with the processes involved in building a world out of others. With false hope of a firm foundation gone, with the world displaced by worlds that are but versions, with substance dissolved into function, and with the given acknowledged as taken, we face the questions of how worlds are made, tested, and known" (1996, 65).

A third pluralism can be attributed to Hannah Arendt, who stresses the "plurality" that stems from the existence of many distinct individuals. Arendt's key term in this context is "natality" (taken from Augustine). Something new comes into the world with the birth of each individual; similarly, human action, performed by individuals, brings new things into the world. She calls action a "miracle," by which she means to suggest that the appearance of novelty both exceeds calculation and is an embarrassment to theory. "Every act, seen from the perspective not of the agent but of the process in whose framework it occurs and whose automatism it interrupts, is a 'miracle'—that is, something which could not be expected" (1977, 169). "[W]e know the author of 'miracles.' It is men who perform them—men who, because they have received the twofold gift of freedom and action can establish a reality of their own" (1977, 171). Humans make both the world and their selves in political action, says Arendt. A commitment to plurality undergirds Arendt's advocacy of a politics that enables the appearance in public of that full individuality which only discloses itself in action before others. But plurality also grounds her basic ethical principle: the reduction of individuals in all their unique difference to types, to instances of general categories, is a violation of their freedom. And Arendt sees a direct link between the failure to cherish plural singularity, a failure that renders the individual "superfluous," and the violence done to whole peoples under general names like "Jew" or "enemy of the revolution."

Isaiah Berlin provides a fourth pluralism, one that focuses on the notion of competing goods. Trade-offs, compromises, and negotiations will always be necessary both because different individuals will prioritize competing goods differently and because many choices are painful second-bests. Berlin's (1969) pluralism is connected to a variant of liberalism that eschews overarching, systematic solutions to social problems in favor of context-sensitive, ad hoc reactions that claim no authority or "correctness" beyond allowing social agents to "go on" (Wittgenstein's phrase) in relative peace and prosperity until the next adjustment is required. All solutions are imperfect compromises that hold only so long as the various parties to the compromise are satisfied enough to restrain from rocking the boat, from demanding a renegotiation of the prevailing terms. I find Berlin the least attractive of all the writers I have mentioned thus far because I think he underestimates the extent to which power holds people to compromises they loathe. So I distrust his reliance on negative liberty, on the individual's ability to withhold consent. But I also don't know Berlin's work as well as that of the other writers, and I am attracted to a view that stresses competing, incompatible, and disparate goods that vary from situation to situation. Berlin, of course, offers one version of liberal pluralism, a version that accords selves more sovereignty as agents than I think they actually possess.[2]

The fifth variant would be the methodological pluralism I am groping toward in chapter 5. Method is certainly too grand a term; it is more like lines of inquiry or characteristic ways of approaching a problem or topic. The goal is to shift our focus from determinate identity, from what a thing or set of relations has been or *is* to what it enables, to how we "go on" from here, to what actions it makes possible. "Things and relations are not read in terms of something else or in terms of where they originate or their history but rather, pragmatically, in terms of their effects, what they do, what they make" (Grosz, 1994, 181). As I suggested in chapter 5, Fou-

2. McLennan (1995, chap. 1) offers a good, quick overview of liberal pluralism and considers the extent to which the various postmodern pluralisms (which usually vehemently deny any kinship with liberal pluralism) retain certain liberal themes of the 1950s. McGowan (1991) argues that poststructuralism often resembles the liberalism it claims to abhor, most particularly in remaining attached to exactly the kind of negative liberty that troubles me in Berlin's work. Berlin certainly embodies the kind of "diffident liberalism" that I explore in chapter 4 of this book.

cault, James, and Arendt all offer hints; other helpful sources of ideas on this score are Paul Feyerabend (1993) and Barbara Herrnstein Smith (1988). The trick is to avoid the Scylla of "methodological individualism" (characteristic of much quantitative social science) with its assumption of sovereign individual choice and the Charybdis of Hegelian holism, which subsumes all particulars under the sign of the general, the system. Relations are crucial (although not the sole) determinants of meaning, as structuralism and other systematic paradigms insist. But relations are contingent, do not necessarily concatenate into ever larger systems of connections, and work upon entities that have substantial properties of their own (what Spinoza called *connatus* in human individuals).[3] Things (persons) are qualified by the relations in which they stand to other things and/or persons, but "constituted" may be too strong a word if we allow it to suggest complete plasticity. There is resistant matter in things and persons; they are not infinitely malleable, as anyone trying to "socially construct" a two-year-old knows. Pluralism searches for a methodology that credits that resistant something without erecting it into the particular's identity and/or essence. The method also has to register how things change, often dramatically, when placed in new relations, new contexts.

Pluralism, simply, sees a world that is full of many different things, of many different contexts (or assemblages of things in relation to one another), and a variety of vocabularies that humans use to position themselves among those things. I want, in the rest of this chapter, to untangle further characteristics of pluralism and to consider some of its consequences. Since I am not ready for a systematic account of pluralism (if such a self-contradictory undertaking is even desirable), what follows is more a set of illustrations meant to flesh out what pluralism claims and where it leads us. Needless to say, the illustrations are meant to be persuasive.

3. Spinoza's concept, *conatus*, does some of the work I am trying to gesture toward here. *Conatus* is "a thing's endeavour to persist in being," the pressure it exerts back outwards toward the world (Lloyd 1996, 9). For Gilles Deleuze, *conatus* becomes connected to what he calls Spinoza's "expressionism." "Our *conatus* is thus always identical with our power of acting itself. The variations of *conatus* as it is determined by this or that affection are the dynamic variations of our power of action (1990, 231)." In this interpretation, *conatus* names that primal something out of which we act toward the world. Unless we posit some such energy or power in the self, we risk seeing the self as an utterly passive recipient of the world's imprint. Charles Altieri (1994) also relies on *conatus* to name "the force driving our investments" (24) and connects it to the concept of "style," which marks each self's distinctive ways of manifesting that "force" (see 85–87). Aaron Pollack and Jörg Schaub, along with Altieri, share the blame for my invocation of Spinoza.

To begin, I want to suggest an interactional model of situations. The pragmatist model of action starts with an individual in a situation. The contrast is to what Dewey (1981, 26) calls "the spectator theory of knowledge," which posits a knower distanced from the objects to be known.[4] The pragmatist self is always already embedded in situations, always already within a society and a culture, always already located in a world that acts upon it and upon which it acts. Knowledge is a by-product of this immersion, not something constituted prior to it or separate from it. At first—and for the most part—the individual acts habitually, minimally conscious of her routine responses within an environment. Matters only get interesting when the routine fails to achieve its usual (expected) results.[5] The individual is pulled up short. An element of doubt has been introduced by the recalcitrance of the world (world here encompasses other people, objects, and institutional arrangements and relations, as well as the agent's own body.) The agent must reconsider her habits and her

4. Arguing against philosophy's obsession with "knowledge" and in favor of a focus on "experience," Dewey writes: "[E]xperience is not identical with brain action; it is the entire organic agent-patient in all its interaction with the environment, natural and social. The brain is primarily an organ of a certain kind of behavior, not of knowing the world. And to repeat what has already been said, experiencing *is* just certain modes of interaction, or correlation, of natural objects among which the organism happens, so to say, to be one. It follows with equal force that experience means primarily not knowledge, but ways of doing and suffering. Knowing must be described by discovering what particular mode—qualitatively unique—of doing and suffering it is. As it is [i.e., in the philosophical tradition Dewey is trying to overcome], we find experience assimilated to a non-empirical concept of knowledge, derived from an antecedent notion of a spectator outside of the world" (1981, 26).

5. This is hardly the place to take up the philosophical debate between realists and anti-realists—a debate that has, I think, hardened into a ritual so prescripted that it has long ceased being productive. But I will note that I am with Hilary Putnam in believing that pragmatist pluralism is compatible with a "direct realism" that credits the commonsense experience of living in a world of material things, persons, social institutions, bodily sensations, and any number of other entities encountered in our daily rounds. One key is that these experiences are unproblematic until something causes us to "doubt" our usual ways of responding to all that surrounds us. As Charles Peirce (1992) insisted, much "philosophical doubt" is singularly unreal; it does not arise out of thwarted interactions with situations and their components. And where "doubt" does occur, action (or "inquiry," but inquiry always understood as action upon the world) follows. Such action aims to readjust our relation to circumstances, so our situation is improved. Another key is that the solidity of these material things is only one relevant consideration among others that influence our judgments and actions. And, finally, as Putnam puts it, comes "the denial that reality dictates one unique description" (1998, 45). Or, as Feyerabend puts it: "The material humans . . . face must be approached in the right ways. It *offers resistance*; some constructions . . . find no point of attack in it and simply collapse. On the other hand, *this material is more pliable than is commonly assumed*" (1999, 145). The reader wanting to begin to explore this pragmatist realism should see Putnam (1998), Peirce (1992), Dewey (1981), and Feyerabend (1999, 131–60).

options. She performs an "inquiry" (Peirce's and [sometimes] Dewey's word) or "reconstruction" (Dewey) that leads to a reassessment of the situation and thus an altered relation to it. What was habitual, routine, unconscious becomes considered, reflective, conscious. Crucial is the insistence that knowledge and action both entail the maintenance or alteration of the self's relation to the situation, of the self's way of being embedded in the world. Hans Joas (1996, 133) calls this pragmatic picture of a self responding to its surroundings "situated creativity," the re-vision of possibilities and strategies in relation to the demands of novel situations.

This account, so far, is hardly at odds with rational choice models or other forms of methodological individualism, including some versions of liberal pluralism. But the pragmatist emphasis on habit does posit large domains of what might be deemed prerational behavior. We will do many things habitually in life—and that's a blessing. When we think consciously about breathing, we usually muck it up. But habit, while always present and sometimes necessary, is never sufficient. And it is when pragmatism turns its attention to the formation of habits, to their insufficiency, and to the processes of their reconstruction that it departs significantly from individualistic models. For a start, habits themselves are not individually generated. To a certain extent, habits respond to the world's regularities. Nature is lawlike because various configurations and events recur. Social arrangements also attain relative stability (relative because no social arrangement lasts forever and because the stability in question may only manifest itself in some circumstances, while not in others). Habits are mapped onto these stabilities and regularities. Routine action generates the expected results because the situation of today is not very novel in relation to yesterday's situation. Actions that have gained the desired end will be repeated until they fail. The world is such that many repeated actions do not fail, so many actions become habitual. Habits, thus, are products of the relations to the world, to others, and to society in which the individual stands, not individually generated.

The pragmatist definition of "world" and "situation" is not limited to an individual facing a nonhuman environment. Because these terms also encompass others and social arrangements, the interactional model cannot be dual (self facing nature) or even triangular (self facing nature and other selves), but quadrilateral (self facing nature, others, and social arrangements). The environments within which we act are (not always, but much of the time) human-made as well as natural, and the results at which we aim include the desired response (approbation, love, obedience, cooperation, to name just a few) of others and (sometimes) the maintenance, reform, or contestation of the social arrangements that structure our relations to others and to nature.

In other words, pragmatism (especially in Dewey and George Herbert Mead) understands habits as socially produced, understands the relations in which agents stand to the other elements of a situation as socially mediated. Habits are not simply individualistic responses to the world; they are also socially instituted, reinforced, and transmitted. Many habits are acquired through a slow process of education. We reach here the place where habits become fuzzily related to norms or ideologies. The unconscious routines of individual agents are acquired through experiences that are not solely individual but are, at least to some extent, social. With Mead we get a pragmatism fully committed to the insistence that the individual herself, the self as the unit of action and organized experience, is socially constituted.

From methodological individualism to a socially constituted self, pragmatism may seem condemned to swing from the fears of fragmentation and anomie that characterize subjectivist interpretations of modernity to the visions of lock-step conformity and social engineering that mark the dystopian visions of Huxley, Orwell, Adorno, Foucault. and other critics of totalitarian, mass, or disciplinary society. Joas is absolutely right to identify "situated creativity" as the talisman that allows pragmatism to escape these unpalatable choices. The analysis of habit is crucial, because it avoids any presentist model of the individual encounter with the situation. The individual enters the situation with a set of habits, beliefs, predispositions, established relations to self and others. The individual is, in a word, experienced—and carries the way of being in the world that experience has forged. The individual is not the blank slate that individualist accounts like rational choice theory or extreme Nietzschean versions of the willful self posit at the momentous instant of action. The pragmatist self has a past—and is oriented toward a future. Action in the present is deeply informed by that past and that future.

Furthermore, the situation itself has a past; it, too, is not simply present. Peirce's semiotics are indispensable to pragmatism's portrait of the situated individual as the site of knowledge of and action in "the world." The individual cannot act in, respond to, a situation unless that situation is named. In other words, action for the pragmatist is conditional on a judgment about what situation I find myself in. And judgment is not purely perceptual (and thus presentist: what I see, feel, and hear now), but also linguistic, conceptual, categorical (Peirce took the word pragmatism from Kant). My judgment processes the raw data and raw feels of the present through the lenses of available vocabularies. The generalizing, categorizing, classifying property of names is crucial. The novelty of situations, the newness of the present, is tempered by judgment.

Crucial to pragmatist pluralism is the denial of infallibility or the singularly proper to this process of judgment and its results. There is a tension between the novelty of what is here now and these generalizing categories carried in our language. Multiple ways of characterizing a situation are possible, each of which singles out a different way of "going on" from here, a different way of aligning our relationship to the other components of the situation. In Shelby Foote's history of the Civil War, he exasperatedly tells us that one year to the day that Robert E. Lee scored his greatest victory of the war by turning Joe Hooker's flank at Chancellorsville, Lee turned both of U. S. Grant's flanks in almost the exact same place in the battle now called the Wilderness. Grant was routed worse than Hooker was, Foote insists, but simply failed to acknowledge he was defeated.[6] Now I think it fair to say that Grant was obtuse. The wonder is that Grant's obtuseness was just about his greatest virtue. Or we might say that his vices became virtues in this particular situation. A better man would have handled the situation worse. If the fact of defeat was a reason for retreat, Grant would look right past the facts and make the situation tell a different story. Famously, the Union troops cheered when they turned right after extricating themselves from the battlefield—right to move further south, rather than left to cross the Rapahannock River and return north.

6. Foote (1974) writes: "'Most of us thought it was another Chancellorsville,' a Massachusetts infantryman would remember, while a Pennsylvania cavalryman recorded that his comrades used a homelier term to describe the predicted movement. They called it 'another skedaddle.'

"If the Chancellorsville parallel was obvious—both battles had been waged in the same thicket, so to speak, between the same two armies, at the same point of year, and against the same Confederate commander—it was also . . . disturbingly apt. By every tactical standard, although the earlier contest was often held up as a model of Federal ineptitude, the second was even worse-fought than the first. Hooker had only one flank turned: Grant had both. . . . *In plain fact*, up to the point of obliging Grant to throw in the sponge and pull back across the river, Lee had never beaten an adversary so soundly as he had beaten this one in the course of the past two days.

"What it all boiled down to was that Grant was whipped, and soundly whipped, if he would only admit it by retreating: which in turn is only a way of saying that he had not been whipped at all. 'Whatever happens, there will be no turning back,' he had said, and he would hold to that" (1974, 188–89, my emphasis).

To invoke a useful term from David Wiggins's work (1998, 124–32), the facts of the situation "underdetermine" judgment and the ways that individuals will respond.[7] Grant's reading of his situation, while not conventional, was possible. The facts do not rule out his chosen course of action. Grant's obtuseness extended to other people as well; he could stomach the slaughter of his soldiers, while the battle of the Wilderness (like the earlier battle of Shiloh) resulted from his narrow focus on his own plans to the neglect of imagining what the other army might do. But that same obtuseness enabled his unconventional judgment of his situation in May 1864. Neither the facts nor Grant's obtuseness were all-determining. There were limits to what he could achieve, but those limits did not reside in one or the other component of the situation. The limits only became apparent in the interplay of all the components as a judgment was acted on and its consequences unfolded. Even Grant had to acknowledge defeat at Cold Harbor.[8] The world bends to will no more predictably than a two-year-old child does. Underdetermining facts are not irrelevant, but neither do they tell one and only one story. They can be read in different ways and there are often many successful courses of action open in any situation.

The Peircean point is that we could not act at all if we did not take the judgmental step of assimilating (through an imaginative leap that processes similarities, analogies, and formal symmetries/asymmetries) this singular present to situations already experienced. The pragmatist emphasis on experiment, on trial and error, acknowledges the highly problematic nature of our judgments. We should always consider these judgments fallible. They are preliminary hypotheses, the first guides to action, but always tentative, always to be revised in light of action's results. William James begins his book, *A Pluralistic Universe*, by pointing to this tension between the need to name things, to assimilate the singular under general categories, and the inevitable inadequacy of any one naming, since some aspects of the singular thing will not be highlighted. No re-

7. I am probably using Wiggins's concept in ways he would deplore. But I highly recommend the work of this moral and political pluralist to literary critics, whose antipathy to Anglo-American philosophy usually means they have never heard of Wiggins, no less read his important and consistently enlightening work.

8. In Foote's (1974, 291–96) account, Grant does not acknowledge defeat at Cold Harbor early enough and thus loses the confidence of his troops, who consistently refuse to obey orders to attack entrenched enemy troops for the rest of 1864. So Grant's failure at Cold Harbor is not solely, or even primarily, reading the facts "wrong," but not getting his army to ratify his interpretation of events. In Austin's terms (1975), Grant's speech act is "infelicitous," because it does not have sufficient "force" to garner his audience's agreement or "uptake."

sponsive action exhausts the potential of a situation. There are always different things we could have done, different opportunities we could have seized. Still, we have a tendency to take our namings as adequate, to neglect pluralism in favor of definitive assertions, so James posits an endless tension between the singular that solicits plural ways of responding and the generalizations that aim to fix that fluttering thing. "Individuality outruns all classification, yet we insist on classifying every one we meet under some general head. As these heads usually suggest prejudicial associations to some hearer or other, the life of philosophy largely consists of resentments at the classing, and complaints of being misunderstood" (1987, 631). Austin (1975) points toward this same tension in his wry comment that "we must at all costs avoid over-simplification, which one might be tempted to call the occupational disease of philosophers if it were not their occupation" (38).

Peirce's semiotic is so important to a pragmatist pluralism because it factors in the social mediation that informs all human encounters with the world without simply locking us into the prison-house of language. While past experience and preexisting (social and linguistic) categories are crucial to our forming judgments in the present, such judgments do not preclude our processing feedback from the real. The expected results of action can fail to occur; we can register the fact of that failure, and we can revise our judgments, beliefs, and habits accordingly. Pluralism, then, resides both in the situation being capable of different descriptions that lead to different responses *and* in the refusal to accord any component of the situation (facts, self, others, or social arrangements) full determinative power.

But even this model of an agent judging a situation in the vocabularies afforded by social categories is too simple. We must also recognize that situations come to us already named and that we judge them in relation to future goals. Here the pragmatist vision of temporality joins with its persistent interactionism and pluralism. As William James memorably puts it, "the trail of the human serpent is thus over everything." (1975, 37). A situation and the elements of which it is composed are not pure percepts because they come to us bearing the histories of their previous relations to humans. Things—and, more generally, the world in the fullest sense of that term—bear the traces of their previous encounters with agents. If one manifestation of culture is transmitted habit, another is this overlaying of history and meaning (carried within language and tradition and serving as assumed background knowledge) that accompanies things. Human action alters the world, and now our relation to that world is mediated through these prior alterations. Situated creativity, then, involves an individual agent, but with an individual and a situation that are both deeply embedded in cultural codings that carry the experiences of the past and motivational/normative orientations toward a desired future. Since the actions of the past and possible orientations toward the future are multiple, there is no single right judgment about a present situation. The present situation affords various possibilities, although not infinite ones. Plural judgments leading to different courses of action are to be expected. That is why creativity is both possible and prized. Successful action is most likely (although there is no guarantee; the world can be, and sometimes is, perverse) when a judgment attentively responds to the various elements in the situation. But few actions will work upon all those elements, while different purposes may be successfully pursued in the same situation. Both the complexity of present situations and the very different pasts that experienced selves carry into situations lead the pragmatist theorist of action to expect multiple judgments and actions in the present and to expect that more than one judgment or action will prove adequately responsive to present possibilities.

This pluralism of response and possibility is meant to counter models that court social or any other kind of determinism. Pragmatist interactionism is another plank—the most basic, ontological plank—in this refutation of determinism. Pragmatism identifies four elements (agent, other people, material things, social meanings and arrangements) in any situation and insists that none of these elements is determinant. Each element has no independent standing, but is an interactional product of the encounters among all four. The identification of the four elements is an ex post facto result of theoretical analysis that rather falsely suggests an independent existence for each one. The ontological claim is that the four only exist (for humans at least) in interaction with each other. The dynamic, ongoing, and inescapable intertwining of the four through time is the environment in which humans find themselves. The human organism thus embedded is continuously adapting to the circumstances of being in the world. Attempts to indicate the causal contribution of any of the four elements to the creation of the situation belie their mutual dependence, the fact that each can only ever act in conjunction. We do not encounter or know any of these four elements in isolation or even in some nondynamic moment of inaction. The pushes and pulls of their coexistence are constant. The world just is the interaction of these four (this is the ontological claim)—and no one of the four is predominant; none gets to call the shots unilaterally. Adherence to this model of complex inter-actions suggests, in Feyerabend's words, that "the dichotomy subjective/objective and the corresponding dichotomy between descriptions and constructions are much too naïve to guide our ideas about the nature and the implications of knowledge claims" (1999, 144).

From this pragmatist perspective, almost all theories of knowledge, judgment, and action are reductive, taking one or another of the four elements as determinative, and thus reducing all action to a reflection of individual temperament (subjectivist psychology), social and cultural coding (ideology theories), natural facts (realism), or the pressure of immediate others (social mores and sanctions). Each of the elements, the pragmatist insists, underdetermines what is now and what will unfold as the dynamic situation moves into the future. Underdetermination is one reason predictions of action are so unreliable. At the very best, some statistical regularities may be identifiable. But individual predictions are hit or miss. The variables are just too complex, since their limited number (four) is joined to the indeterminacy of just how much weight any one carries in any particular situation. Analysis after the fact can offer plausible accounts of how the variables interacted to produce a specific action and specific results. But even these analyses will occupy a realm of plausibility, not exactitude, and will be subject to the pluralism that stems from the different possible ways to name a situation and the different possible identifications of its consequences. So, for example, I think "obtuseness" captures something about Grant that provides a plausible account of his actions, but other interpretations, other judgments of his behavior, are certainly possible.

Situated creativity, then, calls on us to focus on the unexpected and novel ways that a particular person goes about responding to a particular situation. Of course, Peirce and Dewey were both interested in communal enterprises; it is not entirely clear how much this basic model of action would have to be modified to account for communal creativity. Physical possibilities, normative expectations (which carry a range of sanctions if violated), and institutional arrangements all structure the field in which action takes place. But the wild card of the agent remains just that; there are multiple ways to act within a situation—a fact that becomes especially relevant when activity in a field is most lauded when not (fully) routine or predictable. We value novelty and difference more in some fields than in others, but our bias toward individualism seldom leads us to praise slavish imitation and complete predictability.

William James famously shook off years of depression when he put the specter of determinism behind him with an act of sheer assertion.[9] An arbitrary and gratuitous action, by virtue of its occurrence, disproved determinism. Appeals to the wild card of agency can look similarly ungrounded. Recuperation of the singularity of creativity within the generalizing vocabularies of theory is never elegant. To a large extent, the argument rests on empirical observation. Humans continually do unexpected, unpredicted things, and humans also demonstrably alter established routines in response to altered circumstances, altered goals, or altered interpretations. It seems odd to be called upon to prove that one situation differs from another just as one person differs from another. Yet the tendency to assimilate these differences within frameworks that group singularities according to similarities is so strong that pluralism is often on the defensive. But surely our theoretical inability to account for creativity and its plural effects says more about the limitations of our theories than it does about the actual capacities of human agents or the nature of the varied worlds they fashion in interaction with others, things, and cultural meanings.

The pragmatist understanding of situated creativity brings one final embarrassment in its wake: the assumption that agents are capable of monitoring the world and of reflexively processing the information received. In other words, a theory of creative action entails a (however minimal) bottom-line individualism. There must be a point, even in a fully interactionist theory, where the self cannot be reduced to a function of forces external to it (or even of forces "internalized" through some process of socialization). That point in pragmatism focuses on the self's ability to read (to judge) situations. The pragmatist model cannot survive an "error theory," that is, any account of behavior which places the self's ability to know what it is doing into radical question. Pragmatism depends on the fundamental trustworthiness of consciousness (perhaps not immediately, but at some level of reflexive process). Any theory that posits unconscious processes as more constitutive of action than conscious choices cannot be compatible with the pragmatist outlook. If habit is not amendable in response to experience, pragmatism is a non-starter. The pragmatist must

9. See Menand (1998) for a thorough and fascinating—albeit skeptical—account of how James escaped depression and how that escape figures in standard versions of James's life and work.

be hostile to theories of ideology that posit motivations and intentions unavailable to consciousness as the determinants of action. Pragmatism depends on agents who can, for the most part, know what they are doing. The pragmatist need not deny systemic relations and/or effects, just as he hardly ignores inherited social codings, but must deny that agents are systematically and incorrigibly unable to perceive and take into account these relations, effects, and codings. The strongest argument here is that the theorist of ideology has achieved a conscious understanding of these matters. What, in principle, could refute the possibility of all other agents' attaining a similar understanding?

The notion of ideology highlights that there are social heuristics for grasping situations, pre-established maps for how to proceed when meeting situations of this or that type, along with guidelines for seeing that it is this or that type that we face now. Novel interpretations that fly in the face of these heuristics must overcome not only the inertia of habit but also the skepticism of others who are prone to follow convention. The extent to which received categories determines judgment is overstated by most theories of ideology, but that does not mean that the problematic of ideology is false.[10] We process the real according to forms that are neither entirely self-generated nor easy to revise. And even when we manage to break through the crust of convention, we still have the difficult task of persuading others to accept our novel reading of the situation.

The argument against ideology theories is that selves in a culture do not all judge situations in the same way and that experiences of new circumstances can change the terms and categories we bring into situations. Change does happen; our "defaults" are transformed by living a life. Because situations are both complex and novel, there is nothing beyond responsiveness to the particulars of the situation and a knowledge of the semantics of available general terms to guide our namings. Judgment takes place in a setting that is chronically underdetermined, which is precisely what ideology theory, with its emphasis on overdetermination, de-

10. See Ricoeur (1986) and Eagleton (1991) for two useful overviews of ideology theories. Althusser's (1971) highly influential account of ideology is also an "error theory," since it claims that "individuals who live in ideology" inhabit "a determinate (religious, ethical, etc.) representation of the world whose imaginary distortion depends on their imaginary relation to the conditions of existence, in other words, in the last instance, to the relations of production and to class relations (ideology = an imaginary relation to real relations)" (166–67).

nies.[11] Realism, with its search for the "right" name, also denies under-determination. Judgment is not an exact science; its inevitable reliance on analogy links it more to the poetic faculty as described in Aristotle's *Poetics* than to any Adamic notion of a proper naming.[12] Not surprisingly, we get disagreements over labeling all the time. Such disagreements are endemic to pluralistic societies in which selves are encouraged to take individualized viewpoints and in which there are various traditions, various cultural orientations, on which individuals draw.

What consequences follow when someone like Dorothea Brooke refuses "to call things by the names that others call them by"?[13] In art since 1750, we expect and value idiosyncratic namings. We encourage defeating expectations, strive for surprises. Beyond the pleasure of novelty, theories of art since the Romantics have often claimed psychological, social, or moral benefits from the poet's ability to find new names for things. Kenneth Burke, as I discussed in chapter 6, finds these novel namings magically transformative. A new name opens up entirely new possibilities; it is as if a charm has been undone. We suddenly see a way forward that we

11. Critics who complain that pluralism is naïve and over-optimistic usually insist that there is an underlying set of enforced, systematic relations that belie the plurality of options that pluralism indicates. Guillory's (1993, chap. 5) critique of Smith (1988) takes exactly this position, while for Eagleton (2000) pluralism is *the* ideology of capitalism since it celebrates a diversity that is properly understood as the product of a capitalism that ruthlessly divides to conquer and segregates economic winners from losers. "The predatory actions of capitalism breed, by way of defensive reaction, a multitude of closed cultures, which the pluralist ideology of capitalism can then celebrate as a rich diversity of life-forms" (129–30). As Gibson-Graham (1996) argue, granting capitalism such monolithic identity (everywhere the same) and such omnipotence is hardly plausible given the variety of economic forms in the world that result from the interactions between economic and other (social, cultural, religious, and natural) factors.

12. Judgment is a kind of metaphor. Aristotle (1996) defines metaphor as "the application of a noun which properly applies to something else" (34) and tells us that "the most important thing [for the poet] to be good at is using metaphor. This is the one thing that cannot be learned from someone else, and is a sign of natural talent; for the successful use of metaphor is a matter of perceiving similarities" (37). Without attaching too much weight to "proper," we can say that judgment uses a name that was applied in the past and now transfers its application to this situation, thing, event, emotion, etc. in the present. Acceptance that we must use the available stock of words to describe the novel present can be contrasted to an Adamic or Orphic notion of names that capture the essential truth of the thing named. See Aarleff (1982) and Bruns (1974) for discussions of the persistent dream of a language that would speak the world as it is in itself as opposed to a language that uses human terms for nonhuman realities.

13. In Book VI, chap. liv of George Eliot's *Middlemarch* (1997; originally 1872), Mrs. Cadawallader tells Dorothea Brooke, "We all have to exert ourselves to keep a little sane, and call things by the same name as other people call them by." To which Dorothea retorts, "I have never called anything by the same name that all the people about me did."

did not see a moment ago. Such conversion experiences, the sense that "I once was blind, but now I see," capture the exhilaration that attends both acting in and witnessing the drama of creation. Pragmatism shares the Romantic admiration of Prometheus. Humans can re-word the universe, thus altering the received world to fabricate a new one better adapted to human needs and desires. The world admits of plural outcomes and human ingenuity is called to direct the stories down the best possible paths. Pluralism goes hand-in-hand with a heady freedom and with viewing "creativity" as a god-like capacity that should be cultivated and given every opportunity to "express" itself. The plot of history has not been written. The underdeterminative facts can be like putty in our hands. Human desires and imagination are not futile; they can be realized in the here and now. Apparent constraints are more likely psychological (fear or some self-limitation of will and vision) or social (the conformism and lack of imagination of the herd, according to Nietzsche, or blocking forces of coagulated power identified by leftists) than natural, inevitable, or "real" in some human-independent way.

Visions of such absolute freedom have proved terrifying as well as heady, and pragmatism outlines a "situated freedom" for reasons similar to the account of "situated creativity" offered above.[14] For every Prometheus unbound there are five Fausts, characters who come to grief when they find themselves in a world without limits or constraints. Even Nietzsche has to posit "eternal recurrence" to structure what otherwise looks like the formless chaos of total freedom. Romanticism has proved more attractive as an idea than as a daily lived reality.[15] Part of me, I must admit, regrets the continual compromises with total freedom, the careful stepping back from the brink of asserting and living the conviction that everything is possible and we need seek no one's permission but our own. We only require the courage and creativity that such freedom calls for. The fault lies in us, not in the stars. We have proved incapable of drinking the cup of

14. McGowan (1991) includes an extended critique of Nietzschean models of freedom and argues that individual actions are only meaningful within a context of relations to world and others. I still hold that position, even as I consider the appeal of the Promethean here.

15. Of course, Romanticism as a lived reality was always a minority avocation. What the majority seems to like is the voyeuristic thrill of watching Romantics like Byron or Wilde trace out the pattern of forbidden pleasures leading to dramatic falls. This same relation holds in the public's current fascination with the fabulous wealth, beauty, and self-indulgence of celebrities joined to that same public's satisfaction with the failed marriages, spectacular bankruptcies, and various drug addictions of those same celebrities. For a wonderful account of how the Romantic ideal lives on among rock musicians, see Marcus (1989).

freedom to the lees. But perhaps others—the overman of whom Nietzsche dreams?—will succeed where we have failed. There can be humans who are Titans.

In other words, I sometimes suspect that our shackles are self-forged. The language of constraints—of choices dictated by the facts—sounds schoolmarmish to me, a tedious scolding, a droning insistence that those who refuse to restrain themselves will eventually be called to order. How dare you think that you can overstep the limits the rest of us respect? We're watching you, taking comfort in our smug conviction that you will fail, and eager to take pleasure in your fall when it does occur. Such prim and petty reasonableness makes Nietzsche attractive. And when such reasonableness takes the form of political defeatism (the new bosses will never be any better than the current bosses so utopian thinking is "unrealistic"), we should recognize it as a self-serving rationalization of the naysayer's own privileges.

But the adjective "schoolmarmish" jumps out. The Romantic vision is linked to hyper-masculinist codes, as well as to aristocratic disdain for bourgeois mediocrity, with its investment in security, peace, and domestic well-being among loved others. One problem of total freedom is that so often its existence is proved by self-destruction or, much worse, the destruction of others. The abolition of limits, the enactment of full-bore creativity, gets played out through suffering, the infliction of pain on bodies.[16] It is as if we don't really believe we are free, so must do the most unthinkable things in order to prove it. But I don't trust my intuitions here. I can only note the repeated pattern of extreme freedom's connection to suffering inflicted on self and others; the logic of the pattern escapes me. I don't see why or how Romantic freedom would inevitably bring suffering and variants of sadomasochism in its wake, but such is often the case.

So I am returned to the issue of constraints, the discourses of reasonableness. But I think the constraints are more self-imposed than necessitated by any facts. "Self-imposed" isn't right either. "Humanly generated" might be closer. We are in the realm of the evil humans do to humans. Let me start with the liberal principle (from J. S. Mill) of not doing harm to others by my own actions. A limit of that kind on our freedom seems right to me. And so I am now in the position of saying that limits underwrit-

16. Scarry (1985) is the fullest attempt to trace out this connection between creativity and inflicting bodily pain.

ten by morality are justified. How does this acceptance of limits fit with pluralism? I think, in fact, it can, but to get from here (the acceptance of a limit) to there (pluralism) will require a few steps.

The first step is the contention that morality is entirely human. Only someone who begins with certain values and convictions that are deemed moral could ever be in a position to judge this or that new situation as one that involves moral considerations. Nothing in the situation declares it a moral one; it can only be seen *as* moral through the lenses of an agent who has the category "morality" and has some content attached to that category. And while it may seem that morality is a "meta-category," I think the same holds true for lover-level categories like "cruelty." I don't think dogs judge whether situations are moral or not, are instances of cruelty or not. I do not think "cruelty" is a natural kind; it is a socially-generated concept, and individuals receive it as part of their initiation into a culture. That culture cannot fully control how the individual applies the concept once acquired; however, a being without the concept, or at least without the notion that events and actions can be evaluated along the lines of right and wrong, is not going to get to moral judgment just by looking at what transpires in full view. This point seems trivially true to me but, of course, as pernicious and disastrous by those who want the reality of morality to be "mind-independent." It doesn't assuage such folks to add that my position does not lead to "subjectivism," because it places individual acts of judgment within a field bounded by prevailing semantic conventions. The individual lives amid the others from whom he or she first learns moral categories and this individual can no more successfully redefine robbery as morally indifferent as he or she can redefine "dog" as a large gray animal with a trunk and ivory tusks. This concession only moves "truth" from individual to communal processes of determination, and the philosopher committed to realism, objectivity, and mind-independence refuses to go there.[17]

17. One such philosopher is Wiggins, who goes down three-quarters of the road toward a social understanding of truth, but pulls up at the last mile to insist that "objectivity is not mere intersubjectivity . . . . Agreement [among members of a speech community] plays its role in fixing senses. We only have a chance of getting to the point where a predicate has a clear public sense if the users of the language are so constituted as to be able to come to agree sufficiently over a sufficiently large area whether the predicate applies or not; and what senses we invest our language with plays its part in fixing what truths we shall be able to give expression to. But that exhausts the role of agreement—just as the size and mesh of a fisherman's net determines what fish he will catch, if he catches any; not what fish are in the sea" (1998, 249–50). But "cruelty" is not the same as "fish." The extension of "cruelty" is not always self-evident. Even where you and I agree that this man murdered that other

In my view, only a humanly created morality can justify limits. We pass the buck, refuse to acknowledge the full extent of our Promethean powers, if we try to claim the limits are necessitated, imposed upon us, by "reality" or from some other transcendent, unalterable, superhuman location. Modern science—first physics and now biology—gives us such capacities to alter the real that the notion of "natural limits" has become just about meaningless. And the horrors of twentieth-century history have shown, in Berlin's (1996) words, that "men of sufficient energy and ruthlessness could collect a sufficient degree of material power to transform their worlds much more radically than had been thought possible before. . . . Human beings and their institutions turned out to be much more malleable, far less resistant, the laws turned out to be far more elastic, than the earlier doctrinaires had taught us to believe" (9–10). Any limits are going to have to be humanly generated. It is an oddity of our scientific progress that if there are "real" limits to be found, they no longer can be plausibly located in a nature outside of us, but only in "human nature" as figured in intractable psychological and cultural dispositions. But, of course, the new genetic engineering promises to address personality traits the same way it addresses bodily diseases. Our paradoxical situation today is to use human freedom to limit human freedom. We cannot expect some non-human force to counter the conclusion that "everything is permitted." If some things are to be forbidden, we will have to do the forbidding ourselves—and make it stick. To wait for a deus ex machina is only to insure that everything will go forward.

Am I pulling back from full-bore pluralism? Yes, to the extent that I, too, will say with the philosophers that "not anything goes." But I am less confident that something about reality or reason or our inbuilt cognitive capacities keeps anything from going. One lesson of the twentieth century seems to be that humans are capable of doing all sorts of unthinkable acts, that nothing stops them from astounding creativity in imagining and performing actions that call forth the word "evil." My position is that the fact of evil compels every society at some points and some places to forbid certain human actions. Both evil and the attempt to constrain it are com-

---

man, we can disagree whether his execution by the state is "cruel," while the question of the "cruelty" of capital punishment may never even arise in whole societies. What could be read off the "facts" of the case that would provide determinate criteria for judging it "cruel"? Here the prior existence of the concept (as shaped through communal speech practices) does seem required for even the apprehension of its possibly applying to this event. But Wiggins is right to remind us that "cruelty" is used to highlight discernible features of the action.

pletely human. Again, it is hard to think of animals as evil or as groups of animals devising strategies to counteract evil. Setting limits on human action and enforcing those limits is, in the original sense of the word, awful. We have this terrifying responsibility. We cannot shirk it. And we should strive to retain a sense of its awfulness. The use of social power to constrain individuals should only be countenanced by a conviction that it is necessary as a last resort. We should be ever skeptical of rules and the sanctions attached to them, returning again and again to question the necessity of even the most time-honored examples. Complacency about social power is dangerous because such power almost always overshoots its mark, ends up constraining and punishing more individuals than is necessary. The problem, of course, is that determining what is necessary is a matter of judgment and, hence, of possible different conclusions. As Wiggins (1998, 314–22) puts it, the meanings of the moral concepts by which we assess need, establish limits, and judge appropriate applications are "essentially contestable."

This contestability, combined with the awfulness of humanly constructed power used to limit human freedom, makes pluralism in moral matters so important. I believe that we want to encourage disagreement, multiple interpretations and judgments, because we need to combat at every turn the possible ossification of moral precepts and their enforcement. Constant disputes, prompting constant re-examination of even the most basic principles, works against a complacency that loses sight of how awful it is to constrain and, worse, to punish another human being. If untrammeled freedom is linked in some mysterious way to sadomasochism, the link between moralism and a pleasure in others' suffering is all too unmysterious. That's why the talk of constraints in much writing on morality is so often insufferable. The pleasure taken in reigning others in is all too palpable. To put it differently: complacent and dogmatic conformism is more prevalent, I think, than dangerous amoralism. Fear of Yeats's "blood-dimmed tide" of anarchy justified massive state-organized violence throughout the twentieth century—and the willingness of many citizens to go along with and participate in that violence. Reverence toward (or at least, sullen compliance with) received authority is much more common than total and unprincipled defiance.

Pluralism in moral matters, then, takes its stand with disagreements as salutary. They should be encouraged. Consensus in moral matters banishes an uneasiness I think we would be better off never losing. Beware the man convinced of his own righteousness. He will do harm to others with a clean conscience and firm, single-minded, purpose.

Luckily, I think the prospects for quelling disagreement are dismal, although that doesn't stop many from trying. Take the example of a trial for murder. There are the facts of the matter. Did this person kill that person? Sometimes the facts are in dispute. But there is also another, entirely different, kind of question. Does this killing count as an instance of murder? Maybe it was manslaughter, self-defense, or an accident. The facts may be relevant to this second question, but they are under-determinative. Precedent, interpretation of intent and motive, and the understanding of what the general terms available mean will also be relevant. And, if we abandon the courtroom for a moment, we can recognize that morality often faces a third—and still different—question, namely "Was this action wrong?"

My position is that everything from facts to more murky matters of definition, assessment, and norms are potential subjects of disagreement. There are no knock-down arguments about anything that are guaranteed to convince everyone. I do think it is useful in many ways to be clear about different categories of statements, and I think the way you get such clarity is by recognizing what serves as your best evidence in cases of disagreement. I say to my son, "I didn't know Mary's hair was red." He answers, "It's not. Just look at her." That's where the spade turns: if my looking doesn't do the trick, my son has no place else to go, no other evidence to bring forward. (I know of what I speak here, since my wife and I disagreed for years over whether a suitcase we owned was black or blue. We made no progress in this dispute, but also demoted "being right" to a place of minor importance. I will admit, however, that when its zipper broke and I threw it out, the resultant relief made me wonder why I hadn't adopted that solution earlier.) But if I say, "I didn't know Mary was Helen's sister-in-law," my son can't respond, "She's not. Just look at her." Something else will count as our best evidence for that claim. In this case, he might say, "She's not. Just ask her." And even if I am unwilling to accept Mary's self-report on the matter, we have made some progress toward understanding the terms of our disagreement. In other words, we can identify what serves as justification for a claim to "being right." But there is always the possibility that someone will deny the cogency of that justification.

When we get to complex covering terms like "murder," "a virtuous life" or "justice," appeals to the facts, to looking at what is there, can never do all the work, never exhaust our reasons for making the statement that this particular situation is a case of injustice. It is useful, when disagreements arise, to be as clear as possible about the reasons we do have, because, pluralism insists, we have many different kinds of reasons, many of which are irreducible to statements of fact. To label an action "murder" is to set into motion a whole series of responding actions—arresting the person, searching for evidence, considering appropriate punishment etc. Those who argue that the label "murder" was inappropriate in this case are advocating different responsive actions. And, as in the case of Grant in the Wilderness, the facts do not determine fully in and of themselves which set of actions should be undertaken.

We reach here the perils and pleasures of pluralism. My argument is that, while agreement is always possible, disagreement is also always possible. And not only is agreement contingent, but it is also contingent whether agreement is desirable. In many cases, we cherish disagreement over agreement. It does seem easier to reach agreement about some matters than about others, but we lose much that is distinctive and valuable about morality if we try to curb its notorious proclivity for endless disputes by making it more like matters that seem to generate less disagreement. Such a strategy, I am arguing, not only underestimates the potential and actuality of disagreement in these supposedly less contentious matters, but also runs roughshod over the plurality of different kinds of arguments and evidence used to back up claims.

There is no end to dispute and disagreement. But, surely, that is an unhappy conclusion, pointing toward a world of strife and conflict. It seems impossible for there to be any successful living with others if there is constant and continual disagreement. We have to agree on some things to coexist. I think this is true. We put tremendous effort into teaching received commonalities to our children and, crucially, to getting them to agree that those commonalities are "right." The effort reflects our awareness (on some level) that agreement is contingent and that no community can survive for very long without voluntary compliance with some set of groundrules. Sheer coercion won't work. The peril of pluralism is that we won't get voluntary compliance. My argument is that voluntary compliance stems from a variety of considerations: from ties of affection to other members of the community; from fears of others' disapproval; from appreciation of the benefits of peaceful co-existence; and from a sense of the "rightness" or "justice" of certain precepts. But voluntary compliance is just that: voluntary. Nothing in the nature of the facts, or the reasons, or the consequences guarantees compliance. There will always be people who don't comply. And every society has to face the question of how to respond to non-compliance. What dissenting opinions and actions will it tolerate, what ones will it step in forcefully to restrain? My pluralism suggests that we be wary of designating some behavior—and even more opinions—intolerable, and that we try to keep all designations open to re-examination and re-formulation. But I don't think universal tolerance is possible.

Voluntary compliance is so important to us not only because it's easier, more efficient, and less violent, but also because within our tradition we value autonomy and autonomy's off-shoots: distinctiveness, originality, creativity, and innovation. That our individual choices and lives are unscripted, that the facts, other people, and tradition do not completely dictate our responses, is something many of us value. The only thing worse than a world in which no one agreed with me about anything would be a world in which everyone agreed with me about everything. We reach something of a paradox here. I am trying to convince you of my pluralistic vision. Yet total success would be the most dismal failure. (Of course, the prospects of total success are mighty slim; that fact is one of my core reasons for being a pluralist.) Do we really want a world in which moral and other issues are not always open to disagreement and dispute? Be careful what you wish for. Are we so confident in our current formulations that we would not value the person who comes along to challenge them? More likely than not, that person is a pain in the ass, a troublemaker, a gadfly. But grudgingly, sometimes only years after the fact, we honor such people.

Pluralism is both frightening and exhilarating. Disagreement and especially disapproval terrify us, yet complete unanimity would be deadly. The pleasures of pluralism, I want to suggest, are an acquired taste. Cultivation of that taste seems to me a significant part of moral education. Cultivation of such a taste is crucial in a democratic polity.

How does pragmatist pluralism's refusal of fixed, determinant realities connect to the views of intellectual activity and cultural politics offered in this book? Let me approach this question through another moral consideration: what does morality cover? What counts as a morally relevant situation? I assume that most of us accept that various actions are morally indifferent. Whether I eat potato or tomato soup tonight is not a moral matter. But no sooner do I say that than I begin to imagine circumstances under which such a choice might seem morally significant.

This ability to transform the situation from one that is morally indifferent to one that is morally fraught suggests that moral vocabularies are not entirely stable. Attempts to transform what labels we apply to new or familiar situations are rampant. Success of such efforts depends on what we can call, following Austin (1975), "uptake." In other words, one of the effects of pluralism is that people are trying to convince other people of all kinds of things all the time. Not only does human action transform the world, but human interaction transforms selves. All is in motion, all is changed through these dynamic relationships. And so it occurs to me that a significant component of morality is convincing others that some situation is morally relevant. For example, in the novel *Crossing the River*, Caryl Phillips (1993) portrays a slave-trader through his laconic logbook—"bought a strong young man and a small girl today; refused 2 others as too sickly" (103)—and through his love letters to his wife. The effect of this juxtaposition is to suggest that the moral repugnance or probity of slave-trading never occurs to the trader. It's just business. It takes a rhetorical effort, a discursive shift, to see slavery under the sign of morality. (That discursive shift begins with the efforts of Bishop Wilberforce in the 1780s to ban the slave trade and continues through the abolitionist movements of the 1800s.)

We might say the same of eating beef. To the vast majority right now, eating beef is not a moral issue. There are people who are striving to make it morally relevant. Whether they succeed or not is under-determined by the facts of how cattle are raised and killed, and of human needs for protein, although such facts are relevant. It seems to me a matter of some interest to moral theory to consider how transformations in our understanding of the morally relevant occur. And I will admit that I hardly know how to begin to develop such an account. I'll just remind you that the transformation moves in both directions. Homosexual acts were morally indifferent in many ancient societies, became morally significant in much of the modern West, and now many are striving to make them morally indifferent again. The nature of such acts in and of themselves cannot alone decide the case.

Let me try to be very clear here. I do not see how something in the physical nature of homosexual acts can make it "right" to declare such acts moral or immoral. In every case of judgment, I am all in favor of being as explicit and articulate as possible about the reasons I have for making the judgment I propose. But where others read the case differently, I don't see what it adds to say "but I am right." And, in fact, where disagreements occur, I think that saying "I am right" is a closing move. It brings discussion to an end; it marks the point where I will no longer entertain your reasons for reaching a different assessment. We do reach the end of discussion with others; but since we have to live with those others, I am suggesting that we want to be wary of such endings. I want us to try, as long as possible, to accept that the other has as good reasons for his or her beliefs as I have for mine. It is a drastic step to conclude that I am right or reasonable or moral, whereas the other is not.

Pluralism, then, makes cultural politics—the attempt to alter the vocabularies in which we understand our experiences and our world—central. But pragmatist pluralism's affinity with "direct realism," its attention to the recalcitrance of things and people to total determination by the cultural terms through which they are viewed, underwrites the insistence that the centrality of cultural politics should not blind us to the limits of what it can accomplish. Nothing can tell us ahead of time where and how recalcitrance will manifest itself. Our actions and our speech acts aim to alter the world and the relation in which we stand to it, but it should come as no surprise that our efforts are not always successful. When it comes to altering others and their relation to us, we occupy a primarily rhetorical scene, although we have other ways besides persuasive words to refashion others more to our liking.

The ominous tinge of this last phrase points toward the tightrope I have been walking throughout this book. I want speech acts and actions that aim to change the world, others, and myself, yet also to cultivate an appreciation, even a celebration, of the ways the world, others, and even myself, resist my best efforts. Pluralism champions resistance, the extent to which things continue to be their singular selves despite my designs and work upon them. Thus, pluralism suggests that intellectuals will find their work in the rhetorical effort to get people to change the names that they apply to situations. But it also suggests, in ways not fully compatible with that first task, that intellectuals, like teachers, will also direct their rhetorical efforts toward encouraging others to develop their own capacities as judges and to adopt a reflexive attitude toward their judgments after their production. Insofar as intellectuals can embrace this second task and cherish the rather chaotic and messy diversity of orientations and values that follow from it, they are aiding the cause of democracy. Or so I have been arguing.

Readers have complained that this formulation is too abstract, too formal. Doesn't pluralism entail any substantive commitments, any concrete courses of action? The ways I have been using democracy can seem either bloodlessly procedural or vacuously hortatory (as so often in Dewey and even more often in Walt Whitman). I have tried to suggest in chapter 2 some of the ways in which a classroom can model a democratic public sphere and in chapter 4 have considered the need for state action to preserve and foster such public spaces. One of the great frustrations of current attempts to reform voting procedures, to reduce the influence of wealthy contributors in our political process, and to combat the accumulation of the media into a very few corporate hands is that a "general welfare" interest in democracy per se is not a recognized legal ground in constitutional law (at least as currently interpreted by the prevailing majority on the Supreme Court). We cannot get the kinds of institutional structures that promote democratic interactions of the type I have been advocating if we have to argue on the basis of "individual rights." The use of the First Amendment right to free speech to stymie campaign finance reform is only the most dramatic case in point. That a practice is not democratic (a contestable point in each case, to be sure) is no argument against it. So advocates of democracy have their work cut out for them: very fundamental transformations of the United States' political institutions are called for if democracy is to flourish. Aiming for such transformations goes hand-in-glove with, but is recognizably a different enterprise than, aiming to transform American political culture (broadly construed.) The available venues for public deliberation, the quality of the interactions in those venues, and the limit on those able to participate in those interactions all leave much to be desired, much to be reformed.

However, as Eve Sedgwick (1990) points out, an "emphasis on the performative relations of . . . conflicted definition" (of a term like democracy as much as of the terms—homosexual, gay, queer—highlighted in her work) suggests "a practical politics" of "multi-pronged movement . . . without any high premium placed on ideological rationalization" among the various actions taken. "The cost in ideological rigor, though high indeed, is very simply inevitable," she insists. "[T]his is not a conceptual landscape in which ideological rigor across levels, across constituencies is at all possible, be it ever so desirable" (13). In short, even where political agents can mobilize groups and win battles through invocation of the term "democracy," we should not expect immediate or even eventual consonance with other uses of that term in political struggles. The accumulated weight and legitimacy of the term "democracy" makes it worth invoking by all sides in many contests. Pluralism leads us to expect many

contests and many invocations. Resolutions will ideally result from felic-
itous performances that secure "uptake," will pragmatically result from
decision procedures (like voting) that bring acceptable closure in the absence of consensus, and will all too often result from the more powerful
contestants taking matters into their own hands. All resolutions, however
achieved, will be temporary. And we will need norms of democratic procedures and ideals of full participation to challenge the premature and
unequal closures wrought by those with power. The only response to a
resolution one abhors as unjust, illegitimate, or "wrong" is to contest it,
with the choice of the means for such contestation a fateful one. Nothing
external to the contest will save us from it—or secure the issue of it. But
that does not mean we should underestimate the efficacy of principles,
ideals, and norms as resources in the contest.

In the universities where intellectuals mainly reside, pluralism suggests
that individualistic models of scholarly work (especially prevalent in the
humanities) are misguided. Interdisciplinarity should not mean one individual mastering several discourses of inquiry, but teams of scholars
working together on broadly defined topic areas from different perspectives. Collaborative work should not be aimed at overcoming the deficiencies of each individual contributor (although it can and will have that
effect in some cases), but at recognizing the plurality of ways that a topic
can be approached and understood. We should not expect some holistic
synthesis to emerge from such collaborations (although we needn't reject
such syntheses if they occur), since the revelation of differences in results
and the beliefs they engender can be as illuminating as convergence. Current modes of working foster not only ignorance of others' work, but a
defensive contempt of approaches that differ from one's own. Doubtless,
building this kind of intellectual community on campuses will reduce productivity as measured by numbers of articles and books published. Creation of functioning public spheres on campuses places various local
amenities and interactions on a higher level vis-à-vis the more abstracted
interaction with the scholar's national professional cohort than has been
the general rule over the past forty years (at least). A sea-change in academic culture, in the priorities and interests of the academics themselves,
would be required. But that change can look impossible to accomplish if
we see the chore as transforming the culture *tout court* and in one fell
swoop. Rather, in the pragmatist experimental mode, we should be creating local working groups, trying out ways of doing our work differently
and more collaboratively, seeing if we can address and reach different au-

diences than the ones we have habitually written for. From the actual doing will follow the changes in attitudes, purposes, and goals.

I will mention one such experiment in Chapel Hill, sponsored by UNC's Institute for the Arts and Humanities.[18] Faculty members are paired with a member of the community who is working on a project in the arts or in community organizing. The program gives the community member access to the university's resources and to the advice and feedback of the faculty member. It also provides the faculty member with an "in" into the world beyond the campus walls and the need to convert his or her specialized knowledge into something of use for the nonspecialist. In addition, the whole group of ten pairs meets three times a year to discuss what each pair is doing—and various participants have found these cross-pollinating gatherings the most valuable part of the whole experience. In short, Dewey's assessment in *The Public and Its Problems* of democracy's need for vital public spaces remains as true now as it was in 1927 when he wrote it. In our classrooms, but also beyond it on our campuses, academic intellectuals have more opportunities to create such spaces than just about anyone else in American society.

The temptation is to offer a final summary that pulls the various points I have made together under the covering term of pluralism. However, not only would such a conclusion test your patience and insult your intelligence, but it would also violate the spirit of pluralism, which finds the world a messy and complex place, in which all things do not hang together. We have competing demands upon us, must choose among conflicting goods, and creatively chart a course for ourselves, knowing that, for better and for worse, not everyone will approve of our decisions, judgments, and actions; and that the facts of the matter will not make one course of action obviously better than another even as they do limit what is possible. Good luck.

18. Ruel Tyson, the Institute's director, invented this "Public Fellows" program, which I currently administer in my position as the Institute's Associate Director. Thanks must also go to our donors, Robert Hackney and Shauna Holiman, whose generosity makes it possible.

References

Aarleff, Hans. 1982. *From Locke to Saussure*. Minneapolis: University of Minnesota Press.

Abrams, M. H. 1971. *Natural Supernaturalism*. New York: Norton.

Adorno, Theodor. 1978. *Minima Moralia*. London: Verso.

Althusser, Louis. 1969. *For Marx*. New York: Vintage Books.

———. 1971. "Ideology and Ideological State Apparatuses." In *Lenin and Philosophy*. New York: Monthly Press.

Altieri, Charles. 1994. *Subjective Agency: A Theory of First-Person Expressivity and Its Social Implications*. Oxford: Blackwell.

Anderson, Benedict. 1991. *Imagined Communities: Reflections on the Origin and Spread of Nationalism*. 2d ed. London: Verso.

Arendt, Hannah. 1968. *Men in Dark Times*. New York: Harcourt.

———. 1977. *Between Past and Future*. New York: Penguin.

———. 1980. *On Revolution*. New York: Penguin.

———. 1981. *Life of the Mind*. New York: Harcourt.

———. 1982. *Lectures on Kant's Political Philosophy*. Chicago: University of Chicago Press.

Aristotle. 1996. *Poetics*. London: Penguin Books.

Armstrong, Isobel. 1993. *Victorian Poetry: Poetry, Poetics, and Politics*. London: Routledge.

Armstrong, Nancy. 2000. "Contemporary Culturalism: How Victorian Is It?" In *Victorian Afterlife: Postmodern Culture Rewrites the Nineteenth Century*, edited by John Kucich and Dianne F. Sadoff, 311–26. Minneapolis: University of Minnesota Press.

Arnold, Matthew. 1965a. *Culture and Anarchy*. In *The Complete Prose Works of Matthew Arnold*, edited by R. H. Super, 5: 85–229. Ann Arbor: University of Michigan Press.

———. 1965b. "Porro Unum Est Necessarium." In *The Complete Prose Works of Matthew Arnold*, edited by R. H. Super, 8: 348–69. Ann Arbor: University of Michigan Press.

———. 1993. "Democracy." In *Culture and Anarchy and Other Writings*, edited by Stefan Collini, 1–25. Cambridge: Cambridge University Press.

Austin, J. L. 1975. *How to Do Things with Words*. 2d ed. Cambridge: Harvard University Press.

——. 1979. *Philosophical Papers*. 3d ed. Oxford: Oxford University Press.

Berlin, Isaiah. 1969. *Four Essays on Liberty*. New York: Oxford University Press.

——. 1976. *Vico and Herder*. London: Hogarth Press.

——. 1996. *The Sense of Reality*. London: Chatto & Windus.

Bickford, Susan. 1996. *The Dissonance of Democracy*. Ithaca: Cornell University Press.

Borges, Jorge Luis. 1962. "Funes the Memorius." In *Ficciones*, 107–15. New York: Grove Press.

Bourdieu, Pierre. 1984. *Distinction: A Social Critique of the Judgment of Taste*. Cambridge: Harvard University Press.

——. 1993. *The Field of Cultural Production*. New York: Columbia University Press.

Brantlinger, Patrick. 1977. *The Spirit of Reform*. Cambridge: Harvard University Press.

Brown, Wendy. 1995. *States of Injury*. Princeton: Princeton University Press.

Bruns, Gerald. 1974. *Modern Poetry and the Idea of Language*. New Haven: Yale University Press.

Burke, Edmund. 1993. *Reflections on the Revolution in France*. New York: Oxford University Press.

Burke, Kenneth. 1965. *Permanence and Change*. Indianapolis: Bobbs-Merrill.

——.1969. *A Grammar of Motives*. Berkeley: University of California Press.

——. 1973. *The Philosophy of Literary Form*. 3d ed. Berkeley: University of California Press.

Butler, Judith. 1990. *Gender Trouble: Feminism and the Subversion of Identity*. New York: Routledge.

Calhoun, Craig, ed. 1992. *Habermas and the Public Sphere*. Cambridge: MIT Press.

Castoriadis, Cornelius. 1988. "Intellectuals and History." *Salamagundi* 80: 160–72.

Cohen, Jean L., and Andrew Arato. 1992. *Civil Society and Political Theory*. Cambridge: MIT Press.

Coser, Lewis A. 1965. *Men of Ideas*. New York: Free Press.

Curtis, Kimberley F. 1997. "Aesthetic Foundations of Democratic Politics in the Works of Hannah Arendt." In *Hannah Arendt and the Meaning of Politics*, edited by Craig Calhoun and John McGowan, 1–26. Minneapolis: University of Minnesota Press.

Dahrendorf, Ralf. 1969. "The Intellectual and Society: The Social Function of the 'Fool' in the Twentieth Century." In *On Intellectuals*, edited by Philip Rieff, 48–56. New York: Doubleday.

Danielsen, Dan, and Karen Engle, eds. 1995. *After Identity*. New York: Routledge.

Deleuze, Gilles. 1990. *Expressionism in Philosophy: Spinoza*. New York: Zone Books.

Derrida, Jacques. 1988. *Limited, INC*. Evanston: Northwestern University Press.

——. 1992. "Force of Law: The 'Mystical Foundation of Authority.'" In *Deconstruction and the Possibility of Justice*, edited by Drucilla Cornell, Michel Rosenfeld, and David Gray Carlson, 3–67. New York: Routledge.

Dewey, John. 1980. *The Public and Its Problems*. Athens: Ohio University Press.

——. 1981. "The Need for a Recovery of Philosophy." In *The Middle Works, 1899–1924*, 10: 3–48. Carbondale: Southern Illinois University Press.

Digest of Education Statistics. 1998. Washington, D.C.: U.S. Department of Education.

Digest of Education Statistics. 1999. Washington, D.C.: U.S. Department of Education.

Diggins, John Patrick. 1994. *The Promise of Pragmatism*. Chicago: University of Chicago Press.

Douglas, Mary, and Baron Isherwood. 1979. *The World of Goods*. New York: Norton.

Dunn, John. 1996. *The History of Political Theory and Other Essays*. Cambridge: Cambridge University Press.

Eagleton, Terry. 1991. *Ideology*. London: Verso.

——. 1995. *Heathcliff and the Great Hunger: Studies in Irish Culture*. London: Verso.

——. 2000. *The Idea of Culture*. Oxford: Blackwell.

Eliot, George. 1997. *Middlemarch*. Oxford: Oxford University Press.

Eyerman, Ron. 1994. *Between Culture and Politics: Intellectuals in Modern Society*. Cambridge: Polity Press.

Feyerabend, Paul. 1993. *Against Method*. 3d ed. London: Verso.

——. 1999. *Conquest of Abundance*. Chicago: University of Chicago Press.

Fish, Stanley. 1994. "The Unbearable Ugliness of Volvos." In *There's No Such Thing as Free Speech*, 273–79. New York: Oxford University Press.

——. 1999. *Professional Correctness*. Cambridge: Harvard University Press.

Fiske, John. 1989. *Understanding Popular Culture*. Boston: Unwin Hyman.

Foote, Shelby. 1974. *The Civil War: A Narrative*. Vol. 3. New York: Random House.

Foucault, Michel. 1965. *Madness and Civilization*. New York: Random House.

——. 1979. *Discipline and Punish*. New York: Vintage Books.

——. 1980. *The History of Sexuality*. Vol. 1. New York: Vintage Books.

Franklin, Phyllis. 2000. "Recent Trends in Undergraduate Majors." *MLA Newsletter* 32, 3: 6–7.

Fraser, Nancy. 1992. "Rethinking the Public Sphere: A Contribution to the Critique of Actually Existing Democracy." In *Habermas and the Public Sphere*, edited by Craig Calhoun, 109–42. Cambridge: MIT Press.

Frye, Northrop. 1957. *Anatomy of Criticism*. Princeton: Princeton University Press.

Gass, William H. 1985. "The Death of the Author." In *Habitations of the Word*, 265–88. New York: Simon and Schuster.

Geertz, Clifford. 1973. *The Interpretation of Cultures*. New York: Basic Books.

Gibson-Graham, J. K. 1996. *The End of Capitalism (as We Knew It): A Feminist Critique of Political Economy*. Cambridge: Blackwell.

Gilroy, Paul. 1993. *The Black Atlantic*. Cambridge: Harvard University Press.

Goodheart, Eugene. 1978. *The Failure of Criticism*. Cambridge: Harvard University Press.

Goodman, Nelson. 1978. *Ways of Worldmaking*. Indianapolis: Hackett.

——. 1996. "Words, Works, Worlds." In *Starmaking*, edited by Peter J. McCormick, 61–77. Cambridge: MIT Press.

Gouldner, Alvin. 1979. *The Future of the Intellectuals and the Rise of the New Class*. New York: Oxford University Press.

Graff, Gerald. 1987. *Professing Literature: An Institutional History*. Chicago: University of Chicago Press.

Gramsci, Antonio. 1971. *Selections from The Prison Notebooks*. Edited by Quintin Hoare and Geoffrey Nowell-Smith. New York: International Publishers.

Grosz, Elizabeth. 1994. *Volatile Bodies: Toward a Corporeal Feminism*. Bloomington: Indiana University Press.

Guillory, John. 1993. *Cultural Capital: The Problem of Literary Canon Formation.* Chicago: University of Chicago Press.

Gutman, Amy, and Dennis Thompson. 1996. *Democracy and Disagreement.* Cambridge: Harvard University Press.

Habermas, Jürgen. 1991. *Structural Transformation of the Public Sphere.* Cambridge: MIT Press.

Hall, Stuart. 1988. *The Hard Road to Renewal.* London: Verso.

———. 1992. "Cultural Studies and Its Theoretical Legacies." In *Cultural Studies,* edited by Lawrence Grossberg, Cary Nelson, and Paula A. Treichler, 277–86. New York: Routledge.

———. 1996. *Stuart Hall: Critical Dialogues.* Edited by David Morley and Kuan- Hsing Chen. New York: Routledge.

Hardy, Thomas. 1966. *Jude the Obscure.* New York: Harper & Row.

Herbert, Christopher. 1991. *Culture and Anomie: Ethnographic Imagination in the Nineteenth Century.* Chicago: University of Chicago Press.

Herder, J. G. 1969. *Herder on Social and Political Culture.* Edited by F. M. Barnard. Cambridge: Cambridge University Press.

———. 1993. *Against Pure Reason.* Edited by Marcia Bunge. Minneapolis: Fortress Press.

Hirsch, E. D., Jr. 1988. *Cultural Literacy: What Every American Needs to Know.* New York: Vintage Books.

Holloway, John. 1965. *The Victorian Sage.* New York: Norton.

Horkheimer, Max, and Theodor Adorno. 1972. *Dialectic of Enlightenment.* New York: Seabury Press.

Hutcheon, Linda. 2000. "Blame Canada: Where Defense of the Humanities Makes the News." *MLA Newsletter* 32, no. 3: 3–4.

Ignatieff, Michael. 1999. "Berlin in Autumn: The Philosopher in Old Age." *Occasional Papers of the Doreen B. Townsend Center for the Humanities,* 16: 1–53.

James, William. 1975. *Pragmatism.* Cambridge: Harvard University Press.

———. 1987. *A Pluralistic Universe.* In *Writings, 1902–1910,* 625–819. New York: The Library of America.

Jameson, Fredric. 1991. *Postmodernism, or, The Cultural Logic of Late Capitalism.* Durham: Duke University Press.

Jencks, Charles. 1984. *The Language of Post-Modern Architecture.* 4th ed. New York: Rizzoli.

Jenks, Chris. 1993. *Culture.* London: Routledge.

Joas, Hans. 1996. *The Creativity of Action.* Chicago: University of Chicago Press.

Johnson, Paul. 1988. *Intellectuals.* London: Weidenfeld and Nicholson.

Keane, John, ed. 1988. *Civil Society and the State: New European Perspectives.* London: Verso.

Kozol, Jonathan. 1992. *Savage Inequalities.* New York: Harper Collins.

Kroeber, A. L., and Clyde Kluckhohn. 1960. *Culture: A Review of Concepts and Definitions.* New York: Vintage Books.

Laclau, Ernesto, and Chantal Mouffe. 1985. *Hegemony and Socialist Strategy: Towards a Radical Democratic Politics.* London: Verso.

Lasch, Christopher. 1979. *The Culture of Narcissism.* New York: Norton.

Lloyd, Genevieve. 1996. *Spinoza and the "Ethics."* London: Routledge.

Lyotard, Jean-François. 1984. *The Postmodern Condition*. Minneapolis: University of Minnesota Press.

———. 1988. *The Différend: Phrases in Dispute*. Minneapolis: University of Minnesota Press.

Machiavelli, Niccolò. 1975. *The Prince*. New York: Penguin.

Marcus, Greil. 1989. *Lipstick Traces*. Cambridge: Harvard University Press.

Marcuse, Herbert. 1964. *One-Dimensional Man*. Boston: Beacon Books.

Marx, Karl. 1978. "Economic and Philosophic Manuscripts of 1844." In *The Marx-Engels Reader*. 2d ed., edited by Robert C. Tucker, 66–126. New York: Norton.

McGowan, John. 1989. "Can Marxism Survive?" *Southern Humanities Review* 23, no. 3: 241–52.

———. 1991. *Postmodernism and Its Critics*. Ithaca: Cornell University Press.

———. 1998. *Hannah Arendt: An Introduction*. Minneapolis: University of Minnesota Press.

McLennan, Gregor. 1995. *Pluralism*. Minneapolis: University of Minnesota Press.

Menand, Louis. 1998. "William James and the Case of the Epileptic Patient." *New York Review of Books* 45, no. 20: 81–93.

Michael, John. 2000. *Anxious Intellects: Academic Professionals, Public Intellectuals, and Enlightenment Values*. Durham: Duke University Press.

Michaels, Walter Benn. 1996. "'You Who Was Never There': Slavery and the New Historicism, Deconstruction and the Holocaust." *Narrative* 4: 1–16.

Mill, John Stuart. 1965. "The Spirit of the Age." In *Mill's Essays on Literature and Society*, edited by J. B. Schneewind. New York: Collier Books.

Miller, Toby. 1993. *The Well-Tempered Self: Citizenship, Culture, and the Postmodern Subject*. Baltimore: Johns Hopkins University Press.

Morgan, Thais, ed. 1990. *Victorian Sages and Cultural Discourse*. New Brunswick: Rutgers University Press.

Nicholson, Linda, and Steven Seidman, eds. 1995. *Social Postmodernism: Beyond Identity Politics*. New York: Cambridge University Press.

Nietzsche, Friedrich. 1968. *The Will to Power*. New York: Vintage Books.

Oakeshott, Michael. 1962. *Rationalism in Politics and Other Essays*. London: Methuen.

Packer, George. 2000. *Blood of the Liberals*. New York: Farrar, Straus and Giroux.

Peirce, Charles Sanders. 1992a. "The Fixation of Belief." In *The Essential Peirce, vol. 1 (1867–1893)*, 109–23. Bloomington: Indiana University Press.

———. 1992b. "Some Consequences of Four Incapacities." In *The Essential Peirce, vol. 1 (1867–1893)*, 28–55. Bloomington: Indiana University Press.

Phillips, Caryl. 1993. *Crossing the River*. New York: Vintage Books.

Polanyi, Karl. 1944. *The Great Transformation*. New York: Farrar and Rinehart.

Poovey, Mary. 1988. *Uneven Developments: The Ideological Work of Gender in Mid-Victorian England*. Chicago: University of Chicago Press.

———. 1995. *Making a Social Body: British Cultural Formation, 1832–1864*. Chicago: University of Chicago Press.

Putnam, Hilary. 1998. "Pragmatism and Realism." In *The Revival of Pragmatism*, edited by Morris Dickstein, 37–53. Durham: Duke University Press.

Rajchman, John, ed. 1995. *The Identity in Question*. New York: Routledge.

Readings, Bill. 1996. *The University in Ruins*. Cambridge: Harvard University Press.

Rescher, Nicholas. 1995. *Pluralism: Against the Demand for Consensus*. Oxford: Oxford University Press.

Ricoeur, Paul. 1986. *Lectures on Ideology and Utopia*. Chicago: University of Chicago Press.

Robbins, Bruce. 1993. *Secular Vocations: Intellectuals, Professionalism, Culture*. London: Verso.

Rorty, Richard. 1989. *Contingency, Irony, and Solidarity*. Cambridge: Cambridge University Press.

——. 1995. "Demonizing the Academy." *Harper's* 289: 1736, 13–17.

——. 1998. *Achieving Our Country: Leftist Thought in Twentieth-Century America*. Cambridge: Harvard University Press.

Rosenblum, Nancy. 1987. *Another Liberalism: Romanticism and the Reconstruction of Liberal Thought*. Cambridge: Harvard University Press.

Said, Edward W. 1983. *The World, the Text, and the Critic*. Cambridge: Harvard University Press.

——. 1986. "Michael Walzer's *Exodus and Revolution*: A Canaanite Reading." In *Blaming the Victims: Spurious Scholarship and the Palestinian Question*, edited by Edward W. Said and Christopher Hitchens, 161–78. London: Verso Books.

——. 1996. *Representations of the Intellectual*. New York: Vintage Books.

Scarry, Elaine. 1985. *The Body in Pain*. Oxford: Oxford University Press.

Schor, Juliet B. 1998. *The Overspent American*. New York: Harper Collins.

Scott, Joan W. 1992. "Experience." In *Feminists Theorize the Political*, edited by Judith Butler and Joan W. Scott, 22–40. New York: Routledge.

Shweder, Richard A. 1984. "Anthropology's Rebellion against the Enlightenment, or There's More to Thinking than Reason and Evidence." In *Culture Theory*, edited by Richard A. Shweder and Robert A. LeVine, 27–66. New York: Cambridge University Press.

Smith, Barbara Herrnstein. 1988. *Contingencies of Value*. Cambridge: Harvard University Press.

——. 1997. *Belief and Resistance*. Cambridge: Harvard University Press.

Sperber, Dan. 1996. *Explaining Culture: A Naturalistic Approach*. Cambridge: Blackwell.

Tate, Gary, Edward P. J. Corbett, and Nancy Myers, eds. 1984. *The Writing Teacher's Sourcebook*. 3d ed. New York: Oxford University Press.

Taylor, Charles, et al. 1994. *Multiculturalism: Examining the Politics of Recognition*. Princeton: Princeton University Press.

Todorov, Tzvetan. 1997. "The Genealogy of the Intellectual Since the French Enlightenment." *PMLA* 112: 1121–22.

Toulmin, Stephen, and June Goodfield. 1965. *The Discovery of Time*. New York: Harper & Row.

Trilling, Lionel. 1955. "George Orwell and the Politics of Truth." In *The Opposing Self*, 151–72. New York: Viking.

——. 1965. "On the Teaching of Modern Literature." In *Beyond Culture*, 3–30. New York: Viking.

Tylor, Edward Burnett. 1994. *Primitive Culture*. In *The Collected Works*. Vol 3. Edited by George W. Stocking, Jr. London: Routledge/Thoemmes.

Viswanathan, Gauri. 1989. *Masks of Conquest: Literary Study and British Rule in India*. New York: Columbia University Press.

Watkins, Evan. 1989. *Work Time: English Departments and the Circulation of Cultural Value*. Stanford: Stanford University Press.

Weber, Max. 1964. *The Theory of Social and Economic Organization*. New York: Free Press.

Wess, Robert. 1996. *Kenneth Burke: Rhetoric, Subjectivity, Postmodernism*. New York: Cambridge University Press.

Wiggins, David. 1998. *Needs, Values, Truth*. 3d ed. Oxford: Clarendon Press.

Williams, Raymond. 1976. *Keywords*. New York: Oxford University Press.

———. 1977. *Marxism and Literature*. New York: Oxford University Press.

———. 1981. *The Sociology of Culture*. New York: Schocken Books.

———. 1983. *Culture and Society: 1780–1950*. New York: Columbia University Press.

Wittgenstein, Ludwig. 1958. *Philosophical Investigations*. New York: Macmillan.

Wolf, Eric. 1982. *Europe and the People without History*. Berkeley: University of California Press.

Young, Iris Marion. 1995. "Gender as Seriality: Thinking About Women as a Social Collective." In *Social Postmodernism: Beyond Identity Politics*, edited by Linda Nicholson and Steven Seidman, 187–215. New York: Cambridge University Press.

Zemelman, Steven, and Harvey Daniels. 1988. *A Community of Writers: Teaching Writing in the Junior and Senior High School*. Portsmouth, N.H.: Heineman.

Index